ASPECTS OF LOVE
in western society

SUZANNE LILAR

ASPECTS OF LOVE
in western society

Translated with a Preface by
JONATHAN GRIFFIN

McGRAW-HILL BOOK COMPANY, INC.
NEW YORK

LIBRARY OF CONGRESS CATALOG CARD NUMBER 65-19851
FIRST EDITION
37855

THIS EDITION © THAMES AND HUDSON LONDON 1965
FIRST PUBLISHED AS *LE COUPLE* BY
EDITIONS BERNARD GRASSET PARIS 1963
PRINTED IN GREAT BRITAIN BY THE CAMELOT PRESS LIMITED
LONDON AND SOUTHAMPTON

CONTENTS

PREFACE

A serious and lucid study of passionate love—of its vicissitudes in Western history, its present status and the place it might have in an improved society of the near future—responds to a deeply felt need of our time. The wide public won in many countries by Denis de Rougemont's *L'Amour et l'Occident* has shown this. And now, in *Le Couple*, Madame Lilar offers a fresh and, I think, outstanding example of the kind. It deserves from readers of English the attentive hearing and lively discussion already given to it in France and Belgium.

Its writer was born in Ghent; she studied philosophy and law, and practised as a lawyer. She then turned to literature, achieving success as a playwright: *Le Burlador* and *Tous les Chemins mènent au Ciel* did well in Paris. Her *Journal de l'Analogiste* is a challenging essay on the nature of poetry, based on close observation and analysis of her own experience. And so, when she came to the writing of *Le Couple*, she could bring to it a considerable range of knowledge and sympathies. Readers will quickly see this for themselves: in, for instance, the subtle and precise distinction she traces between Rubens' love for his first and for his second wife—and between the qualities of the paintings they inspired; in her balanced account of homosexual love in ancient Greece; in her penetrating comments on the legend of 'patient Griseldis'. There also shines out, from page after page, a passion for justice—which must, one is tempted to think, owe some of its intensity to the fact that a decisive reform of the status of women in her country was steered into law by her husband, who was Belgian Minister of Justice.

It was time for a book of this type and range to be written by a woman. A good many fresh insights have emerged. Above all, Madame Lilar has pinned down and described what seems to be a real difference between the basic ways in which love is conceived by men and by women. To the problems set by this, she puts forward solutions drawn from evidence of bisexuality in human beings of both sexes. At the same time her recognition that the difference is real and grave is the basis for her plea that society's attitude to the human couple should now—a thing not yet tried in Western history—take proper account of the woman's need for fulfilment.

This book is the work of a feminist, who makes no bones about her wish to proselytize—and refuses to evade saying certain solemn things which in her view must be said. This honesty in the author may put some readers off, but it should not. It is very good to find an author who has really something to say and says it frankly; and besides, this is a feminist with a sense of humour. While the desire to convince is constantly in evidence, the humour is unobtrusive. To the reader who is willing to take this very serious book seriously, it offers quite frequently the surprise pleasures of irony.

JONATHAN GRIFFIN

INTRODUCTION

The Phœnix ridle hath more wit
By us, we two being one, are it.
So to one neutrall thing both sexes fit,
Wee dye and rise the same, and prove
Mysterious by this love.

JOHN DONNE

When Bernard Privat asked me to write a book on the couple, I certainly did not expect it would lead me so far afield. The few ideas I had on the subject made me imagine it would be easy. But as soon as I began to go into it, everything seemed against me. I had thought that love and the couple were going through a modern crisis, and I found out that this crisis had already existed in antiquity. I had believed in *eros* as a value, slightly below that of married love, and now I perceived that the most legitimate kind of feminism demands that the two should not be separated. I had thought that my work would be made easier by categories that had become classical, such as *eros* and *agape*, and I soon realised that *agape* had been infiltrated by *eros* so that often the former is defended with weapons taken from the latter. And so on. In short, I was face to face with so new a subject and so far-reaching an undertaking that it would clearly be beyond my powers if I did not limit its scope.

To write the history of love all over again was a task that exceeded my abilities and energy; and yet I was convinced that the couple had factors that were constant: how could these be brought out without comparing different periods? I then thought of making a few cross-

sections in the history of Western society: these would already provide
the beginnings of a verification and might encourage others to explore
them further. But even this plan turned out to be too ambitious. The
cross-sections, unless studied in some detail, would be of only moderate
interest. I found myself obliged to reduce them to two—one for the
period in which a complete doctrine of Western love was worked out,
and the other for the period in which its distortions emerged most
clearly.

I very soon became aware that, from antiquity onwards, theories of
love have evolved around two different questions—that of its absolute
value, and that of its value as a basis for marriage. While opinions
differed on its absolute value, there was something very near unanimity
on the incompatibility of love and marriage. Philosophers and moralists
tended to agree with practical morality in considering a certain kind
of love, known as *eros*, as dangerous to conjugal union. All, or almost
all, defended 'reasonable' love—that is to say, esteem, friendship,
confidence, comradeship, team spirit and, sometimes, tenderness and
its compromises: in fact, everything except real love.[1] It seemed to me,
in fact, that these edifying sentiments were usually masks for much less
edifying motives: all too often, under the pretext of protecting the
family against the dangers of love, the object was to protect the
patrimony and to guarantee the exercising of marital privileges. This
policy was completed by institutions and by a morality that was
strict towards the woman's moral lapses and indulgent towards the
man's, and its result was to exclude love from the woman's destiny.
To me, believing as I do in the civilizing value of love and its power of
salvation, this discovery was a grave one, and I could not remain
indifferent. Not only is it in the *interest* of women to restore the dignity
of conjugal love, but also, for most of them, there is no genuine fulfilment apart from a lasting love. In woman love tends naturally to the
conjugal: 'no tomorrow' is a typically masculine programme; it is
generally on the morrow that a woman begins to establish hers.

I therefore took up passionately the cause of *unreasonable* love as the
basis and foundation of the couple—and by this I mean, of every conjugal union, regular or irregular: what constitutes the couple is not its
formal recognition but its intention. Above all, the intention that it

should last. I am a feminist insofar as I have become aware of the enormous injury and injustice done to women by the traditional politics and morality of marriage; but I depart from the feminist position by persisting in believing in the existence—and this precisely in the field of *eros*—of an 'eternal feminine', which goes beyond the physiological and extends to feeling and to thought—if not to their mechanism, at least to a certain direction they tend to take. This, however, does not mean that a woman is not just as much an individual as a man is, equal to him in dignity. If this difference between men and women could be conceived as the basis for any inequality of rights or treatment, then it would work rather in favour of the woman as the eternal initiator of the man—whether of a Pythagoras or of a Socrates.

I realize that there is something absurd in announcing that one is setting out to defend a thing as flourishing as love. One has merely to open a newspaper to see that, in more or less reputable or more or less hidden forms, this motive continues to determine the conduct of a vast number of men. Not only are there still, as there always have been, innumerable marriages for love, but people commit suicide for love, murder for it, ruin themselves for it and even abandon thrones. And yet there is a great deal of talk of what is called 'the death of love'. I am not so pessimistic: if anything has died, it is not so much love as the honour in which love is held. Our self-constituted guides and masters, those who claim to express the consciousness of our time, are engaged in what amounts to a campaign to denigrate love: the result is a confusion, which is certainly serious and might even destroy love were there not already signs of reaction against the most complete attempt at desanctification ever yet undertaken. For the present 'crisis of the couple' is only one aspect of the crisis of the sacred. If I had to name the principal plague of my time, I would say it was a passion for *demythologization* (the history of the word is well known): it attacks all values, and we should perhaps be glad of it insofar as it will, in the end, have served the very values it claimed to be destroying, by sifting them and by disengaging what is basic and essential in them from what was merely contingent.

The point of view I have adopted is now clear: it is a point of view that implies the dimension of the sacred. But one cannot say 'sacred love' without meaning a complete love, a love that fans out through all the colours of its spectrum and is equally able to refract them and to recompose them: a love that involves *communication*. What I have been led to defend—against any and every formula of evasion—is a whole and responsible love. I soon saw, or thought I saw, that the moment might well have come when the union of man and woman would begin to be fully aware of its majestic symbolism. I caught a glimpse of a new idea of love, a relationship between the sexes that had never occurred till now. Needless to say, I make no claim to have described this theory of love. But I may succeed at some points in making people imagine it, in winning over some minds to the idea of a resanctification of love, and of curing some lovers, either of false shame with regard to their feelings or of a bad conscience about sex. In a world dominated by fear a few men—such as André Breton, René Nelli, Guitton (insofar as his *agape* is enriched with the implications of *eros*) and de Rougemont (at least in the last phase of his thinking)—have come out in favour of love as the means of reconciling humanity with life. This book is intended to take its place in that line, and to be a tribute of gratitude towards those exploring thinkers, those 'prowlers on the frontiers'.[2]

A few words in conclusion on some things discovered by the way. More than once in the course of my reading I have felt: 'I have come across this before'. In the commentaries of Eliade, Alain Daniélou, Grenier and Corbin, so admirable in their different ways, and in the original texts that belong to the main stream of Hellenic or Christian mysticism, I suddenly found myself confronted—usually at the edge of the official religions, in those outer zones where adventurous minds seek their salvation on the frontiers of mysticism and philosophy—by an already familiar form of union with God, of deification starting from love; or again, by a similar transformation of spiritual love and physical love through what has been called at different times 'daimonism' and 'angelism'; or again by identical precepts of chastity, which are really techniques for the economy and storing of sexual energy. At these times I would wonder how other, more learned writers would have treated these parallels between worlds so completely distinct and so remote from one another as Tantric India and Taoist China, as Shiitic and Sufic Iran, as paganism and Christianity; I would dream of a comparative history of religions, and feel sad at the need to limit my scope. These resemblances will be mentioned at various points in this book. Like someone walking among mountains, who at a distance recognizes from certain relations between ridges, angles and peaks the pattern of rocks that reveals the system of their structure and origin, I have sometimes recognized the pattern belonging to a family of myths and have seemed to see emerging the crests of a range that was obscured—or the lost continent of an ancient and all-embracing doctrine. This has given me that serene joy which comes to the intelligence when it meets with coherence and order and thinks it may presume it is in the presence of a law.

In this doctrine—which nearly always implies a belief in beginnings, in a sacred Time of non-duality, of Simplicity, of an original Unity— the love of the sexes is only one mode of a much wider aspiration towards deliverance from duality and towards a reconstitution of the lost indistinction. This concept of sexuality, symbolically represented by the myth of the Hermaphrodite which recurs in most of the great traditional cultures as well as in the sexual rites of so-called primitive societies, has met with fresh favour in modern thinking. It is to be found in the later speculations of Freud and in Jung's *Archetypes*. Some sociologists speak of sexuality as a 'nostalgia for lost continuity', as an 'appetency for the other', or as a 'protoplasmic hunger'. But science is finding that the phenomenon of an *internal propensity towards union* may well go beyond living matter: it may exist in the virus (which is in some respects a bridge between non-living matter and life). At the same time in living species an elementary type of love seems sometimes to make its appearance independently of reproduction and sex: certain infusoria are not prevented by their lack of sexual dimorphism from seeking one another out, moving together, pressing mouth to mouth and finally interpenetrating and exchanging substance in what seems very like an amorous copulation, at the end of which each has become half the other. It has even been suggested that sex is a biological luxury. Sexual differentiation appeared late in the scale of being, as one effect of that law of increasing complexity which governs evolution. Yet life never starts a movement towards difference without accompanying this with an aspiration to overcome the differences.

This aspiration to compensate for the gap between the sexes, to reconstitute the pre-sexual state is love. Hence the myth of the Androgyne is at the same time the myth of the Couple and that of the return to the Paradise of the lost continuity.

A dream? Perhaps. But a fruitful and exalting one. It alone measures up to love, to its religious and cosmic range, and is the only satisfactory explanation of the relation, always rather suspect, between sex and the sacred. I take it as my working hypothesis. Without ignoring the requirements of historical relativism, I shall always try to go beyond this, and shall not content myself with treating as old wives' tales or crazy notions the great mythical themes which, far from having lulled the childhood of humanity to sleep, awoke it to knowledge: they have indeed, with their attempt to represent the truth of things symbolically yet exhaustively, often been more successful than the generally partial approximations of science. I believe that their images survive in the collective unconscious, always ready to reappear and to give men the benefit of their deep-rooted and persisting wisdom.

My hope is that the modern couple, without renouncing the advantages of our own time and the new opportunities it gives to love, will be willing to adopt its myths once more. This is a matter not so much of going against the stream of demythologization, as of rescuing from it the true myths and leaving to it the false ones: it implies, in fact, discrimination—de Rougemont's *Analysis of Myths*, or Eliade's *Metapsychoanalysis*. The term is of little importance: the essential is to bring to life again, in modern man, the bases of a primordial symbolism that has always expressed better than anything the reality of man's existence and of the world. The *érotique* is either sacred or nothing: a theory of love does not deserve the name unless it brings out the connection between the physical desire of a determinate body and the metaphysical desire to escape from all determination and to reconstitute —if only in flashes—the lost unity.

A great love is above all an awareness of a deep-rooted *nostalgia*, which it passionately tries to satisfy. This, whatever may be thought to the contrary, presupposes a strong sexuality, a motive power capable of assuring communication, able to join as well as to transport: it presupposes the *daimonic eros*.

I foresee that this programme will be criticized as Utopian and as esoteric, as reserved for a privileged few and of no concern for the mass of people. But there may well be more understanding of love in the 'mass of people' than in 'society': as René Nelli has said, '*Somme toute, les marquises en ont moins bien attrapé le mystère que les grisettes*'. Incomprehension and cynicism are to be found rather among the 'intellectuals'. But indeed there is no question of expecting 'the man of the people' to comment on the Mysteries of love (it would be like asking the church cleaner to comment on the Mystery of the Holy Trinity), but of once more surrounding love with a fervour, a climate of respect and honour capable of giving support to those who take it seriously and of persuading people that even to aspire towards it is noble, not ridiculous.

What is more, this conception of love is not my invention. It existed already. I am merely asking that it should be extended to the couple formed by a man and a woman. I think, as I have already said, that the woman has no choice—she must aim at conjugal love; yet it may also be thought that love itself has everything to gain by being embodied in the normal couple and by making the attempt at being lasting—what may be called a 'vertical' adventure, may be at least as absorbing as the surface dispersion or horizontal adventure of a Don Juan.

For fulfilment in multiple relationships women have long substituted the convergence of the particular and the universal in the deepest kind of monogamous love. A poet, Aragon, has expressed vividly how disconcerting he found this paradox (which is at the very heart of 'sublime' love and at the starting-point of its dialectic):

The marvel is that I fled from Woman to this woman. A vertiginous journey: thought becomes incarnate, and I am in it and cannot conceive of a greater mystery.[3]

Though great, the mystery is familiar to the humblest woman, provided she is in love and possesses the specifically feminine gift of waiting. I shall be told that the man must also be ready for it—and this brings us back to the love that intends to be lasting. There have been couples that have based their union on *eros*. There have even been some that have tried the two formulae, reasonable and unreasonable love, and have gained happiness from both. It seemed to me that a comparison of the two experiments would be the more instructive if both had been made by a famous man. I therefore place at the beginning of this book two emblems of conjugal love, strongly contrasted, and both of them well known.

RUBENS, *Rubens and Isabella Brant*, Pinakothek, Munich

Two emblems of love

TWO EMBLEMS OF LOVE

Car l'esprit ne sent rien que par l'ayde du corps.

RONSARD

Isabella Brant and Hélène Fourment. As Eugenio d'Ors said of Goya's *Majas*, 'one is almost ashamed to comment on images that have been pawed about so much'. Yet in this case what seems commonplace may not have been completely exhausted and may, if studied more deeply, bring together those who like what they are used to, and those who like a change.

Two marriages, two successes—and yet the first is considered to have been a 'reasonable' one and the second a passionate one. This tradition certainly owes more to the pictures of Hélène Fourment—to her insolent beauty at sixteen and her obsessive presence in the work of Rubens—than to the written sources. The *Life of Rubens* by Roger de Piles does not go into these fine shades of feeling. And the painter's correspondence—at least, what was not destroyed in the fire—confronts us with his official *persona*: in it Rubens shows himself, or rather shows himself off, in his various capacities as court painter, diplomat, courtier, collector, friend and husband; one looks in vain for the thickness, the third dimension; Rubens is deliberately absent from his letters. There is in them hardly more than a fugitive indication of the man—who must, nonetheless, have loved, desired and suffered like another. Indeed, more than another: for after all, this sensualist, this lyricist of the splendour of the flesh and of women must have been strongly predisposed to long for love and to hurl himself into it: he would do so with all the vehemence, temperamental generosity and mental curiosity that came to him not only from the period he lived in, but also from his heredity, from the opulent and luxurious tendencies of a citizen of Antwerp, from his humanist passion for knowledge and from his innate paganism, increased by Italian influences. He lived for eight years in one of those Lombard courts where men were apt to have preoccupations beside art and metaphysics. In fact, one would expect of this young man from Flanders, who was the close associate of a worldy and dissolute prince, a full-blooded love life—the licence of a Cellini or the grand passions of a Michelangelo. Yet there is in Rubens' life no definite evidence of any gallant adventure or of any love affair apart from his two wives: one is astounded, almost disappointed by the apparent steadiness, the regularity, indeed the prudence of his life. It is unthinkable that a man like Rubens should have had no relations with women other than his wives, but (even before his marriages, even when he was travelling to Mantua, Venice, Rome, Madrid and Paris), it is certain that he never led a dissolute life or even got himself talked about. Young, handsome, highly sexed and attractive (Nicholas Peiresc states that 'Rubens was born to please and give delight in all he did and said' and Lipsius wrote 'our Rubens has come home. You know him, one has to love him'), gifted with prodigious vitality and filled with professional curiosity for the mysteries of human bodies, their strange qualities, their aberrations and their blemishes (Delacroix considered that no one had had such knowledge as Rubens of the animality of man and the forms of bestial degradation)—how was he preserved from such a fate? By religion? Italy had taught him that religion is ready for any compromise in favour of love. And besides, he was a practising Catholic free from moralistic tendencies. What kept him from irregularities was an intemperate love of work, together with a fear of disgrace and scandal.

Peter Paul Rubens must have been aware that his parents' lives had been overwhelmed by a love adventure which turned to disaster. In Cologne, where the Rubenses had taken refuge after becoming suspect for having frequented the house of Marco Perez (a meeting-place of members of the Reformed Church), Jan Rubens was first the lawyer, then the lover of Princess Anne of Saxony, the wife of William the Silent. The couple were signally indiscreet, a daughter was born to them, and finally William grew angry. Jan Rubens was shut up in a fortress. Liable to the death penalty, he narrowly escaped it, thanks to the persistent efforts of his wife; but he emerged from prison a sick and ruined man. It was then that Peter Paul Rubens was born. How much did he know of this story? It was certainly the delight of the gossips: the prison had tried in vain to disguise the reasons for his absence, but 'it is too late,' his wife had written to him, 'for in Antwerp as well as here they know only too well where you are.' Peter Paul Rubens must certainly have heard people praising the conduct of that admirable mother of his, who had indefatigably taken journeys and taken steps of all kinds on her husband's behalf during the two years of his imprisonment, ever ready to write letters, forgive insults, beg, invent 'decent' explanations, even to have humiliating meetings with her rival, managing the family's affairs, bringing up her four children as best she could and getting together an enormous ransom, by means of which she at last obtained, after many disappointments, the imprudent man's liberation. Even if the child was told nothing of all this (and it is most unlikely, seeing that opinion had sided against the unfortunate hero of this anodyne story, condemning him and idolizing his wife), he could not help seeing Maria Rubens fighting to restore the family fortunes (heavily strained by the ransom), administering the estate, carrying out deals, recovering inheritances: he lived under her protection. He saw Jan Rubens threatened with being imprisoned again. And he knew that the wrong done to William the Silent condemned the family to obscurity and insecurity and exile. Antwerp, of which he dreamed, was closed to him. It was not till after his father's death that he could return there.

To wallow in bitterness was not part of his generous nature: everything in him turned to the positive. Having experienced the dangers of a dissolute life, he would adopt a policy of prudence. It has been said that his motive was ambition, the desire to 'arrive'. This is wrong: it was his painting that he wanted to see 'arrive'. He knew he was Rubens, and was responsible for his future glory. Having lived in the company of a woman like the strong women of the Old Testament, he would model his choice of a wife on her.

And in fact, almost as soon as he lost his beloved mother, he busied himself with finding her double. Isabella was certainly a woman of the same type, both strong and gentle, one on whom a life, a home, a

career and a great output could be founded—in short, 'a companion'.
And it was as such that, when she died, he was to mourn 'that dear and
revered soul'. He wrote of her then: 'Truly I have lost a very good
companion, whom I could love and was bound in reason to love, for
she had none of the faults of her sex, she was neither morose nor
weak but altogether good and so honourable and virtuous that everyone loved her during her life and weeps for her since her death'; the
words show a sincere distress, but are not very different from those
that would be inspired by mourning for a sister or a mother. Indeed
(or am I wrong?) they are, if anything, more subdued than those a
son would use, than those probably adopted by Rubens himself in
mourning for his own mother. Isabella would certainly have shown
herself capable, just as Maria Rubens had, of forgiving with a smile
('do not go on writing *your unworthy husband*, for all is forgiven') and
even of consoling a sinner, ('God be thanked! in the world as it is, a
man's sin, though very grave, is not considered shameful'). She too
would have shown herself humble, patient and self-effacing, yet
vigilant in administering the family fortune and alert to make up for
her satrap's failings. This type of woman has always been sought after—
at least for marriage (for a man demands opposite virtues from a
woman, according to whether he intends her for his success or for his
pleasure).

The ideal of the good wife, neither extravagant nor lascivious nor
a gossip nor too fond of dressing up, was not, as is often thought,
invented in our bourgeois societies. It is to be found in the Bible and
in Hesiod, and no one has formulated it more elegantly than Xenophon
in his well-named *Economica*. But certainly it has not diminished in
favour, and in Rubens' time it was openly expressed. It was sometimes
even exploited in the form of precepts from the husband to his future
wife. A contemporary, almost a compatriot of Rubens, Paulus Merula,
an advocate at the Dutch Court, did so in a chilly dissertation addressed
by him to his fiancée, Judith Buys.[4] From it we learn how, in 'the holy
and virtuous life of matrimony,' 'the husband guides, instructs and
protects his *huisvrouw*' (literally, his housekeeper, for the wife is an
accessory of the house). 'If she is not wholly perfect, he will reprimand
her in private, with friendliness and politeness.' However, 'should the

husband's fury be let loose, let her remember that he is the master and it is right that she should endure it. . . . Should he be harsh, severe, disobliging, cruel, pitiless, let her then bear it with humility and Christian patience. . . . Above all, let her refrain from all stubbornness or susceptibility, even should she be clearly in the right and even should what she say be the truth.' What is required, in fact, is blind obedience. This surrender of the wife's individuality admits of only one exception, and that is when the husband's ineptitude endangers their common fortune: 'Should the husband administer his property badly,' wrote Merula, who had foreseen everything, even his own failings, 'then the wife will seek, after mature reflection, a remedy to this weakness.'

Here we are at the heart of the subject: this is serious. Marriage is first and foremost an association. A fusion of two bodies, of two hearts? Above all a fusion of two patrimonies. It is the primacy of the purse. . . . As for love, this is clearly mistrusted. True, Merula says he will cherish his wife as 'his own flesh and *sister*' (the nuance should not be missed: this is not the 'bone of his bone, flesh of his flesh' of Scripture, a concept too bold for this Puritan, who indeed confesses that he is a novice in marriage and 'hardly knows what happens in it'. Poor Judith Buys!), but surely the fraternal flesh is already the flesh that has been humiliated. However this may be, Merula goes on: 'One does not marry to satisfy one's passions and give oneself up to pleasure, but to live together in virtue and in conformity with the Word of God.'

In some cases, it is true, this strict doctrine of matrimony was mitigated by humanity and tenderness, and then something like happiness could flourish. The security of the wife, yielding up once and for all to her companion the conduct of their joint life, the loving protection which the husband extended to her, the peace of two people indissolubly linked together and trusting one another—all this is to be found in the moving portrait of Peter Paul Rubens and Isabella Brant at the beginning of their marriage. With his wonderful understanding of correspondences, Rubens has depicted himself with his young wife under a tree, whose calm foliage spreads its shelter over the couple as if the painter had intended it as an image of the withdrawal, of the distance placed between them and that real life which was going on somewhere else, somewhere outside. Everything in the picture expresses the intention to keep well away from risk—and first and foremost the restraint of its technique, the precision, the calculated slowness of the drawing (we are here a long way from the rapid, impulsive, amorous strokes of *Hélène Fourment in a Fur Coat*!). The whole picture reveals a determination to define oneself within a world of convention and tradition, a world in which everything— even that instinct which this couple will clearly manage to tame like a bird in a cage—is regulated and domesticated. The solemnity of the clothes contributes to this impression, especially Isabella's clothes, which perhaps go beyond the effect intended: instead of merely defining, they mask; instead of protecting, they provoke. How can one remain insensitive to the cruelly defensive character of the clothes of this seventeen-year-old bride, who is so bundled up that all one sees of her is the muzzle of a frightened animal? The aggressive stiffness of the busk, of the shoulder pads, of the high collar, of the bodice, a whole sub-structure of cardboard, grosgrain, tarlatan, whalebone and wire whose presence can be felt under the sumptuous but forbidding materials, the lace ruff, stiff and sharp with starch, the rigid velvet of the sleeves and bodice, the wine-coloured velvet of the skirt which seems, like the satin of the brocaded and embroidered bodice-front, to be of the kind that catches one's nail and that one is afraid to touch; everything about this costume, covering that young body with an inhuman carapace, seems to have been put in by the great flesh painter to make us forget the flesh or to discourage approach to it. Everything suggests that this couple, which seems to have taken 'tranquillity first' as its motto, means to guard itself against the dangers and complications of the erotic. Whether conscious or not, that is certainly the intention of the handsome man with the sensual mouth, who has contrived to get a kind of moral solicitude into the symbolic image of the hand he is giving to his wife. Isabella is leaning on it, as on a balustrade. We are a long way from the mystically touching hands of the Arnolfini couple.

This is reasonable love. It is well expressed in the phrase 'to engage oneself *for life*'—that is to say, everyday life. Let us not forget that Rubens had placed his life under the sign of success. He needed a wife of the domestic kind, who would be little trouble and would not interfere with the discipline which that great worker imposed on himself—to rise at four in the morning, paint or draw all day, at five in the afternoon ride along the ramparts on a fine Spanish horse, and then dine early and frugally (but with a few good friends, to whom he would show his paintings or his collection of agates) so as to be in good shape for the next day's work. His calculation might have turned against him: repressed love sometimes takes its revenge and, in richly endowed human beings such as he was, rises fiercely to the surface, as Jan Rubens had found to his cost. But in the harmonious life of Peter Paul Rubens everything came at the right moment, and when that royal temperament, contained for a long time by the hard work that consumed its energy, at length reclaimed its due, Rubens was free. There was to be no conjugal conflict.

This kind of marriage, so convenient for the man and so favourable for his studies, output and career, is not necessarily devoid of beauty. The woman may find in it scope for a destiny of oblation and asceticism. Sometimes she enters into marriage as others take monastic vows. Did Isabella Brant live her life in the contemplation of her god, or did she devote herself to the service of the sacristy? Certainly she has more the look of Martha than of Mary. The portrait of her in the Cleveland Museum is cruel in this respect: years have passed, and the confident little bride of the Munich picture has renounced the so-called illusions of youth. This Isabella, who has made her compromise with reality and now gives the world a little ironical, satisfied smile, was no doubt 'altogether good and honourable' as her husband wrote of her, but she was firmly anchored in material things: that she has compromised is quite clear—she has become a woman free from anxiety, solidly installed in the terrestrial, content to be so, and showing it defiantly. Pity has been expressed for her 'features undermined by sickness': is this face a sick one? It is, if anything, repellent in its freshness (and indeed Isabella seems to have died of the plague and rather suddenly). The sadness is not in the sitter, but in the observer sensitive to the contradiction between the two pictures of her—one of them filled with infinite expectation, the other with this deliberate placidity, this stubborn self-limitation. It is clear that in Isabella something had been extinguished, and—unexpectedly—this something was spiritual. The word *eroticism* always gives rise to misunderstanding: here I am not referring to the sexual life of the couple. While of course not claiming to have uncovered the secrets of this marriage, I am inclined to believe that sexual pleasure was something the full-blown woman of the Cleveland portrait has experienced: what she lacks is the experience of a love that gives sexual pleasure a meaning. She has missed that state of grace in which the exaltation of the flesh is no longer distinct from that of the spirit, in which the path from the one to the other is always open. What makes the last portrait of Isabella disappointing is the absence of the spiritual—to which modestly and in terms of love (the woman's way *par excellence*) the seventeen-year-old Isabella had aspired, or so at least the Munich portrait seems to suggest. This is the commonplace pathos of the reasonable marriage: the woman brings to it her desire for the absolute, and is only required to run her house well.

And certainly Isabella was to prove a skilful manager of the painter's household: she established in it peace, so valuable to that tremendous worker; she smoothed away the obstacles and effaced herself so as to leave intact in him reserves of vitality, temperament and energy which he would then discharge superbly into the fury of his *Battle of the Amazons* and the great *Hunt* pictures. Whatever may be said, the part she played was a great one, perhaps invaluable. All the same, it was an external one. Isabella was never to be, like Hélène Fourment, indissolubly mingled with the painter's work. Rubens' path—a path to knowledge pursued through painting (one has only to think of his passion for knowledge, his wide-ranging scientific curiosity which included physics, astronomy, intaglios, morphology, physiognomy and archaeology)—passed to one side of Isabella, but through Hélène: Hélène, who was scarcely concerned with self-effacement, who was doubtless neither modest nor humble nor (probably) submissive—a far cry from the austere ideal of Councillor Merula. Of Hélène, Rubens asked only that she should be beautiful and allow him to love her; she haunted his spirit to the point of obsession; sometimes dressed as the consort of a Doge, sometimes undressed and more sumptuous still—he would depict her in every kind of rôle, as the Madonna, as goddesses, nymphs, sinners, bacchantes, and would even endow all the women in a picture with her features.

This difference in their destinies is the more curious since, as Fromentin observed, the two women were of almost the same type—a type in which Rubens unconsciously found his ideal of womanhood, since he was already painting it before Hélène Fourment was born. Isabella was like Hélène in complexion, the spacing and colour of the eyes, a certain auburn gleam in her hair, and, above all, the spontaneity of her expression—an almost animal naturalness. When Rubens met her, she was scarcely, if at all, less beautiful than Hélène, and hardly any older. Perhaps she was also equally gifted for love, and all she lacked was the luck of meeting Rubens at the right moment. When Rubens was growing old, any young girl of that type was bound to embody for him the nostalgia for the Feminine, together with the melancholy that is to be found in all great passions. As one meditates over the portraits of Isabella, one is inclined to think that perhaps Rubens did not give her every chance. Sometimes she looks like a younger sister of Hélène Fourment, like a sketch for Hélène, an incomplete Hélène. The poet Gilliams writes that she was *onvolwassen*—that she never finished her growth: he says that when Rubens depicts her with her children, she looks as childlike as they. Childlike, or infantile? It is not rare to find women who compensate for a certain infantilism by the exercise of almost manly virtues. Let us consider the look in Isabella's eyes (an impenetrable look that in a rather curious way, if examined for some time, takes on a mineral hardness, to which the painter sometimes supplies an answering note in the form of a jewelled diadem or bracelet)—and then compare it with Hélène's look in *The Fur Coat*, which is perhaps the most subterranean, experienced, knowing, aware look in all modern painting. Even if we had no other evidence, we would know from Hélène's eyes that this woman has been passionately loved. Eros is like that—bold, insolent, knowing. The child-woman of the *Park of Steen Castle* and the *Walk in the Garden* has become the mistress. This new Hélène is neither innocent nor obscene, but knowing.

Knowing to the point of sadness. Nearly all Rubens' portraits of Hélène Fourment are melancholy—unless she is looking at the painter, and then the sadness gives place to complicity or challenge. What, not happy? this woman who was extravagantly loved by one of the most attractive men of his time, when he was at the peak of his glory as an artist and even of his reputation in society (to which Hélène is known to have been not insensible)? I shall have more to say later about the false problem of happiness, but meanwhile I put my money on Isabella. There is a myth—a minor one—of happiness: it is the myth of the roof. What is happiness if not a sheltered condition? The happy man is not the man who is travelling, but the man who has come home and sees the smoke rising from the chimney of his 'poor house'. '*Avoir une maison commode, propre et belle*' is the first condition of the *Bonheur de ce Monde* in the famous sonnet by Christophe Plantin. 'Two hearts, one hearth . . . and yet the world also exists,' writes Roland Barthes in his denunciation of the modern forms of this myth of happiness as comfort.[5] It is a not very ambitious myth (one thinks also of Chamfort's dictum, that 'it is with happiness as with watches, the least complicated are the ones that go wrong the least often'), a myth of substitution and surrender. To live in that way is merely 'to wait gently at home for death'. Not surprisingly, Rubens improvised brilliantly on the theme of hearth and home. It was during the reign of his first wife that he built in Antwerp the splendid Italo-Flemish residence which can still be visited today. Many memories of Rome, Tivoli and Mantua cling about that baroque portico, those garden vistas, that rustic temple and that cabinet of antiquities with its niches holding statues of pagan gods and philosophers. It is a stage set—and sometimes so absorbing a setting is meant to put people off the scent: the empty scene cries out for couples engaged in trifling or in exotic delights. But for Rubens the setting was a studio where genius could re-create the world. Isabella also was creative, for soon three children of hers were growing up. Yes, a kind of happiness must have surrounded her, though not a very rare kind: modest rather than robust, a sort of custom of happiness. Rubens and she had never been enemies.

One would not dare to say as much of the other couple. There is a lover's supplicating look in the *Garden of Love*, there is Hélène's provocative look in *The Fur Coat*, yet Rubens kept this look of hers where he could see it till his death. And that unclothed body of hers, caught in its false surprise. For the clothes of Isabella seem attached to her skin like a kind of shell or like scales, which could not be stripped from her without flaying her, while Hélène's clothes seem always ready to slide off her, except when they are fancy dress, as in the *Walk in the Garden*. No pompous, stiff materials for her, but soft furs, underclothes and the gracious, conscious disorder of fluffy, opulent hair left free to invade the face. No elaborate jewellery with almost uncut gems, but at the ear a pearl, whose simple drop of light takes up the mother-of-pearl sheen of her delighted flesh that perhaps contains the promise of light. That flesh, gazed at with a lover's eye, a consecrating eye, became for Rubens the place at which all things came together, the most humbly concrete detail and the symbol. How that suggestion of a garter above Hélène's knee must have touched him—one thinks of Degas and his fondness for painting the mark left by a girl's stays. But love was needed to give meaning to these convergences, and to enable Rubens to paint, with such tender pride, a body that was the more moving since it was not absolutely perfect.

Yet nothing in this picture—not the look of the eyes, the long tresses or the knee—is as striking as the bosom. That swollen, heavy, superabundant breast, ostentatiously uncovered, is not merely the sign of the painter's obsession with the flesh: it is also the symbol of Fertility and of Life. The breast is not only the prime attribute of feminine beauty (d'Ors and some friends of his, discussing the renowed beauty of the Duchess of Alba, came to the conclusion that it was due entirely to 'the shape, the volume and the position of the breasts'), but is also the elementary, essential symbol for it. It was the breast that the Amazon was supposed to mutilate when she wished to be virile, and it is the breast that fashions reduce or ban when, conforming to mores, they adopt a canon of beauty that is sexless rather than hermaphroditic, and dress women to look like beardless youths. There is a symbolism of the curve, of the globe, of rotundity, which goes back to the earliest ages of mankind:[6] the Venus of Lespugue and the Venus of Willendorf are nothing but spheres, ovoids and nodoids. In them men were already pursuing—not without reference to the fascinating and formidable magic of the circle—the dream of a return to the Paradise of pre-natal unconsciousness, whose image was Woman as Mother and Woman as Nurse. This dream crops up constantly at the centre of the most religious and venerable conceptions of love (for instance the importance of the breast in the Indian art of love, where its volume symbolizes the divine abundance and generosity), as well as in the more furtive ones (I am thinking, of course, of the cinema). The importance attached to roundness by the sensualist Ronsard (who in so many ways is close to Rubens) is well known:

> *Le ciel n'est parfait pour sa grandeur.*
> *Luy et le sein le sont pour leur rondeur:*
> *Car le parfait consiste en choses rondes.*

He regarded the 'round' as 'celestial', and confessed that he saw women as 'a rounded mirror'. Lascivious? Perhaps; but the disconcerting fact is that the same image that excites and satisfies lasciviousness, serves and sustains (possibly in the same man) the symbol—that is to say, the spirit.

This contradiction will recur often as we consider love, and perhaps it can be resolved. If the breast of Hélène Fourment is to give suck to the whole world, it must be painted by Rubens with all the amplitude of the triple necklace of breasts belonging to the great Ephesian Artemis. And the impression made by this prodigal flesh is not 'materialistic' or 'realistic', like that of Isabella's insignificant flesh in the Cleveland portrait. Indeed Rubens, whom only thoughtlessness and stupidity find facile and only the timidities of good taste find materialistic, was constantly escaping from realism: he escaped from it by the very nature of his view of the cosmos. Taine was right: he was a barbarian and entirely pagan. But he was so by nature, not by deference to fashion: innocently, and therefore genuinely. The nymphs, satyrs, bacchantes and Silenus-figures in his pictures are not products of allegory: they rise to the surface and cover it with the gleams from a multiform Greece that belongs to Pan and Dionysus, a Greece that is, in spite of everything, authentically sacred, the Greece of the Mysteries. But after he met Hélène Fourment, something was added to all this. In his incredibly *coherent* painting, the connections were now strengthened, the repetitions and answering elements became more intricate, betrayed by the signs which that modulating, order-creating brush left behind it. It is as though Rubens had passed from intoxication to knowledge. His view of the cosmos had risen into consciousness.

Even those who minimize Hélène Fourment's influence on the painter recognise that there are certain signs of exhaustion in the pictures he painted shortly before his second marriage. There is more grandiloquence than greatness in the Buckingham Palace *Saint George* or in the decorative series of the Galerie de Médicis. In Rubens' life there was suddenly a moment of uncertainty: it was in vain that he wore himself out in multifarious activities, in diplomacy and travelling. He was adrift. For the first time, he was bored by court life. It was as though he was waiting for something. Rich and animated though his life was, he needed something to happen in it, something even more revolutionary than his visit to the Prado: he needed a great disturbance of the senses and of the heart, in order that his painting might be increased by a new dimension and that there might be added to it a thing Rubens had not yet really understood—poetry. And how that robust Fleming was refined by the ordeal of love, when it came to him! How he succeeded in dominating his titanic nature! From that moment dates the velvety melancholy of his *fêtes galantes*, of his Gardens of Love, the frenzy of his bacchanals and fairs, and the *perpetuum mobile* of his later landscapes—which are like great mechanisms whirling and gravitating through space, celestial bodies perfectly obedient to law, revealing organisation and number as these emerge here and there in the onward drive of a wave or the rotation of a whirlpool, interrupting the eye and drawing it in to descend the spiral way of some invisible funnel. Rubens could now afford to lose interest in his collection of antiquities and agates: something quite different fascinated him, and this was the new level attained by his painting, which had become extraordinarily conscious, thoughtful and controlled. The more he abandoned himself to the demon of extravagance, the more he felt the need to tame it—as though he was inwardly subject to that principle which projects worlds only to call them to heel, which multiplies only to reduce, which diversifies only in order to discover a medium within which Unity can constantly be recomposed. What he must have learnt from this motive power of Eros, which is always ready to bind the particular to the universal, the individual to the absolute, the most humble and profane to the sacred, and what confirmation it must have brought to his Heraclitean vision of a world in perpetual transience! Glory be to the flesh when it transcends itself. Either Rubens never transcended the flesh and remained a 'realist'; or in being a painter of the flesh he was also a painter of the spirit, as those who have taken the trouble to study him closely have seen clearly ('The spirit is Rubens' province,' wrote André Lhote). And in this case he was *bound* to come upon the path of Eros; for Eros is the mediator from the flesh to the spirit, and was the undisputed master of Rubens' soul, as it was of the soul of Socrates. Eros was the purveyor of the divine to that genuinely *religious* soul, which had pursued it for so long in the baroque manner in the multiplicity of forms and had constantly sought Order in extravagance and disorder. The God whom Rubens was to encounter at the end of this *initiation* was—as one might have expected—the cosmogonic God, the God of the Manifested, the Whole, the other aspect of the One, and—looked at more closely—Law. The erotic experience was complete.

The part played by Hélène Fourment has, it seems to me, been often belittled: she has been criticised, even attacked—a great beauty is apt to excite envy. Legend has depicted her as a flighty frivolous child and Rubens as a scolding, preaching husband. Was the Hélène Fourment of the Louvre portrait, with her melancholy gaze, frivolous? Was the lover in the *Garden of Love*, the man who painted *The Fur Coat* and so many other boldly sensual pictures (one of them, in which Hélène is being assaulted by a shepherd, has been described as 'on the edge of pornography') a scolder and a preacher? Quite clearly, Rubens' second marriage has not met with the same approval as the first. The historian balks at admitting its influence on the painter's work. And the novelist is apt to offer us a painful image of an Hélène who is gradually converted to the domestic virtues by the preachings and the carpings of an old fogey whose mere approach would put love to flight. The fault found with this marriage (not openly, but by insinuation, for Rubens was a great man who may be allowed an extravagance) is not so much the difference in their ages (thirty-six years all the same! but men have always claimed the right to marry

RUBENS, *The Fur Coat*, Kunsthistorisches Museum, Vienna

young girls) as its eroticism and the ascendancy it gave to the woman:
as we shall see, these two things are connected. This marriage was an
imprudent one and Rubens must have known it. But no doubt he
considered that he had given strategy its due: his life was nearly over.
On one occasion, as I have said, he betrayed what was in his mind: this
was when he was announcing his second marriage to the humanist
Peiresc, whose good opinion he valued, and after giving a selection of
prudent reasons, he allowed this confession to escape him—that it
would have been hard for him 'to give up his freedom in exchange
for the caresses of an old woman'. The sharp point of the satyr's ear
has been detected in this confession, but the real confessions are in his
paintings. These show that the ageing man threw himself unreservedly
into physical passion. His biographers have not altogether forgiven
him for this. And it is worth while to observe the tone attributed to
him in a novel by Harsanyi, which was the best-seller of its time. In
it Albert, the eldest son of Rubens and Isabella, is worried about the
character of Hélène and asks 'Does she make you happy, father?' To
which Rubens answers:

'As happy as I can be, my child. Naturally, she will never be able to fill the
place filled by your admirable and perfect mother in my heart [the hypocrisy
of this is clear] but I am old and ill and often unhappy. She is the joy of my
old age and I am infinitely grateful to her.'

The edifying story ends with Albert's marriage, a model marriage
served up to the reader as the moral to the Rubens fable. Not only
do the engaged couple refrain from exchanging the tender banalities
proper to those in love, but they discuss marriage portentously and
subject themselves to a two-years' separation—so great is their fear of
yielding to the sentiment of love!

Hélène Fourment might be expected to be somewhat humiliated
by being set between those three exemplary figures, the painter's
mother, his first wife, and his daughter-in-law; but one has only to
look afresh at the radiant image which Rubens has left of the women
he so deeply loved, and the other three are crushed. Certainly Hélène
had merits, if only the merit of having come upon the scene like a
Pomona loaded with fruits in the old age of a Rubens who could
only conceive of beauty as abundant and nourishing; but merit is not

RUBENS, *The Garden of Love*, Prado, Madrid

the point. He and she lived through an experience of which the others did not even catch a glimpse, the experience of a fusion so complete that the couple they formed existed as a living, organic entity independent of them. What distinguishes unreasonable love from the other kind is not that it leads more surely to success or happiness, but that in it the two people are mingled. This mingling is both a miracle and a mystery, and is essentially different from the non-sacred understanding between husband and wife who are friends. True, for these there is the miracle of the child; but it is no longer the miracle of the couple, which is already supplanted and yields place to something else. Procreation apart, all that reasonable love holds in store is solitary successes— even when these are won by the two people side by side. Isabella certainly helped Rubens, but her help consisted chiefly in keeping his path free. Hélène, on the contrary, was right in the middle of the path; Rubens could not avoid her, he was forced to move forward through her. Luckily it was not a love shut in upon itself, but an open love constantly surpassing itself through knowledge. Certainly Rubens was inclined, like all lovers, to see the world through Hélène, but she, instead of blocking his view (as happens in passion), was a lens for him, through which he saw things lit with a supernatural glow. She must indeed have been wonderful—someone has written that, after he met her, Rubens' painting always had in it a feeling of wonder. In spite of what is often said, she never behaved unworthily. Of course she married again: probably, at the age of twenty-six and with five children to think of, she had good reasons for doing so. But it was by the side of Rubens that she wished to be buried—thus showing that she had a sense of proportion as between the temporal and the eternal.

Two centuries later, when certain scholars took it into their heads to inspect the tombs in the church of Saint John in Antwerp, the bones of sixteen people were brought to light. The bill from the weaver who had made the pall for the painter's bier was still extant, and two coffins unearthed on the south side of the chapel had been covered with velvet. They were striking instances of those images often known as *vanities*. By the side of a sturdy man's bones there lay a delicate skeleton with one knee slightly bent, displaying even in death a kind of chilling, macabre grace. Were these Hélène and Peter Paul? What was left now, of two lovers? Of a woman more gifted than any other with love, beauty, glory and others' desire? Not a hue of the flower or the soft flesh of the fruit: merely this small quantity of carbonate of lime and magnesium, the sediment at the bottom of the alembic of transmutation, the rubbish that is called matter.

The more I study the examples I have chosen, the richer I find them in meaning. I wanted to show, right at the start, a great love, equally remote from hedonism and from dolorism, from a superficial eroticism and from the masochistic delight of the lovers of the *Liebestod*. A passion does not have to be *passionism*, a predisposition to suffering. Since all the modern attacks against *eros* exploit that confusion of thought, I am glad to have faced up to it so soon; in contradiction also to 'the great Western myth of adultery,' the love I have just described was a married love.

But the comparison of Hélène with Isabella (and indeed with Maria Rubens who prefigured her) has proved no less fruitful. It confronts us with two types of love, the reasonable and the other, and with two types of couples, the associates and the *lovers*. With two types of women also, the mistress and the manageress. These recur constantly. An extremely ancient policy of duplicity has enabled man to enjoy the first without depriving himself of the virtues of the second. To the one he says:

> Thou art beautiful, O my love, as Tirzah, comely as Jerusalem, terrible as an army with banners. (Song of Solomon, vi, 4.)

While he reassures the other with:

> Favour is deceitful, beauty is vain: but a woman that feareth the Lord, she shall be blessed. (Proverbs, xxxi.)

The second is the one usually preferred as a wife, the one to whom the management of the house is entrusted:

> Her candle goeth not out by night. . . . She riseth also while it is yet night, and giveth meat to her household and a portion to her maidens. . . . She looketh well to the ways of her household and eateth not the bread of idleness. (Proverbs, xxxi.)

She is appreciated for her domestic virtues, for her industry with the spindle and the distaff, and because 'she maketh fine linen and selleth it'.[7] Apart from this, what is required of her is mostly negative. Not too much beauty, not too much knowledge, just enough to make her agreeable. Not too much religion—piety also must be within measure, as Plutarch was to say, as Erasmus was to say, as Montaigne was to say, as Fénelon was to say (before he met Madame Guyon?). Not much conversation: she should, *The Book of Proverbs* stipulates, only 'open her mouth with wisdom', and Councillor Merula echoes this with his 'know much, but speak little'. Meanwhile others pronounced that 'a woman's finest adornment is silence'. Love there should be, no doubt, but of the quiet kind. Even chastity should remain a reserved sort of thing: not a heroic refusal, a source of power and energy, but a kind of non-being, the flesh rendered negative. At the cost of these amputations, the wifely woman would have public opinion in her favour.

Rubens' second marriage, as I have already said, went counter to tradition—a tradition which seeks not so much to eliminate *eros* as to keep it apart from marriage. The moralists and the religions are against his mingling a conjugal life and erotic life. But this mingling is the best fate open to a woman. It may well be the best condition also for love, the fulfilment of which—whatever men may think—requires that it should be lasting. It is for this condition that the present book will be a plea. It will take sides for *l'érotique* against *l'érotisme*, for love taken seriously against what is sometimes called the 'art of love'. An art of love is a collection of procedures or suggestions designed to provoke or reinforce the sexual trance: it is a striving for pleasure which turns away as soon as satisfied. Love taken seriously is the elucidation of an experience: it is a striving for knowledge which presupposes that passionate love be allowed its long and patient gestation. Our civilization has sometimes admitted it. The courtly philosophy of love, Ficino's philosophy of love, and those of D. H. Lawrence, of Georges Bataille and even of Henry Miller are often discussed; but none of these is complete or exempt from prejudice. The doctrine of *eros* achieved its sovereign expression only once. True, the kind of couple which produced so glorious a posterity, was a strange one. Although the story is twenty-five centuries old, we must now go back to that long and passionate liaison and try to re-think it. We owe to it the charter of Western love.

*Two moments in the history
of the couple*

THE PAGAN MOMENT

You who by love brought into being delirium in my heart, O Dion.
PLATO

He did not hurry towards his destiny. Indeed, he gave himself to dreaming on the way. In Egypt he visited the temples, he lingered in Cyrene to work at geometry, and again in Taranto, making notes for his theory of music. At Catania, since Etna had recently erupted, he went to take a look at a river of mud. Everywhere he allowed himself to be detained by the festivals, the shows, the crowded theatres. Perhaps indeed he was hesitating to respond to the invitation of that tyrant who boasted that he had bound Syracuse with 'diamond chains'. He was, of course, looking for a place in which to found his ideal city —this Plato, in whom the radiant Utopia of the *Republic* was already fermenting; but what hope had he of realizing it among these Italiots, famous as they were for their attachment to good living and with, as Plato himself was to say, not an idea in their heads except 'to stuff with food and drink and not to go to bed alone'? When he did finally go, it was with no presentiment of a meeting that was to prove as important to him as his meeting with Socrates—Plutarch considered it 'the verie providence of some god'.[8]

Of what that meeting was like, between the illustrious stranger and the young Sicilian prince who were to love each other for life, nothing is known; but something may be imagined, for Plato has told of similar meetings and has described the kind of suffocation produced by the appearance of a young man 'of admirable stature and beauty', the *cortège* of adorers, the children staring at him as at a statue, the stir of the adolescents jostling to make room for him, and even the agitation of the grown man, did the young man cast a glance in his direction, or did his cloak fall open. It is known that Dion was, to the highest degree, *kalos kagathos*, that with the beauty of body and face he combined that of the soul, and that he possessed the seriousness, the gravity that Plato loved and also the reserve, the modesty and (doubtless) the touch of timidity, cause of those blushes which 'make him seem yet more charming'. He was twenty, only slightly older than was required by the custom of a misogynous society which regarded male homosexuality as the noblest form of love (but no doubt the words of Euripides to the exquisite Agathon when his beard was beginning to grow—'beauty remains beautiful even in its autumn' —were applicable to him). Everything combined to make him what his friend was later to call 'a beloved of royal quality'. Plato himself was, according to Simplicius, as handsome as Socrates had been ugly, and his forty years had matured him for a great and passionate love. He had, of course, been in love before, but in these enthusiasms the soul, in spite of the couplet on Agathon,[9] and even the heart, in spite of the epigram on Alexis,[10] seemed to have played only a limited part. But in his love for Dion it was the soul that triumphed—not that desire was absent from what Wilamowitz has called *'einen rasenden Eros'* (a frenetic Eros), but this desire itself, tamed and controlled, supplied the motive power which brought him, stage by stage, up the whole ascent.

One may deplore that Plato's experience took place in the field of homosexual love: the fact was to weigh heavily on the destiny of love and of the couple in the Western world. I do not agree with Jean Guitton[11] that Plato 'is not interested in the quality of the individual', and it seems still less true that 'sex is a matter of indifference to him': Greek homosexuality was not a line of least resistance, it was a deliberate choice—the militant affirmation of manly superiority, the disavowal of the softness of feminine love, which was regarded as languishing and lascivious. It was because Plato adopted as his own the Socratic ideal of ἀρετή that he could not centre his desire on a woman—supposing he had been tempted to do so. This he certainly was not. From childhood his life was dominated by friendship or love between men. Apart from Socrates (and everyone knows how he venerated him), he had a tender care for his brothers Adimantes and Glaukon (he really loved

Glaukon, and has left a charming portrait of him in the *Republic*). He admired Demos, whose beauty caused a sensation, and above all there was his passion for his handsome uncle, Charmides. But none of this came up to the love he was to feel for Dion—a love that triumphantly passed the test of time: after thirty-five years it could still draw from the now aged philosopher a passionate epitaph, when his disciple was murdered. To the end this love affair remained a perfect example of the peculiarly Greek pattern of love as education: Plato continually formed and fashioned Dion, Dion continually modelled himself on the teachings of Plato. But what took the affair beyond normal homosexual practice was that the experience, or experiment of love was pressed onwards till it ripened into full understanding: this love gradually became a philosophy of love, and it is not surprising to find that the idea of *spiritual fertilization* was present. 'A substitute, an absurd *ersatz* for procreation,' Marrou calls it[12] and says that 'it is clearly the normal instinct for procreation . . . that, frustrated by inversion, goes adrift and seeks fulfilment on the educational plane.' Nothing is less certain. Depth psychology has shown that an identical substitution takes place in normal love. Jung has even presented this spiritual procreation as superior to the other kind. Moreover, the product of this gestation was, after all, the *Symposium* and the *Phaedrus*, two divine and immortal children of Eros.

The *Symposium* (which, like the *Phaedrus*, is an initiation) shows clearly that in Plato love soon took a mystical turn. It was a love that was *travelled through*, and its course and development can be followed in the great themes of the Dialogue—those of prédestination in love, spiritual fertilization and purification. A twenty years' separation did not loosen that long, passionate liaison. In the *Phaedrus*, which was written long after the Symposium,[13] one can still feel the presence of Dion—'his name', as Wilamowitz was to say, 'is almost spoken'. And this hymn of praise to the delirium of love has a freedom, a youthfulness and an eagerness that still provoke our wonder.

At the death of Dionysius the Elder, as is well known, master and disciple met again, and Plato's devotion to Dion involved him twice more in what he himself called his 'mad Sicilian wanderings'. He had some grounds for imagining that his going to Sicily would serve his political designs—for not only Dion, but the Pythagoreans of Italy assured him so, and events at first seemed to confirm this. The triumphal welcome given to him, the royal chariot waiting for him when he came ashore, the sacrifice offered to the gods by the young king as thanksgiving for the philosopher's arrival (and one can imagine something of the devotion and tender pride felt by Dion for the man whom he saw being received like a god)—all this was full of promise. So was the zeal shown at first by the younger Dionysius:

> The wonderfull modestie and temperaunce that was begon to be observed in feasts and bankets, the Court clean chaunged, and the great goodnes and clemencie of the tyran in all thinges, in ministring justice to everie man: did put the Syracusans in great good hope of chaunge, and everie man in the Court was verie desirous to geve him selfe to learning Philosophie. So that, as men reported, the tyrannes pallace was full of sande and duste, with the numbers of studentes that drew plattes and figures of Geometrie.[14]

But this enthusiasm was no more than rivalry: Dionysius, as Plato wrote later, 'wanted me to praise him more than Dion and to set a higher value on my friendship for him than on my friendship for Dion'. There followed scenes and outbursts, after which the tyrant would repent and beg for reconciliation; all this was a long way from philosophy, and caused consternation in Plato. He was separated from Dion, whom Dionysius had ignominiously driven out of Sicily. As soon as the winds and the tyrant allowed, Plato went back to Athens. There he was re-united with Dion, whom he kept close to him, in the Academy, guiding him in his studies and in his choice of friends, continuing to form and direct him as he had done before. Dion, who was very rich, lived royally. At the Academy, to which the glamour of the prince attracted many young men, life had certainly changed somewhat in the direction of the social and the artificial. Did Plato, absorbed as he was in study, see this? In any case, he continued to support Dion's ambition, bringing him into public life and securing his reception with high honours by various Greek cities.

Meanwhile in Syracuse, Dionysius was consumed with jealousy: tyrant as he was, 'madlie caried away with light desires,' he had a sudden impatient longing to see Plato again. Dion, who had left important interests in Sicily, pressed Plato to make the journey ('he begged me to do so', Plato wrote), and indeed there were fresh rumours that Dionysius had developed an extraordinary appetite for philosophy. He had contrived to gather some sages about him, and clumsily, from time to time, he put into action some small reform. But Plato by now had little belief in Dionysius's vocation for philosophy: 'I knew pretty well', he wrote, 'that philosophy often gives rise to such enthusiasms among the young.' He left, nonetheless, full of fear and presentiments. The journey, as is well known, ended badly: Dion assumed the leadership of the Opposition and the two princes became open enemies. Plato, who did not like war, regretted this; yet when he heard of Dion's victories, he could not help feeling proud—'His heart', says Wilamowitz, 'beat warmly at the news of the successes of the man he loved'. But there is a revealing phrase in Plutarch: when Dion had freed Syracuse from the tyrant and was recognized as the most glorious captain of his time, Plato wrote to him that the eyes of all the world were turned towards him; 'but', says Plutarch, 'Dion, in my opinion, had no respect but to one place, and to one citie (to wit, the Academy)'.

The assassination of Dion (by a man from Plato's own circle) cast a deep shadow over Plato's last years and last works. He died five years afterwards, 'looked after by the kind Thracian woman, who made music for him on the evening of his death'. He left neither debts nor fortune—a few personal things (two silver cups, a gold ring, a pair of ear-rings, and a clock and that posterity of thought which he had preferred to the other kind: he was not mistaken in relying on those 'fairer and more immortal offspring' to assure for him 'the immortality of glory and remembrance'.

GREEK LOVE

To Ménard—who cannot be suspected of anti-paganism—the *Symposium* and the *Phaedrus* seemed the two most immoral books in Greek literature, and Michelet's judgment was that they are 'austerely licentious'. Someone else, more acutely, has written that in them morality exists at its saturation point. Before enlarging on this, we must make quite sure that we are free from the crude but not uncommon confusion between paganism and impiety. No people has had a more

lively, youthful sense of the sacred than the Greeks, no people has felt
more strongly the power of the irrational than this people, whose
self-appointed mission was to control it. Behind the 'human, all too
human' form with which the Greeks endowed their gods, they
perceived the presence of something that went beyond reason, even
beyond forms: this, certainly, was not specifically Greek, but went
back, by some local connection, to the most ancient fund of beliefs
common to humanity. What was certainly Greek was the will to
bring it within the field of thought. This somewhat militant conception of the sacred (for in it the divine had to be perpetually won
back from the human, moderation from immoderation, order from
disorder) remained attached to the ancestral notions of the pure
(*katharos*) and the impure, of a sullying and a purification (*katharsis*).
Purity to the Greeks (unlike the Christians) was not a sexual purity—
or only became so incidentally: essentially, it was the absence of
mixture. The sullying was something added, and to purify oneself
was to get rid of this. To wash, to separate oneself from a material
impurity, was an act that was both concrete and religious, that is to
say, a rite.

Ritual purification very soon acquired a national importance, while
on the scale of the individual the idea of catharsis became the basis
for a religion of salvation. Socrates seems to have been the first to use
the expression *katharein* for the cleaning of the soul. In Plato's thought,
to purify the soul was to separate it from the excess which was burden-
ing it, by means of an art akin to sorting—for which the *Timaeus*
suggests terms like 'to sift', 'to filter', 'to winnow' and 'to card', and
the *Republic* offers that wonderful image of the sea-god Glaucos,
covered with seaweed, mud and barnacles, who had to be scoured
to be recognized. What is the excess that burdens the soul? Plato's
answer is its *corporeity*. Does this mean that to him the flesh was
altogether evil (as the Gnostics held) or altogether illusion (as in
Hinduism)? The Greek cult of physical beauty proves the contrary.
True, the spirit is *opposed* to the flesh (Plato came near to saying, like
St Jerome, that the spirit desires against the flesh and the flesh against
the spirit), but the nature of love is, precisely, to be the intermediary
between things opposed: love is a *daimon*. And the Platonic world is

a world of connection and recuperation, in which the contraries attract one another, instead of excluding one another. Love can, of course, *pervert*: this happens when the flesh usurps power and abuses it, dragging the soul down with its weight and turning her aside from her own proper movement. A pure soul is a soul that goes straight—like Apollo, god of purifications and archer-god, she aims straight and always hits her mark. In the light of catharsis, *eros* is separated radically from eroticism. Such love is no less opposed to licence than Christian love is: it is a love that is essentially controlled—but solely with the aim of remaining constant to itself, to its own movement towards rectitude, in conformity with that straight line which is, for the soul, the shortest way towards the state to which she aspires.

For these pagans, as for the Christians, the soul came from and returned to God. Plato thought that she retained the memory of this original condition, a memory which Socrates strove to reawaken through *anamnesis*. When a man met with 'some divine face, successful imitation of beauty, or a body similarly well-made,' he was filled with the memory of the true beauty and with the desire to possess this. And this transport was Eros: Eros was the love of the divine. Unfortunately, only a small number of souls had retained a sufficient memory of the original condition and of the beauties contemplated there; the others, deprived of memory and powerless to draw nearer to the gods, lost their wings and fell heavily to earth. It was for the former that Plato, when the time came, wrote his *Symposium* and his *Phaedrus*, developing—through the speeches of Aristophanes, Diotima, Alcibiades and of Socrates (whose arguments were so firm that, as Hierocles put it, 'like dice, whichever side they fell, they came to rest')—a doctrine of love, which, though degraded in transmission, has gone so deep into our culture that one finds traces of it even in the language of the man in the street.

To explain the element of predestination in love, Plato has recourse to that most venerable of the symbols of the couple, the myth of the Androgyne (which by means of ingenious variations he contrives to accommodate to the love of boys). In the *Symposium* Aristophanes, taking up a tone of fantastic fabling and a theme from the anthropology of Empedocles, tells of a prehistoric world in which there were three sexes, the male, the female, and a third composed of the other two. When Zeus decided to punish these Androgynes for their intrepidity in proposing to scale the heavens, he cut all human beings in two, 'like a sorb-apple which is halved for pickling, or as you might divide an egg with a hair'[15] and gave to each of these halves the desire to find and be reunited with its other half: since the division, the desire for one another has been implanted in us, 'reuniting our original nature, making one of two, and healing the state of man'. Each of us, when separated, 'having one side only, like a flat-fish', is complete. Men who belong to what was once androgynous are lovers of women, but

> they who are a section of the male follow the male, and while they are young, being slices of the original man, they hang about men and embrace them, and they are themselves the best of boys and youths, because they have the most manly nature. Some indeed assert that they are shameless, but this is not true; for they do not act thus from any want of shame, but because they are valiant and manly, and have a manly countenance, and they embrace that which is like them. And these when they grow up become our statesmen, and these only, which is a great proof of the truth of what I am saying. When they reach manhood they are lovers of youth, and are not naturally inclined to marry or beget children—if at all they do so only in obedience to the law. . . .

But love is not merely the desire for bodily completion: if a man encounters his other half,

> the pair are lost in an amazement of love and friendship and intimacy, and one will not be out of the other's sight, as I may say, even for a moment: these are the people who pass their whole lives together; yet they could not explain what they desire of one another. For the intense yearning which each of them has towards the other does not appear to be the desire of lovers' intercourse, but of something else which the soul of either evidently desires and cannot tell, and of which she has only a dark and doubtful presentiment.

Aristophanes, anticipating Diotima, tells us that what they desire is the return to the original condition—unity. But Diotima, the priestess of purification, tells us much more about this: we learn that love, that great daimon, mediator between the mortal and the immortal, seeks not so much to win back the lover's other half as to restore a state in which they were not distinct and to achieve delivery from all finitude. Eros is the aspiration of our mortal nature towards immortality, and is therefore impatient to procreate. But there are two kinds of procreation, one according to the body and the other according to the spirit; and Plato, like Jung, places the second well above the first. The peculiarity of Platonism is that it confines this to male homosexuals: the myth, it is true, applies in theory to both sexes, indeed to all three; but in practice only those who desire to perpetuate themselves physically turn towards women. As for the others, 'truly divine mortals' whose fertility resides in the soul, if one of them feels the longing to procreate he turns teacher, goes in quest of a beautiful adolescent boy and in his company 'brings forth that which he had conceived long before' and 'tends that which he brings forth', so that

> they are married by a far nearer tie and have a closer friendship than those who beget mortal children, for the children who are their common off-spring are fairer and more immortal.

This is still the stage of non-sacred explanation, of *instruction:* from it Diotima goes on to the more austere and difficult part of what she has to say. Here Fable gives place to Mystery, and we move from the mythical to the mystical, to that initiation by love at the end of which —at least if the spirit has not stopped by the wayside—it is given to perceive the true Beauty, which is then *revealed.* All this part of the dialogue is very fine and is bathed in the strange light of the Eleusinian rites. Following Socrates, whose guide is Diotima, we rise—but to rise is also to go down into oneself, to dig deeper and deeper towards the *epopteia.*

This philosophy of love is one of catharsis. Stripping off impurity after impurity, it proceeds from the beauty of a single body to a de-individualised beauty, and then to beauty disengaged from the corporeal (the beauty of the soul), then to this beauty in turn delivered from the individual person, and so at last, beyond all representation, to 'beauty absolute, separate, simple, and everlasting', in its unmixed purity, the divine beauty in the oneness of its form. This oneness remains a mystery—not an *arcanum,* an explicable mystery, but an *arrhēton,* an ineffable one (Plotinus later said that it was beyond the intelligible, which must be passed before it could be contemplated). This double transcendence, high point of the mystical approach, is a gift, is grace, even if the lover has made the greater part of the journey by his own efforts; but it is a grace that is always present, constantly given: God is not only our final state, but is also, and permanently, our deepest nature, absent from us only insofar as we absent ourselves from him and linger in the superficial regions of our soul. There are, of course, impure souls that remain bogged down at the surface: sometimes *eros* will contrive to save them, for the passion of love is an access to the divine—it is a *way*. This is the discovery Plato owed to Dion: he might never have made it, had he not met him. Eros is grace —for some people the only grace, the one chance of salvation. Later, in the *Phaedrus*, Plato returned to the subject of grace, and made Socrates say that the superiority of love lies in its being a *divine madness*. The beloved is the vehicle of this divine intervention, and allows it to appear supernaturally through him; and it is for the lover to respond to this call, to this divine incantation, and—without letting himself be deceived or lulled—to recognize the true object of his desire and to approach it by the method taught by Diotima.

But love is not the only madness—it is merely the best—now the only form of purification. To the Greeks there was also a form of purification in which the god swept down on men and made them divine by a kind of violation of the soul. This was the Dionysiac way —that of the orgy, of the bacchantes, maenads and corybantes, the way of frenzy and unmeasure. It was as Greek as the other—one has only to reread Euripides' *Bacchantes*. It implied a magical experience of dispossession followed by divine possession, which was favoured by drink, whirling dances, wild leaping, the shrill sound of the flutes and the clash of the cymbals. Transported by the god, who led them where he wished, these frenzied people were no longer themselves and they achieved automatically a *purgation*.

Plato distinguished more clearly than anyone between the two methods, the active and the passive, the critical and the drastic. The author of the *Phaedrus* ranks the corybantic orgy as an authentic divine *mania* and recognizes its homeopathic effectiveness; yet it is clear that his preferences go not to the way of intoxication but to the way of mastery, self-control and intelligence. This has been called the Western way, but it was really that of a synthesis of Eastern and

Western mysticism—Plato being one of the two summits of this, the other being Plotinus. It does not underrate the power of the irrational but submits it to the perspective of the intelligible; and it contrives to introduce into divine possession the purifying control of thought—of thought exercised not against the god but against the constantly threatening mixture of impurity.

In this living intellectualism, which was constantly remaking itself, refining itself yet never becoming abstract, the intelligible hovers at the almost imperceptible point where it separates from the sensory: the result is a very strange conception of the flesh—as impure and troubled, but like a liquid that must be made to clear—and a still stranger conception of chastity—as something that is to be won at this burning frontier where the two worlds are divided. This is why we find, in the characters in Plato's *Dialogues*, that passionate rivalry in maintaining themselves on the perilous ridge, that delight in describing embraces and caresses and that familiarity (which some have found troubling) between his wise men and certain young men of evil life —such as Phaedo, a redeemed slave and perhaps a prostitute, whose excessively long hair Socrates stroked, or Alcibiades, the handsomest and most admired of the Athenians, but also perhaps the most debauched. In this connection nothing is more significant than the scene (sometimes frowned on but in fact extraordinarily beautiful) of the temptation of Socrates. (Mme de Rochechouart was so shocked by it that she refused to include it in her translation of the *Symposium*.) As the result of a ruse by which he was certainly not taken in, Socrates was finally lying in the same bed as Alcibiades, who had slid under the *tribon* (the poor man's cloak of rough material which the philosopher used to wear), and Alcibiades tried—in vain—to seduce this lover of beauty and of beautiful boys. He embraced him:

> And there I lay during the whole night having this wonderful monster in my arms. This again, Socrates, will not be denied by you. And yet, notwithstanding all, he was so superior to my solicitations, so contemptuous and derisive and disdainful of my beauty—which really, as I fancied, had some attractions—hear, O judges: for judges you will be of the haughty virtue of Socrates: nothing more happened, but in the morning when I awoke (let all the gods and goddesses be my witnesses) I arose as from the couch of a father or an elder brother.

It has been remarked that at no stage did Socrates exhibit that horrified revulsion which is to be expected from a man who is naturally chaste. He remained lying in the arms of Alcibiades, and one imagines that it was with a smile that he resisted him. This sureness of himself—for after all, it was the young, wealthy and beautiful Alcibiades who was offering himself to the elderly, ugly and poor Socrates—has been considered so contrary to commonsense that it has been used as an argument to show that the Platonic conception of *eros* was a figment, whereas it is precisely this situation that gives the whole scene its character, the fantastic light of a world turned upside down.

For here, unquestionably, we are in the realm of enchantment and prodigy—one cannot help being reminded of certain techniques of chastity belonging to Tantrism or to the Tao, and even of *cortezia*. In it the figure of Socrates, completed by the next part of Alcibiades' speech, shines out in a supernatural aura. With apparent abruptness Alcibiades goes on to describe Socrates' insensibility—like that of a yogi or a guru—to fatigue, hunger and intoxication. In battle his appearance was such that it frightened enemies away. His resistance to cold was incomparable. One day on campaign, when the frost was terrible and no one went out unless with 'an amazing quantity of clothes' and with 'their feet swathed in felt and fleeces', Socrates 'with his bare feet on the ice and in his ordinary dress marched better than the other soldiers who had shoes'. On another occasion the soldiers saw how, from early dawn till noon, he stood thinking about some problem of which he could not find the solution:

> And at noon attention was drawn to him, and the rumour ran through the wondering crowd that Socrates had been standing and thinking about something ever since the break of day. At last, in the evening after supper, some Ionians out of curiosity (I should explain that this was not winter but in summer), brought out their mats and slept in the open air that they might watch him and see whether he would stand all night. There he stood until the following morning; and with the return of light he offered up a prayer to the sun, and went his way.

Nowhere does the figure of Socrates appear more strange than here—more magical, more daimonic, more like a genius or glorified hero or even a saint (as Fr Festugière has called him)—in any case, one of those intermediary figures with which the pagan world has peopled the no-man's-land between Man and Principle.

The strange perspective created by this scene—it is a perspective of prowess—makes the question how far philosophical *eros* was physical appear pointless as well as sordid; and yet the question requires to be asked, since it is raised by the philosopher himself. Must we agree with the recent thesis that philosophical *eros*, while its aim was to free itself from the fleshly, was firmly rooted in the sensual? I think the accent should be slightly shifted, so as to bear not perhaps on the aim— which was sometimes missed—but at least on the general purpose, the passage from flesh to spirit: Platonism is essentially this movement from the sensible to the intelligible, and to *root* it in the physical is as great an error as to cut it off from the physical. In Platonism, amorous desire is the motive power of purification, raising the soul upwards and literally 'giving her wings'. This is illustrated in the *Phaedrus* by the boldest metaphors. The consequence is a kind of familiarity, of friendliness with the flesh, and an indulgence towards its weaknesses. Without 'seeming like some gross sailor', it is possible to agree with Plutarch that the winged chariot of philosophical *eros* sometimes overturned. And this was not treated as tragic: did not Plato himself say frankly that in certain cases it was good for the beloved to accord his favours to the lover? The fate of those who started with pure love and succumbed to pleasure was by no means miserable: though they failed to reach the supreme blessedness reserved for the wise and perfect, they gained a kind of second prize. The *law* did not condemn them to embark on the subterranean voyage of the condemned: instead, it allowed them to spend a luminous existence, to travel to- gether—though as yet without wings—and to be happy. So their destiny was settled in accordance with the principles of justice. 'Souls', says the *Phaedo*, 'go where their resemblances and their tastes carry them.' Or, according to the Upanishads: 'What a man thinks, he becomes. That is the ancient secret'.

Thus the specifically Platonic doctrine consists not in despising the flesh (like the Manichees and the Gnostics, who regard the body as the 'raiment of shame'), but in *converting* it by involving it in the dialectical movement of a dualism that is constantly being surmounted and reborn—and in regarding chastity as a sovereign stage in the domination of the sensory world.

This ethic of mastery required an unbroken vigilance. Since it demanded that man should always regard himself as *egregoros*, as a sentinel on duty (one of the sentences pronounced in the Mysteries was: 'The sojourn of us men is, as it were, a watch'), it implied something very like saintliness. Although this radiating influence was of benefit to the whole of the Greek world, it was practised only by a few wise men. Meanwhile the majority of men thought only of eating and drinking and making love, of enjoying life lightly in the respite between two wars. Plato himself tells us that there is, side by side with the *divinizing eros* of the philosophers, a love aiming not at the sublime but at pleasure, and side by side with the *Uranian Aphrodite*, the *Pandemian*—and it was she, unfortunately, who presided over men's love affairs with women. The kind of love that leads to salvation is not conceived by Plato as possible with the opposite sex. And yet he has left proofs that are sufficient to clear him of any suspicion of anti-feminism. He sketched out a reform of education favourable to women. He admitted women—not Athenian ones—into his Academy. Better still, he placed the most esoteric words of his whole work in the mouth of a woman; and this woman, so advanced in knowledge that Socrates himself was afraid he might not be able to follow her thought, was not depicted by him as a bloodless symbol but was chosen out of a line of philosopher-priestesses that very definitely existed, holding an eminent position in the religious life of Mantinea.

In Plato, then, there was no personal misogyny—nothing comparable to the attitude of Hesiod, or of Aristotle, or even of Euripides (who puts into the mouth of one of his characters a terrible diatribe against women, that 'great plague', *cacon mega*), or of the early Church Fathers—of Chrysostom, for instance, who was always ready to let fly against 'the sovereign pest'. Plato treats the inferiority of women as a fact because he was judging from what he saw—because in classical Athens there were far fewer women like Diotima than like Xanthippe. Uneducated, shut in, brought up in obscurity (while the young men were flourishing in the pure light of the gymnasia), and devoting her time, according to her rank, either to dress and cosmetics or to household drudgery, not even appearing at table, always considered as an inferior and treated as a slave, the Athenian woman had the slave's defects: she was idle and lascivious, both talkative and incapable of conversation. 'Look, Critobulus', says Socrates in Xenophon's *Economica*, 'we are all friends here: are there any people with whom you have less conversation than with your wife?'

The question has often been asked, whether misogyny led to homosexuality, or homosexuality inspired the contempt for women. There is a third explanation—that men who were not naturally misogynous turned away from women in proportion as their type of love aimed at a level to which women were incapable of rising. The Greeks of the classical period were certainly not incapable of normal love (indeed most of them were ambidextrous like Alcibiades). Flacellière has pointed out that a Greek was very apt to take fire if he met a foreign woman who was beautiful, intelligent and brought up in freedom—as is proved by the case of Aspasia, the Milesian woman, with whom Pericles fell passionately in love. What is impressive about Greek homosexuality is the quality of those who practised it: certainly not the whole of Greece was homosexual—not by a long way—but incontestably its *élite* was. The names include: Solon, Aeschylus, Pindar, Theognis of Megara, Aristides, Themistocles, Sophocles, Agathon, Aristotle, Xenocrates and Zeno.[16] The classical Greek was homosexual in proportion as he desired, or claimed, to be heroic, ascetic, soldierly or philosophical and aimed more at intellectual exchanges than at 'pleasures'.

The *Symposium* and the *Phaedrus* are known to be the *fruit* of a homosexual experience ('all this', wrote Gomperz, 'is not merely Platonic doctrine but Platonic experience'). Yet in similar circumstances the homosexual poets of the *cortezia* and of the Renaissance disguised their inclinations and 'platonised' on the theme of the *Lady* or the *Amie*. In Athens Uranism did not go unquestioned, but was obliged to take some precautions and make a case for itself: it was not without reason that it always adopted the appearance of chastity and laid claim to educational value, besides expressing itself in the form of dialogue, which eludes precise attribution. Several laws, not so very different from our own, attempted to suppress it. Solon himself, 'emerging from the gales and tempests of the love of boys,' had thought fit to legislate with a view to limiting its spread. A woman could get a divorce for her husband's homosexuality, not for adultery. Violation of a child or an adolescent, whether free or a slave, and prostitution or debauching of minors were severely punished. Access to gymnasia and palestrae was restricted. And law apart, male homosexuality— though it was the ideal of an aristocracy and sometimes the object of a snobbish cult—still aroused the disapproval of many citizens: there were Greek cities in which, to be admired, it had to give proofs of virility and courage. It took the heroism of the sacred battalions of Thebes, composed of lovers who at Cheronea stood their ground and were all killed where they stood, to extract from Philip of Macedon the cry: 'Cursed be those who imagine that such men could do or submit to anything shameful'. It took glorious acts like the assassination of the tyrant Hipparchos by Harmodios and Aristogiton, like the charge of Cleomachos at the head of the Chalcidians and many other feats of arms and acts of sacrifice, to make their fellow-citizens raise monuments to these heroes—honour hich to some extent shed reflected glory on all the partisans of love tween men. Even so, they remained targets for popular ridicule and for wdy jokes by the comic writers.

In short, to base a major philosophical doctrine on the love of boys required more boldness than is usually thought—quite apart from the fact that one of the charges that led to the condemnation of Socrates was that of corrupting youth. But to base it on the love of women *would have seemed, quite simply, improbable:* this is the fact we must keep constantly in mind if we wish to understand anything about this history of love and of the couple in the Greek world. The habit of treating a woman as a mere instrument of pleasure (when she was not confined to household work) meant that such love as could be felt for her was bound to be at the opposite pole from the superb discipline which was integral to Platonism.

It was on a more modest level that the defence of conjugal union was in due course made. Certainly Aristotle cannot be reproached with having fallen into the snares of the sublime. In contrast with Platonism and its constant process of communication, Aristotle's world is astonishing in its division into watertight compartments, and its stagnation. Modern thinking is only just freeing itself from this 'tenacious apparatus of logic' and from the rigidity of its classifications. Everyone is familiar with Aristotle's conception of an isolated god, cut off from the world, with his odious political system of class and castes, anti-feminist and justifying slavery, with his morality of the just mean, firmly grounded on the earthly (not to say, the earthy), and his mediocre hedonism (which is to blame for the reputation for hedonism often attached to the wisdom of the Greeks).[17] Even the famous *catharsis* to which the name of Aristotle is wrongly linked (for the relevant passage in the *Poetica* is no more than a rather pale reference to that orgiastic purification which went back to the pre-Hellenic cults) has about it, as used by him, a feeling of the absence of any impulsiveness, ecstasy or motive force.

Aristotle was indeed a strange figure, one whom it is difficult to like. His contempt for women was so great that it weighed down his scientific theories. A woman was, for him, merely a 'sterile male', a 'crippled male'; only the male possessed the generative element, and the female was merely matter or medium. The male was 'divine', his sperm contained the principle of the soul, and it was because her seed contained no soul that the female was a mutilated male; this was why she could not engender alone; her nature should be considered as a natural imperfection—and so forth. One gasps at such misunderstandings of *eros*, of its mystical urge, and at such indifference towards the great process of critical purification which is at the heart of Platonism. Moulinier says that Aristotle 'was not in the least interested in the purification of the soul' and that 'he had not even any personal opinion on the subject of purity'! Certainly there was less morality than moralising—indeed Pharisaism—in this Puritan, with the anxiety he showed to preserve women from incontinence and lasciviousness, with his recommendations that women should be spared the sight of wanton pictures and that the too frank images of certain gods should be kept for the eyes of men, and with his admission that he detested the Old Comedy (that is, the robust, lusty, magnificent vitality of Aristophanes), preferring the suggestive subtleties of the New Comedy (perhaps because one could always pretend not to have understood them?).

I know it may seem surprising to apply the word 'puritan' to this pagan, who was probably a homosexual (at least early on) although he condemned homosexuality and, once converted to having dealings with women, felt the need to make public his satisfaction (but at the same time proclaimed his return to the official morality!). And it is true that one finds in him a fascination with sexuality—but of the mind that is often found associated with a stupefied astonishment of the mind at the servitudes of sex. Aristotle was one of those who are scandalised because love makes use of the organs of excretion. His obsession with this is well known. The spirit of scientific enquiry is not enough to explain his predilection for the study of the sexual organs, of the modes and even the positions for procreation, and his insistence on comparing them with the functions of excretion. The number of pages—entire treatises!—devoted by him to the description of sperm, menstruation and excrement is astonishing. If I am not mistaken, there appears in Aristotle a kind of wicked pleasure in pinning love down to the dissection table (like the hedgehogs and cuttle-fish whose uterus or testicles he cut out), and show it in its most repellent medical aspect—never in its exalting activity. He can be said to have wallowed in obscenity. A certain irritable envy of Plato is part of all this—one has only to compare his often malicious criticisms of his master's theories with Plato's own attitude of veneration towards Socrates, as shown in the *Apologia*, the *Symposium* or the *Phaedrus*. This merely added intensity to that rabid incomprehension of sublime love which is sometimes to be seen in those who know they are incapable of such love. If such natures are more ashamed than others are of certain acts that seem similar in both cases, this is not because their souls are more lofty, but because what they are in fact doing is more base and commonplace, since they are incapable of freeing themselves from it. The Puritan is constantly exploring this difference between love and the dark ways it is obliged to take: he experiences this gulf as a fault in nature, and is pained by it because he cannot conceal it. These souls lacking in the daimonic are logically led to be ashamed of love, and either to yield to it only with a bad conscience, or to refuse to yield to it—like Hypatia discouraging her lover with the words: 'See what it is you adore, Archytas—this foul matter, this corruption, with its secretions, its excrements and its infections'. (But Archytas gave the sublime answer: 'It is not matter I love, but form'. Of the two, it was not Archytas who was the materialist.)

All Aristotle's intelligence was unavailing: his was a nature hopelessly divided into compartments. In him there was no communication from flesh to spirit. This powerlessness to love was a religious impotence: his want of the will to connect things together, his lack of the sense of the sacred, is plain. By what paradox did he become a great doctor in the Church? In all fields he exercised his influence in the direction of laicization. But, of course, it was in proportion as love ceased to be sacred, ceased to aim at becoming divine through purification and, cut off from its proper connections, was no longer the marvellous risk by which it could be either salvation or perdition—in fact in proportion as love was reduced to its physiological purposes and to the expediences of practical life, there would surely remain no obstacles to its being introduced into marriage and shared with a sex for which Aristotle had, otherwise, little respect. All that was required was to tie it up with friendship and give it the accompaniment of a solid moral codification.

Aristotle set to work to do so. First of all, one does not marry for pleasure—at least, the woman does not; for the man would not marry without getting sexual pleasure (and Aristotle was not insensible to it, although at the same time he feels the need to run it down and calls it somewhere 'a vigorous itch'). One marries to procreate, but also for economic reasons—to have a partner in the pursuit of the means of subsistence, to share the work and, above all, 'to pool the advantages proper to each'. Such would be the principal achievement of this kind of marriage, in which, as Aristotle puts it so prettily, 'the useful is combined with the agreeable'. The union can even, at a pinch, be based on *arete*, provided it is remembered that virtue is not the same thing for the two sexes. Socrates thought there was only one virtue, and that temperance; courage and justice were the same in a man or in a woman. But Aristotle knew that there is one virtue for the governing and another for the governed—the one is all command and the other all submission. Just as there are slaves to serve as living tools, part of the property of the free man, so there are human beings born to command and others born to obey. Women are of the latter kind. Their adornment is silence.

Here, obviously, we are a long way from love. Let us take Aristotle's most human saying about the couple—'Mutual affection between man and woman seems to be an effect of nature'—and complete it with the rules he gives immediately afterwards for proportioning this affection in accordance with justice: in conjugal *philia*, as in any friendship in which an element of superiority comes in, 'to re-establish equality the inferior must give a proportional compensation to the superior', and 'the better must be loved more than he loves' (and the better is, of course, by definition the man, since the woman cannot even lay claim to *kalokagathia*). Aristotle dots the i's and crosses the t's: 'to the better the more advantages', and thus 'each obtains his due'.

But *eros* also was based on an inequality, and in pagan love reciprocity was rarely total; it was the better of the two partners, the elder, the *erastes*, who loved the more strongly and, far from feeling injured by this, considered that he had the best of the bargain—'a lover is more divine than the beloved, for he is possessed by the god'. There is no clearer indication of the immense gulf between Plato's *eros* and Aristotle's *philia* than this reversal. It is the gulf between the sacred and the profane.

We should, therefore, protest with the utmost vigour whenever it is said that Aristotle rehabilitated conjugal love. What he rehabilitated was not even reasonable love: it was that *conjugal association* of which Xenophon, a few years before Aristotle was born, had sketched out the features with exceptional felicity.

As far as I know, it is in Xenophon's *Economica* that husband and wife are first called associates. For twenty-four centuries people have extolled the delicacy of feeling of that well-to-do Athenian, the charm of the conversations with his young wife and the debonair authority exercised by him over her. One is tempted to take a closer look. It begins well. Socrates—a decidedly dull Socrates, with his Attic salt carefully removed—meets Ischomachos in the market-place and asks him what he does with his days: 'In any case you don't spend all your time shut up in your house, to judge by your healthy look'. Ischomachos laughs and reassures the philosopher: no, he does not stay at home at all, 'for, as regards household affairs, my wife is quite capable of looking after them by herself'. It emerges that one day, after Ischomachos had reprimanded his young wife for making herself up with ceruse and alkanet and had recommended her to give up those artifices which are only appearances and not really beauty, his wife (I hope, not without irony) asked him what she must do 'to be really beautiful'. Ischomachos then advised her—not to take the air, no, but to carry out tours of inspection in the house, going from the weaving-room to the bakery and from the bakery to the still-room: in this way she would get on with her work and take her exercise at the same time.

> Another good exercise, I told her, was to moisten the dough and knead it, to shake out and fold the clothes and the linen. If she exercised herself in this way, she would find more pleasure in her food, feel more healthy and acquire a better colour.

All the rest is in keeping with this.

To understand the full significance of the anecdote, one should remember that to the Greeks life in the open air amounted to a cult. To the Greeks—as Henry Miller has understood so well—light is a kind of holiness. Even the poor were allowed to share in its purifying virtue—Plato somewhere gives us a glimpse of a 'poor man dried and roasted in the sun'. It was forbidden only to women. That is the meaning of the 'stay at home' which comes as a refrain in every paragraph of Ischomachos' sermon.

Ischomachos is as proud as Punch of having himself educated his young wife: he discourses at length on the excellence of the training, at the end of which 'he had only to speak a word to be obeyed at once'. Complacently he recounts his first conversation with her after marriage:

When she had got used to me and was tamed enough for a talk, I asked her these questions, more or less: 'Tell me, my wife, do you now understand for what purpose I have married you and for what purpose your parents gave you to me? Neither you nor I was at a loss to find someone to sleep with: you know this, I am sure, as well as I. But after both I on my behalf and your parents on yours had given much thought to the best *associate* we could take to us for our house and our children, I for my part chose you, and your parents, it seems to me, chose me from among the possible partners.'

And when his wife (who was fifteen!) asked in agitation

'What can I do? It all depends on you. My mother has told me my business is to be good.'

Ischomachos replied:

'The duty of a good man and wife is to keep their property in the best possible state and to increase it as much as is possible by honourable and lawful means.'

This tells us where we are: what Ischomachos taught was merely the art of getting rich. The famous virtues which he was anxious to inculcate into his wife were no more than the qualities of a good manageress: sobriety, docility, industry, parsimony and, above all, orderliness—orderliness in the storing and conservation of possessions and provisions, orderliness in the working out of the budget and the regulation of expenditure, orderliness in the distribution of tasks and the supervision of servants and slaves (including a watch over the bolt on the door between the men's apartments and the women's, for the slaves must not have a child without permission). The whole economy of that marriage was dominated by a share-out of functions. And Xenophon was not afraid to justify this by a theology which was more crafty than naïve: it was divine Providence that, after careful examination, had adapted the nature of the male to work out of doors and that of the woman to the work of the house. Was it not, in fact, necessary that there should be one person to plough, sow, plant and take the cattle to pasture—things that must have kept the rich Ischomachos busy!—and another to store the provisions, bring up the new-born children, weave the cloth, send off the servants whose work was outside, give out the money for the purchases and, when wool was brought in, see that it was used to make clothes for those who needed them.

I am surely not mistaken in comparing her to that other manageress-wife in Judaea, who 'riseth also while it is yet night, and giveth meat to her household, and a portion to her maidens', who 'is like the merchant's ships; she bringeth her food from afar', who 'seeketh wool and flax, and worketh willingly with her hands', so that 'all her household are clothed with scarlet'. And Ischomachos' young wife would be wrong to complain of having to work harder at managing her husband's fortune than if she had been one of his servants: she would find pleasure in some occupations—in doubling the output of the slaves, rewarding the servants whose conduct was good and punishing the others. But no pleasure would be equal to that of becoming a good associate, more and more respected by her husband as she grew older, 'for it is not grace and beauty, it is the virtues useful to life that increases goodness and happiness among men'. Here again the Biblical echo comes in answer: 'Her children arise up, and call her blessed; her husband also, and he praiseth her', for 'favour is deceitful and beauty is vain'.

To this institution, designed for the management of a patrimony, and of material possessions, Aristotle in his turn brought the support of a political and moral philosophy which, though in fact not very consistent, helped nonetheless to establish the confusion between family virtues and domestic economy. Aristotle did not, of course, invent the marriage of reason, he merely added to it his niggling rules and his meticulous eugenic prescriptions (on the ages proper to procreation, on the intervals to be observed, on the seasons and winds favourable to the sexual act, on political limitation of births, on obligatory abortion in certain cases, on the exposure of malformed infants). The institution was grounded in custom, and in due course (since philosophy is made by men) all the schools came to approve it: whether mystics or moralists, upholders of *eros* or puritans, philosophers of the Academy, of the Lyceum or of the Garden, all these people in time agreed on one point at least—the incompatibility of Eros and marriage. In some cases the very loftiness of the aims adopted by the philosophy of love worked against the inclusion of women in that love; in others it was fear or hatred, not only of love but of anything that exalts and goes beyond the ordinary. But whether Eros was being defended against marriage or marriage was being defended against Eros, the result was the same, the dissociation of conjugal union and real love.

These doctrinal attitudes were supported by harsh laws. In Athens the repudiation of an unfaithful wife was obligatory (the husband was deprived of civic rights if he did not repudiate her), it was lawful to kill the lover if he was caught *in flagrante delicto*, and an adulterous wife was forbidden to approach the altars, to dress according to her rank or to wear jewels and other adornments. In addition, public opinion was as pitiless towards the slightest lapse on the part of the wife as it was indulgent to the straying of the husband. If we remember all this, we can see that the system was admirably organized for reserving love for men. The system was not peculiarly Greek: it was a long-standing result of the ascendancy gained by the masculine sex. The man had no intention of depriving himself of sexual freedom because he was master of his wife: he amused himself with his slaves and with hetaerae, or even went in for polygamy. The distinction between the woman who was an instrument of pleasure and the domestic woman seems to have asserted itself very early on, and from early ages men were reluctant to mix up the two functions and so give the companion in marriage the formidable advantages of the mistress.

In Greece the system found support not only in the laws but in religious custom. It was the girl's father or, failing him, her brother who chose her husband from among the suitors—she must take no part in the choice. She must be a virgin when she married. And she must promise strict fidelity. This triple padlock should, it seems, have sufficed to banish love from the lives of women. In fact it did not: in spite of the severity of the laws and the seclusion to which women were subjected (it was with them in mind that Phidias represented the Venus of the Eleans with her foot placed on a tortoise, signifying that their duty was to remain at home and keep silence), not all of them resigned themselves to effacement. There was also the unforeseeable: wars, the hunting of captives, abductions, not to speak of the ingenuity of lovers. The Iliad is the epic of a rape, and already in Homer there are two kinds of love. There is the love for the woman who is a prize of war—how many cities were pillaged and countrysides were laid waste in campaigns whose zest lay in hunting women as well as slaves and cattle! Sensual, voluptuous, greedy for physical, never for spiritual delights (one has only to think of the famous scene in which Helen, guided by Aphrodite, enters the tent where Paris, like a lover in the *Arabian Nights*, is lying exquisitely adorned, on a perfumed couch), this was already romantic love. Side by side with it there was regular love and the woman who was a man's companion. And while the general or the soldier besieging Troy, or the sailor chafing on a ship detained by the winter storms, no doubt sighed for his wife, there lay behind this longing another, stronger one—for the hearth (whether a house or a palace) of which his wife was both the guardian and the servant, both an accessory and a symbol. What made Odysseus unhappy with Calypso (who nonetheless managed to keep him for seven years) was not only the thought of Penelope, it was 'the desire to see the day of return to his own dwelling'. Certainly, as Achilles said, 'every man that has a heart and a brain loves his wife and gives her his protection', and so he wept for Briseis; but the great lamentations were for Patroclus, and it was to avenge him that Achilles went towards his death. Does this mean that no man in Greece loved a woman passionately? Far from it. But they did not boast of it, and no one dreamed of complimenting them on it. As soon as a Greek abandoned himself to the passionate love of women, he was lost to the community, since he was making himself unmanly—like Paris, who was regarded as merely effeminate.

What redeemed love in the eyes of the Greeks was the conception of the woman as chattel. A warrior was not thought to demean himself by love-as-recreation—any more than he diminished himself by taking a wife, provided he commanded her, was her chief, dictated his law to her, as was the rule in the primitive families described by Homer. So married love was expected to be reasonable love—at least on the part of the husband, for legend preserved and celebrated the devotion of Alcestis to Admetus. The woman's spirit of sacrifice, far from damaging, consolidated the system. No man was likely to

blame the Pythagorean women for carrying devotion to the husband
to the point of a mystical cult of marriage. Such a policy involved
either prostitution (for sexual licence with another man's wife or
daughter would compromise the prevailing institutions) or the
practice of homosexuality, and the Greeks had both of these. But a
policy sometimes recoils, and the effect of this one was to deprive the
West of a heterosexual philosophy of love. It is the degrading conception of the woman as a chattel that must be blamed for the
monstrous fact that the doctrine of exalting love, of love as the *way*,
was worked out apart from, if not against, women. This brought
with it the dissociation of the conception of love and the sexual function
—nothing less than the disintegration of love. The event was one of
the utmost gravity—and a strange one since Platonic *eros* was
essentially daimonism, communication, unification. From whatever
direction the facts are looked at, what we have here is the first, the
precocious disintegration of *eros*, and it was the more formidable since
it took place on the level of the sublime.

This is not all. The fact that the Greeks, actually in proportion as
their love aimed high, were reduced to a type of relationship that was
never wholly accepted by opinion, put the philosophers in a false
position. Socrates and Plato knew very well that the chastity they
preached (and probably practised) was for others only a show. Did
this mean that those others must be rejected and considered as lewd
animals? Plato's answer[18] was definitely: No, at least not if they are
joined by true love. Nonetheless, the commentators wavered and
were often anxious to make the verdict a harsher one. Misunderstood
Platonism was destined to load the Western conscience with the
dualistic condemnation of the flesh, and here bourgeois false idealism
had its origin. From that moment began the triumph of the opinion
that it is nobler to love with the heart or the brain than with the senses,
to love 'platonically' than to love totally—whereas the central idea of
Platonism, stated again and again in the *Symposium* and the *Phaedrus*,
had been that 'stirred by amorous longing a man can rise, starting
from the senses and the flesh'.

Platonic purification no doubt remained a privileged experience.
Most of the Greeks did their loving under the aegis of Pan rather than

of Eros. But Pan, the son of Hermes, has a double nature. One part is rough, bristling, earthy (derived from the goat) and turned towards men; the other is smooth, soft and turned towards the gods. Socrates was not afraid to pray to him: 'Beloved Pan . . . give me beauty in the inward soul; and may the outward and inward man be at one.' And as for Plato himself, as Flacelière has said,[19] 'even in low life he saw the shining of the promise of pure love'.

The same policy that excluded women from *eros* and favoured male homosexuality was also propitious to love between women. Well before Socrates and Plato, a woman's voice had to some extent anticipated their doctrine. The Greeks compared Sappho's *art of love* with that of Socrates. Hers, like his, was first and foremost an education. The much mutilated surviving fragments of her work are enough to establish that Sappho was a great poet of passionate love; but do they really allow us to go further and speak of Sappho's philosophy of love?

Socrates, Plato and the Emperor Julia ll praised her, Strabo called her a marvellous prodigy, and Antir r a feminine Homer. She was a widow and a mother, she pre ued over a great school, and she brought up young girls to dance, sing and play the lyre. Mario Meunier and André Bonnard consider that she was simply preparing them for marriage and that her school was a kind of Saint-Cyr. For—unlike what is happening in the case of Plato—the tendency of recent opinion is in favour of the purity of Sappho's morals. For my own part, I think this point, which is anecdotal, is of little importance: the real question—as with Plato—is concerned not so much with purity as with purification. It seems hard to deny that Sappho knew all there was to know of Eros, 'breaker of limbs'. It is no less evident that she went beyond lust, conquered the flesh and attained something that can safely be called divine. We have clear evidence on this in the argument of Jérôme Carcopino's fine book on the pagan basilica of the Porto Maggiore in Rome. The fact that the leap from the Leukadian cliff was depicted above the altar of the austere Pythagorean sect as a symbol of regeneration, of new birth, assures us that, perhaps by an arduous path, Sappho had reached the term of her initiation. And yet her work too sets its seal on the separation of the sexes, on the rupture between Eros and the couple, on the dissociation of the sexual function and exalting love.

There were Greeks who realized the danger and tried to defend normal love. The most considerable effort was made by Plutarch. In the desire to recover *eros* for the benefit of marriage, he undertook to prove that women are as capable of inspiring and experiencing love as boys are. And although the position of women was improved, the care devoted by Plutarch to supporting his reasoning with quotations and examples shows that this was no foregone conclusion, even at the beginning of the second century A.D.

In his *Eroticos*, Plutarch pleads for a marriage of love, criticizing the marriage of reason and attacking those men who have little concern for loving or being loved—of whom

> some use the bait of a small fortune to attract unfortunate women and then throw them, together with their money, into household work and, scolding them all day long, control them like servants, while the others get with child the first woman who comes along and, more anxious to have children than to have a wife, behave like the male cicada who drops his seed on an onion or any other vegetable.

The scene is at Thespiai at the moment of the Erotides, a festival of Love which was celebrated every fourth year, and we learn at once that Plutarch had in the past come to this place to sacrifice to Eros with his young wife. In spite of these favourable circumstances, the dialogue never rises to the plane of the sacred. It does, however, convey something of the atmosphere of superficial religiosity and animation characteristic of places of pilgrimage; and the animation reaches its climax when the crowd abandons the traditional gatherings and rejoicings to mass in front of the house of Ismenodora, a young and beautiful widow who has just carried off an adolescent boy with whom she is in love. Of the characters in the dialogue (two of whom are *erastes* of the boy) some take the side of homosexuality and treat with scorn 'that other love, effeminate and bastard, enervating and stay-at-home, clinging to women's dresses and beds, and always in search of transports and delights unworthy of a man', while the others, Plutarch among them, cast doubt on the disinterestedness of love between men:

> If the love of boys rejects pleasure, this is because it is ashamed and is afraid of punishment; because it needs an honourable pretext for approaching beautiful boys, it brings to the fore friendship and virtue. It covers itself with dust in the arena, takes cold baths, and is always frowning; outwardly it gives itself the airs of a philosopher and a sage, because of the law, and then at night, when all is quiet, 'sweet it is to pluck the fruit when the watcher is away'!

But if unnatural physical love still allows of loving tenderness, then, says Plutarch, *a fortiori* the love of man for woman must do so. And indeed there is only one love. Let Eros, therefore, triumphing over individuality, unite the souls of the two partners in a fusion so close 'that they no longer wish to be two nor believe that they are so'.

In this way he attempts to extend Plato's sublime theme of complementarity to conjugal love. Had he succeeded, it would have been a considerable event—the reintegration of all the elements of love, the restoration of the myth for the benefit of normal love, the rehabilitation of marriage and of the couple. Unfortunately, though overflowing with good intentions, Plutarch lacked genius—and this in two ways. He was certainly not a great philosopher. Nor was he, like Socrates or Plato, a 'daimonic' person—less than ever at the time when he wrote the *Eroticos*, within ten years of his death. The liberty of his early works had been replaced by a dualism not far from that of the Gnostics, a dualism which he mistakenly thought could be deduced from a passage in the *Laws*. The high priest of the official polytheism had ousted the initiate of Eleusis, the theologian had replaced the mystic. It is in vain that, throughout the *Eroticos*, he refers to Plato's thinking, recalls the themes of winged love (Eros-Pteros) and love as remembrance, and evokes the theory of the four madnesses—but by what strange degradation does the divine *mania* come to be associated here with Ismenodora's act of violence in carrying off a young man, who has hardly reached the age for marriage, in the hope of imposing their marriage on public opinion? Something essential is lacking to Plutarch's conception of *eros*, and this something is the great Socratic and Platonic discovery of amorous longing as the spring-board to purification and knowledge—the 'daimonism' of exalting love. And so the attempt to extend the Platonic philosophy of love to the couple may be considered to have failed; it envisaged a love deprived of its metaphysical and mystical dimension, a love which most couples would be content to do without. It is nonetheless regrettable that normal love never dared or was able to avail itself of the high Platonic doctrine.

Yet Plutarch's love was an advance on Aristotle's *philia:* it was a genuine love of the senses and the heart. Where it failed was on the spiritual or mental side. Plutarch did not practise the method of Diotima. He did not raise himself gradually from the sensual to the intelligible and on to something still more august. And yet, though failing to explore this region of communication, he was aware that the mystery of love lay there: 'Physical union with a wife' he wrote, 'is a source of friendship and, as it were, a shared participation in great mysteries'. The resemblance between this *hieron megalon* and St Paul's *mysterion mega* has caused astonishment, and it is true that the co-incidence—for it is no more—is striking; but Plutarch's thinking falls short and leaves us unsatisfied. Plato found other words and tones to transport us and introduce us into the very heart of these Mysteries. The *Symposium* and the *Phaedrus* have never been equalled, and the fact remains that it is to the love of boys that we owe the one and only great Western philosophy of love. All the same, Plutarch has the merit of having treated the love of man and woman with honour for the first time.

Was it really the first time? Was there not a mystical cult of marriage and of the heart, known to the Greeks and practised among them? And was not this sacred ethical doctrine largely the work of women, and therefore deeply interesting?

There was, in fact, a Pythagorean mystical cult of marriage. It was not a cult of love or of the couple, but a *cult of service.* Although the surviving fragments of treatises or letters attributed to the Pythagorean women[20] are late, the great themes of that School—order, proportion, harmony—recur in them. The Pythagorean sects, like the Platonists, made use of the mystical image of the sentry post, from which no one, any more than a soldier, has the right to run away; but Pythagorean pessimism put the stress on the idea of subordination and service.

This idea was to weigh heavily on the wife, in spite of the liberal element in the Pythagorean attitude to the condition of women. For following the example of the cosmos, the family (like the State) must be governed, and this function of governing belongs to the man by natural right and divine mandate. As for the woman, she will be the priestess of that holy temple which, in the Pythagorean view, a family hearth is.

Things had not changed much, it is clear: from whatever direction it was approached, the woman's lot was always submission. But since, this time, the man was not ruled by sordid considerations of expediency disguised under the deceptions of a conventional religion (as in the case of Ischomachos, forcing his young wife to promise before the gods 'to become such as she ought to be'), but based his actions on a genuine and living religion in which the wife could feel she had her own place (though a modest one); since, also, Pythagoreanism would give her subordination a mystical justification, the woman could and would rally to it with enthusiasm. And indeed she went one better and, in a kind of rivalry in asceticism, worked out the most austere of all the conjugal catechisms.

All the commonplaces of the traditional ethics reappear in it. The woman's function, though dignified by being regarded as sacred, was nonetheless to be subject to restraint, reserve, modesty. It reminds us of those dwarfs (mentioned by the author of the *Treatise on the Sublime*) who were shut up in boxes to prevent them from growing. In the Pythagorean woman, even knowledge and religion were kept on a tight rein; should she aspire to philosophy, it must be with the aim of acquiring a more correct awareness of her conjugal duties; if to intelligence, then to *applied* intelligence; if to piety, then piety towards the traditional gods, the founders of the city, the 'sober gods'. For there prevailed in these strong women the idea of the weak sex, which needs to be both sustained and restrained: Phintys taught that there were different virtues for the man and for the woman, and different occupations—an all too clear relapse from Socrates and Plato. It was for women to watch over their houses, to remain at home, to wait for and wait upon their husbands. Phintys enumerates the cases in which a woman may go out of her house: 'It will not be at nightfall, nor towards evening, but when the market-place is full, and then she will leave her house openly, either to be present at some solemnity or to do the household marketing, decently accompanied by a maidservant or, at most, by two'. To seclusion was added silence. Pythagoras had enjoined women 'to utter only salutary words'. But Theano teaches that the speech of a decent woman must not be audible to everyone and that she 'should be as reluctant to let her voice be heard by all as she would be to undress in front of strangers'. For, he says, 'in the voice there appear the feelings, character and disposition of her who speaks'.

Honour the gods, said Perictione, and no doubt parents too were to be honoured; but a woman's principal duty was to the marriage couch. She had to endure whatever might happen to her husband—whether he met with adversity, or fell short through mistaken judgment, weakness or drinking to excess, or even had affairs with other women. Such failings were allowed to men, but not to women, and for them the punishment was always ready. A woman had to remember this customary concession to men; she must not let herself be carried away by jealousy, and furthermore she had to endure her husband's anger, meanness, complaints, jealousy and reproaches, and any other defect he might have by nature.

Phintys likewise preaches piety towards the marriage bed, decency in clothing, restraint in the matter of going out of doors, abstention from the orgiastic festivals and from those of the Great Mother, exactitude and moderation in religious observances; but the first principle, which includes all the others, is to 'keep herself incorruptible in regard to her bed'. What is weakness in a man becomes a crime in a woman. Phintys recalls that in certain cases the law—rightly—punishes it with death.

There exist several letters of consolation addressed by Pythagorean women to friends of theirs whose husbands have fallen in love with courtesans. In all the theme is the same: the virtue of a wife consists not in spying on her husband, but in being his indulgent companion and patiently supporting his folly. Pythagoras, however, had recommended reciprocal fidelity. He had also advised women to observe simplicity and discretion in their behaviour and in their clothes; but here again the Pythagorean women went further. Perictione applied this principle to food, clothes, baths and hair style:

> Women who love food and drink and who dress too expensively are prone to stray into complete perversion and to conduct themselves ill with regard to the marriage bed and to many other matters. Therefore it is right, as regards hunger and thirst, to aim only at appeasing them, and this by frugal means; and as for cold, it is enough to provide against it with a fleece or with a hair tunic. To dress in clothes that are too thin and in colours derived from the dye of a shellfish or in any other sumptuous colours is a great folly. All that the body demands is not to be cold and, for decency's sake, not to be naked, it needs nothing else. . . . Therefore a woman will not wear gold or any stone from India or from elsewhere; she will not dress her hair with excessive artifices, nor anoint herself with scents that exhale the perfume of Arabia, nor make up her face to look more pale or more rosy, nor blacken her eyebrows and eyelashes, nor dye her white hair, nor, certainly, take frequent baths. The woman who pursues such refinements is seeking an admirer of feminine excesses. The beauty that comes of moderation, not that which results from these cosmetics, is the one that pleases women of good birth.

Phintys reinforces this with a characteristically Pythagorean meticulousness:

> A woman must be dressed with simplicity and without superfluity. She will succeed in this if, to clothe her body, she never uses transparent, striped or silken veils, but only modest white materials. In so doing she will avoid ostentation, luxury and coquetry, and will never cause a perverse jealousy in other women. She will absolutely renounce the wearing of gold or emerald. . . . Her face must not be heightened by a borrowed and foreign colouring, but by the natural tint of the skin, washed in water only. Modesty will be a better adornment for it, and in this way the woman will draw respect both to the companion of her life and to herself.

At the same time,

> a woman will utter and will listen to none but honourable words, will adapt herself to her husband's parents, will have no friends but his. She will live in conformity of opinions with him, and will regard as sweet or bitter the same things as he does. . . Lastly, she must live in such perfect conformity with usage and with a heart so sincere that *she must have no thought of her own.*

Oblation, submissiveness, seclusion, silence, absolute fidelity, effacement and circumspection (even in piety), simplicity of behaviour, sobriety, decency in speech, austerity in clothes, unlimited generosity with regard to the husband's failings—I wonder if some part of this lofty and severe conjugal morality did not pass into the conception of the Christian wife. One is reminded of the Epistle to the Corinthians and the Epistle to Timothy, and again of St John Chrysostom's homily on the choice of a wife—except that there is more serenity in the Pythagorean women: the comparison brings out the nagging tone of the early Church Fathers. And yet the morality and way of thinking which we have been discussing were purely pagan: they were in conformity with early Pythagoreanism. This had been transmitted without a break, orally, secretly and faithfully, through the confraternities; yet the subjection of the wife had become more severe. Had these women, in intensifying it to the point of asceticism, felt that they were asserting themselves, rather than submitting? Did they by these means persuade themselves that their dignity had been saved? In any case, the principle remains clear: the divine order demands *that the woman be subordinated*. To submit is, for her, the natural way of regulating her life by the Law and respecting the Oath. I was right, surely, to use the phrase 'a cult of service'.

Pythagoreanism, like Platonism, took as its essential aim union with God through purification; but the Pythagoreans did not, like Plato, put their trust in love as the agent of purification. As is well known, they practised a mysticism of numbers; but this was accessible to a few disciples only. The rest obeyed the *acousmata*, which were a kind of precepts regulating meticulously the details of life—and sometimes of love: one should have children in order to provide servants for the gods, one does not make love in a temple, or have a child by 'a woman who wears gold' (that is, a courtesan), and one should make love in the winter rather than in the summer. But a morality subject to an external law is not a *pure* morality: purification is essentially separation, elimination; and so a thing that is added, even if it is a rule of conduct, is already to some extent a compromise with the lie of matter and may even help to lend its negativeness a kind of structure. Time showed that Pythagoreanism had in it a tendency to degenerate into moralism, and its mistrust of human nature made this moralism an austere one. Plato, the philosopher of love, thought that 'our worst desires are impulses towards the good, which we direct badly'; but when the

Pythagoreans asked the ritual question 'What is the truest thing that can be said?' their answer was 'That men are wicked'. This mistrust took women as its target: in spite of its disinterestedness, of the purity of its intentions, Pythagoreanism—undergoing a degradation like that of Christianity, a degradation that seems characteristic of religions— became a servant of policy. It gave its blessing to the matrimonial system in which the woman is oppressed and humiliated. And in due course the perfect Pythagorean wife took as the object of her mystical striving a situation in no way different from that of the wife-as-associate: 'Thou shalt not found the friendship which thou owest to thy husband upon the perfection of his virtue', says one of these fragments, 'for it is the well-being of the association that is its principle'.

It is not perhaps always realized that Pythagoreanism—in this also like Christianity—imposes subordination on the wife, not on woman. As Jesus surrounded Himself with women so Pythagoras admitted them into his *hetaeriai*. In his list of illustrious Pythagoreans, Iamblicus names seventeen women: they must have been unmarried, for how could they, as wives, have reconciled the semi-communal life of the Brotherhoods with the rules of seclusion? In this, Pythagoras was not departing from the beaten track: even fifth-century Athens—where the status of a woman was no more enviable than that of a metic— admitted priestesses of purification and women-philosophers, celibate and preferably foreign. What was undesirable was the ascendancy which love might give to a wife or mistress, especially should she happen to be a brilliant woman. Pericles learned this to his cost: his love for Aspasia and their perfect union were never forgiven him. He himself was not free from the prevailing prejudice: he relapsed into it when he was no longer blinded by love, as is shown by his conduct towards Elpinikë, Kimon's sister, an intelligent and courageous Athenian woman who, braving public opinion, took part in politics. He ridiculed her, as Marie Delcourt has discerningly pointed out, 'in the same way as his enemies had denigrated Aspasia, and he treated her arguments as the mumblings of an old woman'.

The austere Pythagorean morality did not exclude a certain kind of conjugal love. From the beginning, the Pythagoreans had taught women that it was right to love one's husband much more than one's parents (and in that sect parents, as is well known, received veneration on a par with the gods). To men they recommended that they should cherish their companion, respect the pact made with her and, in marriage, hold everything in common with her. In fact, conjugal affection was thus incorporated into the splendid communal conception of Pythagorean friendship. It was a decidedly unamorous kind of love, nearer to what the Christians later called *caritas* or *agape* than to the *eros* of the philosophers, and it was gravely deficient: it was a consecrated but not a sacred love—in contrast with *eros*, which far from deriving its religious character from a rite or ceremony, is itself a sacrament, not merely sacred but sacral: that is to say, able to communicate sacredness. In Pythagorean marriage, as in the Christian sacrament, the consecration results from the commitment entered into before God. To be operative, it requires the sincere and sustained adhesion of one, at least, of the two partners. The morality developed by the Pythagorean women demonstrated that, through constant sacrifice, conjugal affection may become religious by a path other than *eros*. But this ascetic discipline was essentially a solitary achievement, that of a quasi-monastic vocation accomplished in marriage. Once again, it was a cult of service, of commitment, of obedience to God— anything but a cult of love.

Legend has it that Pythagoras himself was frantically in love with Theano, his wife and disciple, the daughter of his spirit. However this may be, we owe to Theano a strange recommendation. According to Diogenes Laertius, 'she advised a woman, when she must be united with her husband, to put off her reserve at the same time as her clothes, but to put it on again when she rises, together with her clothes'. There is here a contrast, if not a clash, which smacks of the art of love rather than of the philosophy of love. It shocked Plutarch: 'A woman', he said, 'must clothe herself in her reserve, even in love-making. The more tenderly husband and wife love each other, the more they show each other a respect which is the guarantee of that tenderness'. So it was in the name of a man's respect for his wife that he could get drunk with another woman or have fun with a servant girl.[12] Plutarch's idea of respect covered a multitude of sins.

In drawing attention to some similarities between pre-Christian and Christian ideas I may have laid myself open to misunderstandings. My intention is not to establish a parallel between paganism and Christianity, but to show that *their conflict about love cannot be reduced in an elementary way to the opposition between pagan and Christian*. It seems to me that the division that existed within pagan morality should itself discourage any simplification of this kind.

To resume: Greece worked out a complete and coherent doctrine of total love, or *eros*—in other words, a philosophy of love; and I believe I have shown that this marvel of civilized thinking based itself constantly on primitive, sacred, pre-religious conceptions of the *pure*, the *impure* and *purification*. I have pointed out also that, in consequence of historical circumstances which can only be deplored, women were excluded from this philosophy of love, and so there came a rupture between sexuality and spirituality. In the course of time Platonism, imperfectly understood, led Western thought into an ill-founded idealism of escape and evasion.

In opposition to the Platonic philosophy of love, there was the marriage of reason. This institution contained variants, ranging from mere economic association to pious Pythagorean marriage, and one constant—the principle of woman's subordination. And this, which certain Pythagorean women carried to the pitch of abnegation, led in due course to the first repercussions of an anti-erotic cult of marriage. *Eros*, when introduced into Pythagorean marriage, was bound either to triumph over its moralism or to be defeated by it and moralized out of existence.

Thus paganism knew the two kinds of love—the reasonable, and that other which was never allowed to wives. Sacred, sacral, purifying and exalting, *eros* was above all daimonic, binding together the lower and the higher, man and the divine, spirit and flesh. The flesh was necessarily present, if only at the stage of aspiration, desire, delight and motive force; for without the flesh, love would find nothing on which to exercise its purifying activity, and the soul would not feel itself engaged in the universal movement, moved by the Law, confronted with the divine. This salutary tension between spirit and flesh conferred on the flesh a function which it was the characteristic of

Platonism to recognize—and which Christianity was never to concede to it. Suspect to the Christians, but capable of being sanctified by the sacrament of marriage, the flesh became—to the Manichees and the Gnostics, and, later, to the Cathars—an evil in itself, which nothing, not even the sacrament, could render legitimate. The morality of these extremists was bound to be either a desperate abstention or a recourse to the orgy, in which the body, that 'vesture of shame', was 'trampled underfoot'. These were the alternatives imposed by a rigid dualism and pessimism, from which Platonism was better able than Christianity to escape. In the secrecy of the Platonic soul, the flesh itself leads to the divine.

If Eros is all that we have said, and not a dead god or a philosopher's exquisite invention, it could not disappear. Even in a world subject to the absolute primacy of an anti-erotic religion, it would find some way of surviving. It would have its avatars and its epiphanies. Let us now choose a period and a society profoundly impregnated with dogma, and let us there see if we can follow the vein of *eros* within the hard grain of the marble of Catholicism.

THE CHRISTIAN MOMENT

I am carnal, sold under sin.
In me (that is, in my flesh) dwelleth no good thing.
ST PAUL, Romans, vii, 14 and 18

HÉLOÏSE, OR EROS IN REBELLION

Insufficient thought is given to the fact that modern love was born not with Tristan but with Héloïse and Abélard. And it was a conjugal love, though this husband and this wife were persecuted (for not all marriages run smoothly). Re-reading their wonderful letters, one finds that they speak directly to our time. The fable of Tristan teaches us the way out of life (out into nothingness, not into being): it is a great myth of death but no true myth of the couple, only a kind of romantic decoy, set up for the rivalry of lovers and constantly moving away as they approach. But the love of Héloïse and Abélard was greedy for reality. Héloïse, even more than Abélard, was determined to live her love temporally: she hurled herself into it and committed herself wholly to it. It is the first existential love: Iseult belongs to legend, but Héloïse is one of the most exalted figures in history. She was the first in modern times, in partnership with Abélard, to analyse love—before Dante, as Nordström has observed, making this one of the key points in his refutation of Burckhardt. She was the only woman of her time to proclaim a morality of love, uttering from the cloister, to which Abélard had relegated her, the most rebellious cries yet heard from a woman: 'If it is a crime to live in this way, then I love crime, and I am now innocent against my will'. Again, 'if I suffer because of [my sins], it is not because I have committed them, but because I am no longer committing them'. And again, 'as for me, God knows I would not have hesitated to follow you or to go before you into hell, if you had ordered me to do so'. And all this in the first half of the twelfth century, when Héloïse was an Abbess!

She had at first refused to marry him, but her reason for this is clear beyond doubt—it was to avoid damaging Abélard's career (for marriage, though not forbidden to a cleric, a canon of Notre Dame, was far from being considered creditable). It shows, in fact, how far she was already his wife by virtue of her concern for his glory, and of her submission to his decisions—whether these involved marrying him, leaving him, rushing to clandestine meetings with him, or shutting herself up in a convent. As for Abélard, he was so much a husband that he could naïvely write that she 'took the veil spontaneously at my command' (*illa tamen prius ad imperium nostrum sponte velata*). To be fair, he could also be her husband in a more generous way: he gave over to her his beloved Abbey of the Paraclete, and never ceased to protect her, direct her and draw her upwards towards those spiritual heights which he himself in the end attained. She, however, remained fiercely faithful to human love: the only sacrifice he succeeded in obtaining from her was silence.

It was a great sacrifice from a woman whose culture and intelligence were exceptional (they even astonished St Bernard) and who was considered as a prodigy of learning, capable of holding her own with the greatest theologians. Yet from the day when she met Abélard she subordinated all this to him. It was a subordination that had nothing servile about it. When she humiliated herself before him ('you possess surpassing knowledge, and I have only the humility of my ignorance') and when she describes herself as his servant or assures him that to her it is less sweet to be called wife than to be called his mistress or even his wench, one can see at once that this is not to be taken at its face value: these pretences of abasement are the simple tricks of feminine love, designed to increase by illusion the distance which love has to cover and to test its strength. But they are all the more striking, and they provide clearer evidence of the purely loving nature of her submission, if the woman who is thus humiliating herself is of exceptional quality. In them, in fact, Héloïse was exemplifying the woman's situation, and was demonstrating that the great concern of a woman is to love one man and one only. This is the supreme goal. To achieve it everything else should be sacrificed and subordinated.

The love between Héloïse and Abélard was a physical passion fully lived through. The letters leave no doubt of this—indeed certain confessions in them are astonishing. I cannot help seeing a certain pride in Abélard's contrition, when he wrote to his wife: 'We omitted none of the steps of love, and we added to them the strangest joys that love could invent.' And what is one to make of his striking Héloïse 'from love, not from anger'—blows which 'far surpassed the savour of any balm'? Or of the sin they committed 'in the most shameful manner possible' in the refectory of the convent at Argenteuil, a most venerable and sacred place? Their great love lacked only one dimension, the mystical. Héloïse and Abélard remain realists—great and powerful characters, but earthly. In time Abélard found his way to God— through reasoning, not through mysticism. As for Héloïse, she was afraid that, by taking the path to God, she would take something from a love which she was determined to keep entirely for Abélard. In Héloïse there is not a single utterance that is really Christian. The tragedy of that passionate soul was that it could not approach God except through human love. And that way was barred to her. Abélard, using his triple authority as husband, as superior in the hierarchy and as theologian, ordered her to turn her back on love and committed her to the monastic life, for which she had no vocation, only resignation. For Héloïse truly sacrificed her life to the man whom she called 'my only one'. Sometimes one sees in the Abbess of the Paraclete a kind of despair at the thought of having made a bad bargain: 'What have I left to hope for, now that I have lost you?' 'Not piety, only an order from you has delivered me up so young to the rigours of monastic life', she wrote lucidly to her husband: 'if by this I have not acquired a new merit in your eyes, *judge of the vanity of my sacrifice*'. And again: 'I can expect no divine recompense, since the love of God was not my motive'.

Unfortunately there was no common measure—there never had been—between Abélard's love and that of Héloïse. Abélard always subordinated love to his career and his own glory—there was an element in him of intolerable self-satisfaction ('My talent for theology equalled my genius as a philosopher', he said, and his wife of course replied: 'What king, what philosopher could equal your glory?'), and he was constantly denying his past, rejoicing that he had been saved from the foulness 'in which he had plunged as though in mud'. Meanwhile Héloïse subordinated everything to love and, though she was an Abbess, considered herself as having been hurled headlong down from a sublime rank—that of Abélard's loving wife. Fate, after having brought her to 'wonderful delights', had made her 'the most miserable of beings', for 'the higher we rise, the heavier is the fall'. In vain Abélard tried to inspire her with enthusiasm for her new condition—Héloïse told him, once for all, what her piety was worth:

> They praise my chastity, not knowing how false I am . . . I burn with all the flames kindled in me by the ardours of the flesh. . . . The amorous pleasures we have tested together are so sweet to me that I cannot bring myself to detest them, nor even to drive them from my memory. Wherever I go they present themselves to my eyes and awaken my desires. The illusion of them does not spare my sleep. Even during the solemnities of the Mass, where prayer should be more than ever pure, obscene images assail my poor soul and fill it more than the service fills it. . . . Not only our acts have remained deeply engraved in my memory together with your face, but also the places and the times that witnessed them, so that I am again with you, repeating those acts, and find no rest even in my bed. Sometimes the movements of my body betray my thoughts and revealing words escape me. . . .

Abélard set to work to persuade Héloïse that the acts and gestures, whose memory was so dear to her, were infamous. But with her deep sense and understanding of love, Héloïse could not help regarding that memory as sacred and venerating it as she venerated Abélard himself. Because of the strength of her love, she was torn in two. The more Abélard tried to make her have a bad conscience, the more she rebelled, blasphemed and declared herself incapable of any repentance:

> Besides, can it be said that the soul repents (however great the mortification imposed on the body) when it clings to the relish of sin and burns with its old desires? . . . True continence is more a matter of the spirit than of the flesh. Men recite my praises, but I have no merit in the eyes of God, Who penetrates the heart, and to Whom nothing remains hid. I am thought pious, it is true; but in our day, for the most part, religion is only hypocrisy, and a reputation for holiness is accorded to the person who does not go against the

accepted prejudices . . . What is the good, indeed, of abstaining from evil if one does not really do good? 'Do good and eschew evil', says the Scripture. But it is vain to follow this counsel, even to the letter, if this is not done for the love of God. In every station to which life has led me, God knows I have feared to offend you more than Him. It is you, not Him, that I have sought to please. It was at your command that I took the veil, not by divine vocation.

She reminded him of this so often that he harshly told her to cease 'that old complaint' and to 'stop her recriminations'. Héloïse never loved or served anyone but Abélard.

Her confession of this is a tragic one, the confession of an utter defeat. For the love she refused to deny was doubly doomed. It was doomed in its earthly vocation: when she became pregnant she was forced to leave Abélard and to hide her condition under a nun's habit; her son was taken away from her and soon died; she could never be known by her husband's name, for Abélard's reputation demanded that the marriage be kept secret. It was condemned also in its super-natural vocation or sublimation. Every soul that is truly in love is already, by that fact, committed to the adventure of God, an adventure of communication and union, and this was true of Héloïse as much as anyone. Hers was no inert soul, incapable of effusion and transports, but a passionate and generous nature, to which was added a mind devoted to truth and knowledge: she was, in fact, one of those whose vocation it is to move forwards through human love. The tragedy of Héloïse—and it was much worse than that of Abélard, for Héloïse was mutilated in the spirit—was to find that way blocked. Every-thing combined to discourage her from seeking God in the way her heart indicated; everything combined to hide from her the existence of any way out, by which human love could find an opening into the other love. Abélard's ascendancy over her was added to the all-pervading Catholicism of her time. Héloïse was at no stage a heretic, and she never questioned the basis of that doctrine which Abélard embodied with such authority—an authority reinforced by her love. Also, she was in charge of the Convent of the Paraclete—she was com-mitted to a life in the Church. And so, rebel as she was, she became a supreme example of the conflict between *eros* and Christianity, of the agonizing choice which that involved.

Nordström was right, the letters of Héloïse inaugurate a new period in the history of Western man. They prefigure the two basic attitudes of modern love. When these are made into a method or a doctrine, there arise the libertine spirit and masochistic indulgence—two major deviations of *eros* when repressed by Christianity.

A RELIGION OF LOVE

How was it possible for a religion of love to put up a barrier against what was most religious in pagan love—its daimonic side, its relation to God, its mysticism? Was not Christian love—like that of Socrates, that of Plato and, later, that of Plotinus—seeking to become as like as possible to God? Is not this what Paul was showing and developing in his great allegory of growth, in which love is treated, as in the *Symposium*, as a means of drawing closer and rising higher?[22] But when Paul recommends the imitation of God, he is careful to propose a model in the person of Christ; and it does not require long reflection to see that there is a great distance between love according to Plato— which at any rate begins with the choice of one person, venerated in his scandalous uniqueness, and relies on the impetus of amorous desire, on the madness it produces in us, to make us remember God and bring us to the inner experience of the divine—and love according to Jesus, a love of God which we are commanded to extend to all men, to enemies even more than to friends. To put it shortly: the starting point of Christian love is detachment, and *caritas* (*agape*) goes against our nature from the first. In contrast, *eros* starts by going in accordance with nature, it lets itself be enchanted and captivated by the flesh before sublimating it, and detachment is progressive—is the effect of that erotic purification whose stages Diotima described. *Caritas* (*agape*) begins with and is based on the love of God, while *eros* leads to this. *Caritas* exists in virtue of the law, *eros is* Law. The one skirts passionate love, while the other passes impulsively through it.

The mystery of the Couple lies in this 'going through' and in the reversal of values produced in the course of it. It is there that, as the flesh is delivered from the spirit, promotion takes place from the profane to the sacred. Christianity could not be altogether unaware of this mystery, which is mentioned once in the famous passage in the Epistle to the Ephesians. But a word, however radiant, cannot take the place of a doctrine, and the word *mysterion*, which the Christians though they were to give it a new meaning, owed to the Greeks, was destined to dazzle rather than illuminate. One cannot help thinking that this word encouraged the confusion between the Christian mystery and the mystery of *eros*, between love of one's neighbour and passionate love— a confusion that was often exploited. Every time anyone wished to give to *agape* a little freedom on the sexual side, the Apostle would be quoted:

> For this cause shall a man leave his father and mother, and shall be joined unto his wife, and they two shall be one flesh. This is a great mystery. . . . (Ephesians, v, 31-32.)

Paul, however, was careful to define his meaning: '. . . but I speak concerning Christ and the church'. The mystery here is that of *caritas* (*agape*)—a mystery of love, no doubt, but not of the Couple, and, considered as a basis for marriage, a second best. Such misunderstanding of *eros* is specifically Christian. The love of the sexes is practically absent from the Gospels: it may be glanced at, sidelong, here and there, in the course of references to marriage, to chastity (which is always preferred to it, as appears from the passage in St Matthew about the voluntary eunuchs, a passage which Origen had the misfortune to take literally), to adultery and to the sanctions of the Mosaic law.

Plato had taught that the love whose object is the perpetuation of the species is sacred, though in a lesser degree than the love that aims at spiritual procreation. But in the Gospels marriage is, at most, an honourable condition which does not enjoy any great favour (any more than do family ties); human love, even if sanctified by the Sacrament, remains a secondary way; as for love outside marriage, there is no question of its having access to the divine. Nothing is more foreign to the spirit of the Gospels than to admit that the desire of the creature may be, basically, desire for God and capable of leading us to God—nothing, unless perhaps one thing: the strange, perplexing familiarity of Socrates with the flesh, his conception of love as a militant chastity on the frontier between the pure and the impure, his practice of a sexual self-control constantly tested by temptation. This attitude of challenge was destined to make its appearance sometimes in the Christian world, but it was always held to be heretical.[23] It is remarkable that, in Christ's Temptation in the desert, the Devil made no use of the temptation of the flesh. Christ appears there as the anti-Socrates.

True, Jesus surrounded Himself with people of low fame, with women who had sinned generously, as Socrates with dissipated boys; but Jesus had no choice in regard to the social flotsam which He collected as a magnet collects iron filings. And although He was, on the whole, less severe towards prostitutes than towards other sinners, this may be because they showed less arrogance, or because they were already harshly treated by the Law. It has, at least, to be admitted that there is, in Jesus, no sign of any tentative interest in the sin of the flesh, of any predilection for its ambiguity, its fundamental contradiction, its power to offer a choice between perdition and salvation.

And so the basic difference between the Christian and the pagan conceptions of purity became established, the former being abstention and the latter emulation and recuperation. But what began by being abstention soon became repression in St Paul, in his obsession with the flesh, his pessimism and his hatred of women. The Gospels had raised, if not the condition, at least the dignity of women (for Christ, by giving to women, as also to slaves, better reasons for obeying, in fact gave His blessing to the subordination of women as well as to the submission of slaves); but St Paul condemns Woman harshly, laying on her the responsibility for original sin. The theme of the woman as temptress and corruptress came to serve as a pretext for a debasement of her condition. It was not Adam who was seduced, but the woman, so let the women keep silent and remain veiled; moreover, the man was not created for the woman, but the woman for the man, and therefore she should bear on her head a sign of her dependence.

Another hardening of the morality of the Gospels took place: the sin of the flesh became the sin of sins. It was Paul who established a graded distinction between the sins committed outside the body and the far graver sins committed with the body. To him, the body was the temple of the Holy Spirit:

> Know ye not that your bodies are the members of Christ? shall I then take the members of Christ, and make them the members of an harlot? God

forbid. What? know ye not that he which is joined to an harlot is one body? for two, saith he, shall be one flesh. But he that is joined unto the Lord is one spirit. Flee fornication. (1 Corinthians, vi, 15-18.)

This antithesis between spiritual union and physical union considered as a source of corruption led straight to dualism, with the addition of a new idea—that the body does not belong to us. 'Now the body is not for fornication, but for the Lord; and the Lord for the body. And God hath both raised up the Lord, and will also raise up us by his own power . . . Glorify God in your body' (1 Corinthians, vi, 13-14, 20). The meaning is clear: physical love is profanation, and the condemnation is extended to every sexual relationship—even in marriage, thought Tertullian in his commentary on the Pauline text. 'It is better to marry than to burn', preached Paul to husbands and wives, 'and come together again, that Satan tempt you not for your incontinency. But I speak this by permission, and not of commandment. For I would that all men were even as I myself.' 'It is good for a man not to touch a woman.' 'Art thou bound unto a wife? seek not to be loosed. Art thou loosed from a wife? seek not a wife.' 'So then he that giveth her [his virgin] in marriage doeth well; but he that giveth her not in marriage doeth better.' 'The unmarried woman careth for the things of the Lord, that she may be holy both in body and in spirit: but she that is married careth for the things of the world, how she may please her husband.' So long as the Apostle confined himself to teaching that marriage was not favourable to the spiritual vocation, he was still true to the Gospels; but when he went on to the degrading conception of a prophylactic marriage, when he treated carnal sin as the essence of sin and allowed his hatred of the flesh to overflow in insults, imprecations and threats against the 'fornicators', then he was forcing the Gospel spirit and transforming a religion which ignored passionate love, which did not take the way of *eros*, into an anti-erotic religion.

Unfortunately, Pauline theology became Christian doctrine, and, from among its teaching, it was precisely the crude dogmatism of *Romans* and *Corinthians* that got the better of the ample symbolism of the Epistles from captivity. The narrow spirit of the former too frequently inspired the teachings of the early Church Fathers. St Jerome, St Ambrose and St John Chrysostom, going beyond the Pauline

severity, engaged in a bitter struggle to gain recognition for the
absolute superiority of virginity and widowhood over the married
state. St Jerome's attacks were so violent that he was accused of
Manicheeism. All this is a long way from *eros*; but in addition the
quarrels of the theologians, their exchanges of mocking or acid letters
(deplored by St Augustine), take us a long way from *agape*. What had
been new and without precedent in the Gospel teaching—love (not,
of course, that of the couple, but 'By this shall all men know that ye
are my disciples, if ye have love one to another')—was forgotten or
smothered in the ardour of polemics. It is hard to avoid admiring the
vigour with which the Fathers drew up their horrifying picture of
conjugal life. St John Chrysostom enumerated the afflictions of
marriage—pregnancy, birth pangs, giving suck, the consequent
painful illnesses, love losing its savour, physical union ending in disgust.
And again St Jerome: 'The breast swells, the child cries, domesticity
keeps the nerves on edge, household cares allow no rest, and in the
end all the imagined blessings are mowed down by death.'[24] These
criticisms of the married state were invariably aimed at discouraging
its adoption, and were always supplemented by a passage in praise
of monastic asceticism. And so there arose, in the Christianity of the
Fathers, an undervaluation (to put it as charitably as possible) of love
and of conjugal union and an overvaluation of chastity (that diapason
of Christian morality, now set up as the norm). It was a generalized
chastity, regarded as normal and natural—not, as in Platonism, an
exalted stage in that domination of the sensory which, while it should
certainly be the aim of everyone, could and should in fact be attained
only by a few sages, often at the end of their lives. 'Know that virginity
is the state of nature—marriage did but come afterwards',[25] wrote St
Jerome to Eustochius, mingling in his robust way coarseness and gusto
with poetry—not only 'Be thou the cicada of the night, let thy tears
water thy couch, watch, and be as the sparrow in the desert', but also
'when thou risest at night to pray let it not be indigestion that maketh
thee belch but inanition'. The tempered asceticism preached by Socrates
and Plato and, a century and a half before St Jerome, by Plotinus—
an asceticism designed 'not so much to constrain the body as to avoid
directing attention to the body'—was now replaced by long drawn out

mortifications that did violence both to the body and to the soul. The exaggeration of fasting was aimed less at training a man to dominate his appetites than at weakening these and allowing less purchase to concupiscence. 'Not that God finds pleasure in the rumblings of our intestines, in the emptiness of the stomach and in the burning of the lungs', wrote St Jerome, 'but that, without these, purity could not be safe.'

A religion that set out not to control the body but to torment, break and crush it, was bound to provoke terrible reactions. The excesses that arose, from the earliest Christian centuries onwards, within the ranks of those who were vowed to celibacy (monks and 'virgins') as well as among the *agapetai* (denounced by St Jerome as a plague, *agapetarum pestis*), prove that asceticism had not stifled the vitality of the Christian masses: side by side with the exemplary mortification of a number of saints, martyrs and anchorites and a minority of the faithful who were constant and sincere, it caused an extraordinary increase in the numbers of debauched and licentious people—and, above all, of hypocrites. There had, of course always been disorderly and shameless people, as well as heroes and sages; but in the endless conflict between flesh and spirit the gap between the two terms had now been considerably widened, and the believer found himself divided between the demands of his own nature and those of a fierce anti-naturalism. As a bow discharges the more violently the more tightly it has been stretched, the believer often swung suddenly from austere virtue into base sin. Some men preserved the appearances and braving the threat of damnation, fornicated under cover of them; but others called in question the very teachings of the Church and drew the most aberrant conclusions: as early as the second century Christianity was surrounded by a festering abundance of Gnostic heresies. Disciples of Simon Magus, Montanists, Messalians, Adamites, Carpocratians and Gnostic Barbelites and Borborites drew a distinction between the absolute excellence of the spirit and the ignominy of matter and the flesh, of procreation, of marriage and of the Sacrament which was its deceptive sanctification.

In principle the Gnostics, like the orthodox Christians, recommended total continence; but for the Gnostics the real sin was to mix the spirit and the flesh and bind them together. That the Gnostic conception is opposed to Platonic daimonism needs to be stressed, since Gnostics, Platonists and neo-Platonists have often been treated as akin (a confusion of which Plotinus made short work). In many of the heretical sects the idea soon spread that the sexual act, provided it does not imply pro-creation or involve the spirit or encroach on *gnosis* (knowledge), is a matter of indifference—may indeed be moral, since it not only consolidates the dualistic separation of evil and good, but humiliates the flesh, tramples it underfoot and procures for man a healthy feeling of his degradation. The man who has sinned is considered to have received the illumination of his own spirit.

This way of darkness is to be found in other religions, sometimes in the form of a heresy, sometimes recognized as orthodox (as, for instance, the Shiva-ite way of the left hand in Hinduism); but in some of the Gnostic sects it became exaggerated and harsh—both more ascetic and more abject. A new view of the world then appeared, a world of degradation and perdition in which sin acquired a positive value; and a tragic tone made itself heard, that of oriental pessimism, which Greek wisdom had proved better able to ward off than had Christianity: now it surged in, carrying away in its flood the great mystical landmarks of Greek thought—Eros, Apollo and Dionysus—as well as the popular divinities of polytheism. What distinguishes Christianity from paganism, even more than its doctrines, is its dramatization of religious feeling. St Paul was already prefiguring the baroque when he exclaimed: 'Who shall deliver me from the body of this death?' Plato also had thought that to purify oneself meant that the soul should strip itself of the corporeal; but this stripping was mental: the Platonic soul was delivered as soon as thought had put things in their places. With St Paul the tone is debased from thought to cry, from serenity to pathos—to that pathos which is so foreign to Platonism (to, for instance, the fervent yet restrained account of the death of Socrates in the *Phaedo*) and is possibly the result of a meta-physical insufficiency. A fierce, harsh and static dualism of Eastern origin was now raised up in clear opposition to the critical dualism of Platonism which always contained the possibility of conversion. In Platonic thinking there was no melodrama, no agonized doubt of salvation, for evil was already dominated by the mere fact of being discerned and known: in Christianity, on the contrary, all is drama, expiation, damnation, redemption, passion; sin is not error but disobedience and revolt. And as soon as the sin of the flesh became the exemplary sin and the sexual act a profanation (except for a resigned concession to marriage), with virginity considered as the state of excellence, the full weight of terror fell upon the flesh and upon love. So we have the paradox of a religion that both despises the flesh and cultivates the obsession with it (as in various of St Paul's confessions, in his 'thorn in the flesh', for instance, and in the dreams of St Augustine). Even in marriage, physical love became subject to indiscreet laying down of the law by the Church and was obliged to conform to its commands. In the world which issued from Christianity, *eros* was essentially tormented, torn to shreds between religion and its own law. Love became a problem. Instead of a sacred doctrine of love, instead of a philosophy of love, there was now a casuistry.

While the new religion failed in its struggle against licence, it triumphed in its conflict with philosophical *eros*. But in raising its barrier across the purifying and exalting way of *eros*, it threw man back upon the creature, with the result, usually, of making him face human nature with demands it could not meet. Hence, in the Catholic world, that latent despair of any 'great love'. We have already listened to decisive evidence of this despair, the evidence of Héloïse rejected by God precisely insofar as she was called to Him. In the last of her love-letters the theme of suffering predominates, and there appear at the same time nihilist and masochistic images: 'The thought of your death is already for us a kind of death.' 'Remember certain words which pierce our soul with a sort of death.' Fate 'has emptied his quiver to shoot at me—had he a single arrow left, he would have searched for a place in me for a new wound.' Frequent words like 'strike', 'wounds' and 'blows' alternate with great self-conscious lamentations: 'O unhappiest of all unhappy women! Among the unfortunate the most unfortunate! . . . I consume myself in plaints . . . I yield to the bitterness of regret, my joys end in an overwhelming sadness.' Héloïse had discovered the pleasure of suffering. And here our knowledge ends: the letters after this are strictly and ostentatiously professional. Is this the sign of a final repentance? Of a vocation that came late but came at last? If so, she would have told Abélard, who had urged her to it. It seems clear that the Abbess was doomed to aridity. The joys of sublime love—when it frees itself from every obstacle to union—were to find other great feminine voices to express them. But these would not be within the framework of human love. It was the Divine Bridegroom whom the women in love would join in the Marriage chamber. And yet—from the flesh to the spirit—Eros was present, whole, under the Christian disguise. Love, to avoid dying, went into hiding.

HADEWYCH, OR EROS UNDERGROUND

What is this sound like the belling of a stag in the night, this voice sometimes so limpid that it becomes the song of a nightingale, sometimes hoarse and stifled as though exhausted and yet quickly resuming, more and more monotonous and obsessed? It is Hadewych, singing of *Minne*, of love—but the lover to whom she appeals is that Other whom we seek, the celestial double of our earthly being, the means by which we aspire to recompose the mystical Couple before sinking into Unity. Her soul was so fervent that she moved forward intrepidly where none of her people had dared to go, so fervent that she invented, to celebrate her adventure, a quite new language, whose passionate alliterations no translation can render. She came a hundred years before Ruusbroec and nearly fifty before Eckhart, and she represents gloriously the great Northern school of mysticism—one province only of the universal mysticism, but strangely well defined.[26] The greatness of this figure is only beginning to be realized, standing out as it does against the background of the agitation of the *beggards* and *béguines*. The movement was a feminine one, and this may have something to do with the predominance in it of the visionary and ecstatic. It is represented in Flanders by a series of inspired women, Marie d'Oignies, Christine de Saint-Trond, Ludgarde de Tongres, Beatrys de Nazareth, Bloemardinne the Heretic, and in the Rhineland by Hildegarde von Bingen, Elisabeth von Schönau, Mechtilde of Magdeburg and Margaretha Ebner, but none of these figures has the purity and rigour of Hadewych.

Little is known of her life. She appears to have directed an assembly of two thousand *béguines* at Nivelles, and to have been able, like St Teresa of Avila, to combine the exigencies of active life with those of asceticism and contemplation. She was a writer of genius, an out-standing poet with a bold intelligence and a turbulent, impetuous soul; she was also a creature of flesh and blood as determined to live as to abase herself and, like Héloïse, at grips with a devouring love—but this time a lawful love, not opposed but authorized by religion, a love which attained its difficult but glorious development, in fact a happy love. There is no masochistic tendency in Hadewych, even though she wrote that 'the sweetest part of love is its violences'. What she was savouring here was not so much the pleasure of suffering as the pleasure of knowing that one is being used by love. It was the experience of love, God apprehended in the form of *Law*.

Some writers—notably Anders Nygren (in *Agape and Eros*,[27] one of the books that opened the modern debate on love)—hold that all mysticism is erotic and of pagan origin, but in that case there is no such thing as a mysticism of *agape*. Was St Paul no mystic? Or, if he was, was he an erotic, a pagan? I do not mean to enter into that controversy. And I am not making the case against mysticism—on the contrary. That case has been made, both in the name of science and in that of orthodoxy: the champions of science have tended to fall into the error of reducing all mysticism to pathology, while those of orthodoxy have been led by their purism to impoverishing the religion which they wished to purge of what seemed to them a survival or revival of Greek thought (but why not a strengthening encounter with it?). Others have made fine distinctions, holding that there are two mysticisms, one that is orthodox and to be commended, the other heretical and to be detested. Unfortunately some of these writers (for instance Aldous Huxley) have proscribed as erotic the sensualist and emotional kind of mysticism, which is often expressed in the form of an epithalamium or in the image of a marriage. Others (such as Denis de Rougemont) connect, on the contrary, the mysticism of the Marriage with the Christian *agape* and go on to condemn an intellectualist, unitive mysticism derived from *eros*, which they arbitrarily connect with Eastern mysticism and the Cathar heresy.

In point of fact, nuptial mysticism and unitive mysticism are not mutually exclusive: the one has often served as the point of departure for the other. But, as I said, I shall not intervene in this controversy: it is enough, for my purpose, to show that one authentic branch of Christian mysticism coincides with the Platonic philosophy of love (or with Plotinus' exegesis of it). By so doing I am perhaps disturbing some reluctant minds into recognizing the exalting and daimonic power of *eros*. If the too brief account of Hadewych which follows succeeds in carrying the reader's conviction on this point, it will justify its place in a book that is intended to be somewhat provocative in its pleading for a *resacralization* of human love and of the Couple.

Nothing could be easier than to begin by taking advantage of the analogies between the vocabulary of human love and that of divine love: some of the images borrowed by the one from the other have often been found shocking, especially certain confusions of the carnal with the spiritual, which have an unprepossessing sensuality in the cases of Marguerite-Marie Alacoque and a number of other saints or nuns. It must be admitted that the *Song of Songs*, or rather the use made of it, has helped such confusion. Guitton maintains that it was the spelling-book of those who refused to separate human love from divine love. St Bernard made it the dominant theme of medieval mysticism; but the idea of the soul betrothed to Christ is to be found already in the Gospels, and reappears in St John Chrysostom and St Jerome. The imagery of the mystic marriage, which was to meet with such favour, is already fully present in the letter to Eustochius: 'Ever may the secrecy of the chamber keep thee, ever may the Bridegroom joy with thee there within. If thou prayest, thou speakest to the Bridegroom. If thou readest, he speaketh to thee. Then, when sleep will have overwhelmed thee, he will come up behind the wall, he will pass his hand through the grating, and will touch thy body. Then shalt thou rise up trembling, and thou shalt say, "I am wounded with love", and afterwards shalt thou hear his voice saying, "It is a closed garden, my sister and my wife, a closed garden, a sealed spring".'

St Jerome chose the boldest images from the *Song of Songs* to celebrate virginity. It would be wrong to see harm in this: much later,

St John of the Cross, who is above suspicion, took sexual symbolism far further, but the theme of the Marriage, even of deflowering, can be treated on different levels: it can be grossly sensual or purely allegorical and abstract, or (in contrast to both) re-lived concretely and yet transubstantiated into mystical experience.

What makes the case of Hadewych interesting is that, without falling into the confusion of the carnal and the spiritual, her experience *assumes* the carnal. There is in her, it is true, hardly a trace of the facile eroticism which would deprive the demonstration of all value: if this ever was present, she immediately went beyond it. The eroticism of Hadewych is an eroticism in the Greek sense, that of sustained thought on a basis of feeling. And so, in her case, the theme of marriage is always in the end *purified* (so that it is sometimes said that her mysticism is not a true mysticism of the Marriage), and yet Hadewych went through the various stages. Sometimes it is experienced as a physiological reality, sometimes it is expressed allegorically (a concession to the language of her time, to the courtly style) and sometimes brought to the high temperature of the furnace of *union*—so that the path from the flesh to the spirit and beyond the spirit was constantly being traversed by that soul, a soul passing tirelessly from the sensory to the intelligible and from the intelligible to what Hadewych herself (before Eckhart) called *Gottheit* (deity distinct from God) or (like Plotinus) *Einigkeit* (Unity).[28] Nothing could be more sensual and passionate at its base, nor anything more stripped and rarefied at its summit. The extent of this difference is seen most clearly in the *Visions*, which she wrote for one of her spiritual advisers; they form a kind of ɛ ɔn-by-step account of the sublime, leaving out none of the torments and joys undergone by the arduously tried body as the intelligence moves boldly forward to its conquest, staking its claim to attention for a moment in a still-human concern for awareness before sinking into *union*.

Already in the first *Vision*, these two phases are distinguished:

> It was a Sunday in the Octave of Pentecost that Our Lord was brought to me secretly in bed because I felt within me a great travail of my spirit such as I had not felt equally outside among the people. And this need which I had in me was to be one with God and to joy in him.[29]

But Hadewych understood only later: she was still too young and too impulsive for so high a dignity. From that day, however, she entered upon a privileged experience:

> When I had received Our Lord, He in His turn received me into Heaven in such fashion that he ravished me in spirit beyond all foreign things, that I might enjoy Him in unity. And I was transported, as it were, into a field, into a plain, which was called the plain of perfect virtue.

Like Plato's 'plain of truth', Hadewych's plain was the place where, the errors of the senses being abjured, the soul attains God in spirit, *not beyond the spirit*. For *union* was not consummated. And, far from sinking into that nameless abyss without methods or reasons, into that fruitful death in which knowledge, sight and hearing are extinguished, Hadewych was singularly lucid and resisted the immersion. She listened and looked about her, and she describes the place, developing in the manner of her time a great allegory of the virtues figured by the trees, plants and flowers.

This first Vision was only, as it were, an organ prelude. 'One day in May, during the Mass of St James and at the exact moment of the reading of the Epistle' (Hadewych always has recourse to concrete landmarks to 'make fast' her Visions, as St Teresa of Avila later put it), her senses appeared to be sucked out of her 'by the violent pulling of a terrible spirit'. Let us note in passing the resemblance between this spirit and the *genii* of neo-Platonism and Socrates' *daimon*. This fourth Vision is full of magnificence with its Apocalyptic scene, its stars and planets, immobilized, one after the other at the beating of the wings of the Angel; it tells us that the mystical life is identification with the Lover by elimination of everything that separates us from him—a reminder, this, of the theme of purification. But it was in the fifth Vision, and, even more, in the sixth, that Hadewych consciously crossed the space dividing the two degrees of ecstasy. And the care she takes to instruct us positively about the first is equalled only by her prudence in governing or qualifying the second, in defining it only by what it is not, in ringing it round with negative significations. Having attained Him whom she is seeking, 'having contemplated in Him the order in which all receive their due and everything is in its place, having seen Heaven and the blessed, Hell and the damned, and the insulted greatness of God and His humility raised up again and His immensity contained in all things and His presence hidden, having heard His reasons', Hadewych is so filled with wonder that she loses consciousness and, escaping from the spirit and from herself, indeed from all that she had been allowed to contemplate and from 'her terrible and ineffably sweet lover', she was lost 'in the fruition of his loving bosom'.

> I remained there, as though submerged, unconscious of everything, of knowing, seeing or understanding, except of being one with him and joying in him. I remained thus for close on half an hour.

Even when her vision begins by being spotted with sensuality, even when Hadewych personifies it, a rare thing with her, as she does in the seventh Vision, the passage to the metaphysical plane takes place infallibly. With that clinical concern for exactitude characteristic of the great mystics—the lucid ones—Hadewych comments:

> My heart and my arteries and all my limbs palpitated and trembled with desire and, as has often happened to me, I felt myself so violently and so fiercely tried that it seemed to me that, should I not give satisfaction to my lover and should he not respond to my desire, I would die of fury and die furious. I was so terribly and so painfully tormented by loving desire that it seemed that my limbs were melting away bit by bit and that each one of my arteries was in travail. My desire was so ineffable that no one could express it. All that I might say of it could still not be understood by those who have not experience of love or of its weariness through desire. Nevertheless, this I will say: I desired to possess my lover wholly, to know him and to taste him in all his parts, his person joying in mine and mine remaining there, careful not to fall into imperfection, in such manner as to content him, who is perfection itself, in all and fully.

Hadewych's lover is usually formless, an abstraction. Or else a splendid angel, as in the fourth Vision. But here he appears in the form of Christ:

> Then he came. Gentle and beautiful, splendid of countenance, and approaching me submissively, in the manner of one who belongs wholly to another. And he gave himself to me, as was his habit, in the form of the Sacrament, then made me drink from the chalice. Then he came to me himself and took me altogether in his arms and clasped me to him, all my limbs felt the touch of his as completely as, in accordance with my heart, myself had desired him. So was I outwardly satisfied and slaked. For a brief moment I had the

strength to endure it, but soon I lost sight of the forms of that fair man and saw him wholly disappear, vanish and melt away so suddenly that I could neither perceive him outside me any more nor discern him within. At that moment we were united without any difference [the second degree]. Thus it was: to see, taste and feel outside me [first degree] as we taste outwardly the Sacrament which we receive, an outward perception like that of the lover with the beloved, each given to the other in the full content of gazing, hearing and mingling. After that, I remained mingled with my lover until I melted entirely into him [second degree] so that of myself there remained nothing.

Quite clearly this effusion of Hadewych's is an amorous one. *Minne* is not *agape*, but *eros*, whose way the Northern mystics had freshly discovered; and if the two converge to the same point, their courses are different. Hadewych, whose orthodoxy[30] is nonetheless unquestioned, was moved like Socrates and Plato by amorous desire and used the same cathartic method to reach the object of her desire. She arrived there by the gradual and systematic stripping away of all that clothed and masked the divine, constantly present in her soul: hence a ceaseless activity of sifting and rejection, a critical activity.[31] This nuptial mysticism became, by its self-purification, an intellectualized mysticism. But it moved on higher still. I have purposely quoted an extract from the seventh Vision, which is the most carnal, in order to illustrate the transmutation that was constantly taking place in that mysticism, and that there may remain no doubt of the physiological, indeed sexual origin of the ecstasy that led it to the reconstitution of the mystic Couple; but Hadewych never lingered in sensualism—something drew her away from these preliminaries and drove her towards the heights. This was *onghedueren*, an impatience of limits, a longing for what is at the same time reminiscence and destiny. This is why, in her, we find none of that indulgence in describing caresses or *minebette* which we find in Mechtilde of Magdeburg. Nor do we find any of the wonderfully concrete images like that of the dart which pierced St Teresa of Avila, or like this from Ruusbroec: 'Make thy dwelling in the hollows of His wounds, as the rock-pigeon in the cliff'. Hadewych was always alert to separate herself from the corporeal and to replace it by the mental. And this intellectualism, far from spoiling her mysticism, results in deepening it and bringing out the ruggedness of all that long stretch which she traversed with such constant vigour from the flesh to the spirit, from the sensory to the intelligible.

Yet this was only one of the stages of the ascent: Hadewych's aim was not merely to be united in spirit in the perfect Knowledge, that summit of the intelligible—it was to go beyond the spirit and the Essences and, far from knowing and understanding all, to go where she would no longer know or understand anything. For Hadewych the highest Heaven—*de hogere hemel*—was not a Fra Angelico Paradise of angels and blessed spirits holding one another by the hand and dancing in meadows thick with flowers: it was a harsh bare peak, one of those deserts of high altitude where the soul is drunk up by the sun in the dazzling metaphysical illumination of Night that has become Day. This was the highest point of the spiritual life; and what seems truly marvellous is that this Flemish mystic in the first half of the thirteenth century should have constantly, in her experience, cut across the main line of Greek mysticism and even its metaphysical expression. The two degrees of *Union* in the experience of Hadewych correspond to the double transcendence, in Platonism and neo-Platonism, first of empirical reasoning by pure thought, then of thought by ecstasy—the reality of the One transcending the Essences. Not only does Hadewych bid farewell to *intelligence with its calm desires* and attain that final peak, not only does she verify the distinctness of the three orders by her attitude and ease in moving among them, but her movement also issues from the same force and is exercised according to the same method of purifying negation. Like Plotinus when he refers to one of the rites of the Mysteries and compares the soul divesting itself to the initiates (who strip off their garments one by one as they move upwards towards the sanctuaries), Hadewych also— and with almost obsessive repetition—uses the image of denudation: God is continually present,[32] and to find Him it is enough to rid oneself of all else. It is the presence of absence: 'know', says Hadewych, 'that nothing can be told of it except that we must rid ourselves of the tumult of reasons, form and images if we would inwardly not understand but know all things'.

> *Those who will not disperse themselves in other*
> *works than that which is here told of,*
> *return to unity in their Principle,*

and this unity which they possess is such,
that nothing like it can come of two beings here below.

In the secrecy of the One, these souls are pure and
naked inwardly, without images, without figures,

set free, as it were, from time, uncreate, loosened
from their limits in the silent breadth.

And here I cease, finding no longer any end or beginning
nor any comparison that might justify words . . .[33]

Unity? The One? Was there then no specifically Christian feature in the supreme experience of this orthodox Christian woman? The great boldness of Hadewych's mysticism lay in postulating that the soul can, at the summit, join with the divine unity even beyond persons. To Christians the problem is whether the soul must go beyond even the humanity of Christ (it set Fénelon and Bossuet against each other). The answer given by the Northern mystics was generally in the affirmative (though they held the humanity of Christ to be the way of excellence): to them, as to the neo-Platonic thinkers, the summit of spiritual life was participation in an absolute simplicity, which could no more be defined than it could be named. And so we find in Hadewych no great fervour, nor even any real interest, for the historical Jesus. In her work there are few allusions to the Passion, few references to the Gospels (even to the Synoptic Gospels), no mystical cult of the Child Jesus or of the Man of Sorrows (neither tenderness for the one, nor pity for the other), no masochism of the Cross, wounds and blood. Even the word 'God' appears only occasionally in her work, and then commonly in a context that deprives it of significance: *goddank* (thank God), *god geve* (God grant), *god weet* (God knows). On the other hand *godheit* (Deity) is apprehended (well before Eckhart) as the basis of things, along with admirable images derived from the word *gront* (later taken up by Master Eckhart in the German word *grunt*). Hadewych, like Eckhart, plays on the double sense of this word, as basis (or solidity) and as depth (or abyss); she speaks of *godheit* as a *grondeloze gront*, a foundationless foundation or a bottomless gulf that must be climbed, and the image conveys the kinesthetic experience of an inner space and of a depth in reverse.[34]

Hadewych, like Plato and Plotinus, steps out into the paradoxes of the negative way. The Principle escapes us as soon as we try to seize it: it must be ringed round with negations—and this method even leads Hadewych on one occasion to call it the Nothing.

> *She is cut off in the shoreless eternity,*
> *dilated, saved by the Unity which swallows her up,*
>
> *intelligence with the calm desires,*
> *doomed to be wholly lost in the wholeness of the immense:*
>
> *and there a simple thing is revealed to her,*
> *which cannot be revealed,*
> *a pure and naked Nothing.*

But this Nothing is also the One, in whose secrecy souls are, as it were, *increate* (for the One is before us but also behind us, it is our origin, our deepest condition and our end), loosened from their limits in the *silent breadth*. Here liberty receives a name, and is found exactly where Plotinus found it.

Who are those who hasten towards this exalted joy? They are those whose *desire pierces ever further forward into the high knowledge of pure love*, those who desire in order to *know* that which they desire, those who *love* in order that they may feel themselves moved and driven by God, by His Law. These, says Hadewych in another poem, are the same who experience the madness of love, the *orewout*—a splendid word meaning 'original fury', in which the prefix *or* (in German *ur*) presents the dimension of myth.

The mystical genius of Hadewych succeeded in doing what, even today, the best philosophers and historians find very difficult—in assimilating the deeper meaning of the Platonic and neo-Platonic doctrine.[35] It is a matter of kinship and coincidence, rather than of influence. The extent to which pagan influences were transmitted to Hadewych through Dionysius Areopagites and Guillaume de Saint-Thierry has been much discussed (Father van Mierlo even speaks, rather wryly, of Orphic influences)—but inconclusively, and the meagre result of these researches suggests strongly that they are on the wrong track. As soon as the way of love is accepted as a natural and authentic way, not as a system that has sprung fully armed from the brain of a philosopher, there is no need to be astonished at seeing it crop up again in some fresh place. Moreover, Hadewych was not the only woman of this Northern school (though she was its most attractive figure) to have adopted this way. The phenomenon may be correctly described as a return of *eros* to the scene under cover of Christian mysticism. The teaching of the great Greek philosophy of love was that all love is already virtually love of God; and so, in recovering *eros*, religion was essentially resuming its own. It cannot be reproached for this, only for having repudiated its origins.

COURTLY LOVE, OR ESCAPIST EROS

Though unitive mysticism did recover *eros* for the benefit of religion, it gave its blessing to the separation between the flesh and sublime love and contributed to the idealist prejudice. The notion became more than ever prevalent, that it is nobler to love with the spirit or with the soul than with the heart or with the senses (and the confusions to which mysticism led at this point are easy to guess). Meanwhile another avatar of *eros*—courtly love—had also, for about a century, been working towards the dislocation of *eros*.

To enlarge on this strange and important phenomenon is tempting, but there are two strong reasons for restraint: one, that a great deal has already been written about it; the other, that it is vast and complex —so much so, that one is forced either to treat it thoroughly and write a whole book on courtly love, or to place many different, even divergent tendencies arbitrarily under the same heading. Writers have at various times included in courtly love the ritual of feudal life and amorous scholasticism, Provençal lyric poetry and the judgments of the Cour de Champagne, the so-called 'Platonic' cult of the *Lady* and the realistic poety of Marcabrun (with his crude praise of pleasure and his diatribes against women); Rudel's *Amour de princesse lointaine* and André le Chapelain's rites of physical approach and *amor interruptus*, St Bernard's mystical cult of the Virgin and the *essentialist* mysticism of the North,[36] the heresy of the *béguins* of St Francis (who claimed that they were training the flesh for the good fight by going to bed with a naked woman) and the rude, severe authority of the *perfects*, and, lastly, not only the *Liebestod* lovers but the existential love of

Héloïse. If this is realized, the diversity of the phenomenon is equally apparent: the least one can say of it is that it is not a good field for strict deductions.

Our astonishment grows when we see how one of the richest, most highly esteemed books of this century attributes the invention of passionate love of the Tristan and Iseult type to the courtly civilization, dating its birth from the passion of Abélard and Héloïse.[37] Denis de Rougemont's thesis—that love was born in the twelfth century and was connected with the well-known heresy of Catharism—is familiar, and I shall not undertake a critique of that fascinating book: it would require an authority and a range of knowledge which I do not possess and those who are interested will find profit in the splendid pages which Sartre has devoted to it in his *Situations*.[38] I shall merely say that it is entertaining to see de Rougemont admonished by Sartre for an excess of historicism. Those of us who do not consider love as a historical phenomenon or do not believe that at any stage men had to invent it, but hold on the contrary that it is one of the 'primitive data of the human condition', are not in danger of falling into the sophism of reducing the eternal *eros* to historically conditioned passionism, an error which leads to the unfair use, against the former, of arguments that are only valid for the latter. Nor shall we fall into the error of assigning to the love of Héloïse and Abélard a place—and that the first—in the courtly phenomenon represented by Tristan and Iseult. This phenomenon, as we have seen, is involved, heterogeneous and confusing. If, however, there is any constant discernible in it, this consists of two essential points: it is anti-conjugal, and it speculates on chastity. That beautiful legend of fatal passion which de Rougemont has called 'the great Western mystery of adultery' is certainly anti-conjugal; so is André le Chapelain's *Tractatus de Amore*. So was the jurisdiction of the Courts of Love—as in the famous judgment of Marie de Champagne:

> We do state and assure by these present that love cannot extend its rights to two married persons. In fact lovers accord all things to one another mutually and gratuitously without being constrained by any motive of necessity, while husband and wife are bound by duty to submit their wills reciprocally and to refuse nothing the one to the other.

But Héloïse and Abélard not only married, they had a child. When Héloïse realized that she was pregnant, she announced this to Abélard with transports of joy. In Abélard's interest, Héloïse was willing to do without marriage—her love had no need of any consecration; yet she did not repudiate the Sacrament. Far from regarding a religious marriage as devoid of sanctifying value, Abélard and Héloïse constantly drew support from it. Abélard: 'We are one in Christ, one flesh by the law of marriage'. And Héloïse: 'You know what bond ties us together and obliges you, and that the nuptial sacrament unites you to me in a manner that is all the more close because I have ever in the face of the world loved you with a love without measure'.

Courtly love included also a most curious magical ritual of chastity. But the love of Héloïse and Abélard was strongly physical. It is an unpleasant thing to say, but must be said, that Abélard's championship of chastity became evident chiefly when he was forced to be chaste. He regarded the flesh as sin when indulged in with perversity or in an extravagant manner, in a consecrated place or in contravention of the vow of chastity: there is no sign in Abélard of veneration for chastity in itself, or of any interest in its feats of prowess—any predilection for those situations of risk in which the soul's resistance is rashly tested. On the contrary, there is a passage in the letters denouncing 'those mad virgins infatuated with their bodily purity, who parch themselves at the fire of temptations'. Abélard expresses pity for 'those who thus deprive themselves of earthly sweetnesses and lose both time and eternity'.

That great couple is by itself sufficient evidence that there existed, right in the midst of courtly love, another love—passionate, no doubt, but not passionist. This fact ruins de Rougemont's thesis. Passionate love was not an invention of the twelfth century.

It is true, however, that modern love has in it an element of drama, of torment, which is not to be found in the Greek *eros*. Indeed love could not be expected to appear in exactly the same form in the Athens of the fourth century B.C. and in the deeply Christian France of the twelfth century A.D. The effect of history on love is confined to this action of conditioning and morphological specification. Both Christianity and Gnosticism affected love: the discredit cast upon the flesh, the drama of sin, the pessimism of the Fathers, the trenchant and fierce dualism of the heresies, were bound to produce at least a distortion of *eros*. This deformation was carried to its extreme in dolorist and masochistic passionism. The result was that the genealogy of love became more and more difficult to establish. The difficulty was increased by the efforts that were made to falsify the nature of pagan love, soften it and sweeten it and reduce it to the Anacreontic image of the winged child. Considering that to Plato (and to Heraclitus, Hesiod, Empedocles and Parmenides before him) love was not only the individual principle of the soul's reunion with God but also a cosmic principle, the Law of the world, cosmogonic Eros, one gasps when one reads that to the Ancients 'Eros was a winged god, charming and secondary'.[39] It is almost like reducing God the Father, Son and Holy Spirit to the 'little Jesus' of the Sunday School.

But the routines of the spirit are so compelling that the most free and honest writers are sometimes caught up in them. Nelli states, astonishingly, that throughout Graeco-Roman antiquity there is no record of a single case of passionate love, except as a 'pathological case'. But the Greeks made long and costly wars for love: countless warriors gave their lives to win a mere glance of admiration from their beloved (battalions of lovers were formed, so great was their valour); others killed or assassinated to defend or to avenge their beloved (history, it is true, has modestly disguised these *crimes passionnels* as civic or patriotic exploits); others again committed suicide from despair of love, as we read in Plato and Aristotle.[40] Some Greeks compromised their popularity and the success of their policy by passion—for instance Pericles, whom (as we have seen) the Athenian people never forgave for his love of Aspasia. A Greek woman noted the somatic symptoms of passion with such a clinical precision that Racine (and he was not the first), no doubt considering that it could not be done better, made use of her work to describe the paroxysms of Phaedra. And it was a man of Athens who, carried away by the love he had vowed to a young prince who was both handsome and wise, worked out what is our only sacred doctrine of love. Plato, it is true, valued love only insofar as it could help a man to purify himself and to draw near to the divine. It is also true that the Greeks would have held it perverse to seek suffering, though they recognized its purgative value: they knew all about love, about the subtlest wiles of the flesh and the most unexpected revenges of the spirit, but dolorism and masochism were foreign to them. And perhaps they would have regarded Tristan with contempt. Not for having desired Iseult carnally, not even for having possessed her. Not for having known the madness of love, but for having destroyed himself through it. For having preferred hallucination to presence of mind, madness to wisdom, magic to the sacred. For having sacrificed *philosophy* to the strange new pleasure of self-destruction. (They would also have been astonished that this great passion was inspired by a woman.)

But Tristan is an extreme case of surrender to magic. The courtly ritual had the effect, precisely, of appropriating for magical purposes the sexual power and, above all, the maleficent power of Woman. Nelli, who has written so well of the courtly phenomenon,[41] says that this religion of love codified, under the superficial form of feudal ceremonial, beliefs that were far older. Thus the *merci*—a kind of exchange of hearts through the kiss, through an exchange of breath and saliva—corresponded to a very ancient rite of animistic communion, in which the man's heart was supposed to lodge in his mistress's bosom and the woman's heart in his, so achieving protection. Sometimes this exchange remained symbolic; sometimes it postulated a more intimate union, playing over a ground of sensuality. André le Chapelain considered that love could be extended to include gazing upon the lady naked and caressing her boldly, provided only that the act which kills love should never take place.

In any case the ancestral, recurrent idea (it appears in the most dissimilar civilizations) that the sexual urge, when held back, increases a man's power, emerged afresh in that astonishing Christian twelfth century, both in the troubadours, who exposed themselves to contact with the naked limbs of their mistresses, and in the heresy of the *béguins* of St Francis. Nelli writes that, if Chrétien de Troyes had been more aware of the Provençal secrets, he would surely have placed Lancelot (the Lancelot of the *Conte de la Charrette*) in the damsel's bed. He also compares this heroism with that of Socrates lying beside the beautiful Alcibiades.

Analogous practices were known to Taoist China, to Sufism and, above all, to both Buddhist and Vishnuite Tantrism. Sometimes the method is bound up with control of breath, of thought and of the semen, and its aim is to attain a mystical transposition of sexual union: consider for instance the *maithuna* of Tantrism, with its precise instructions (the man is to serve the woman like a domestic servant for the first four months, to sleep in the same room, then at her feet, then for another four months in the same bed, on the left side, then for four months on the right side and then to sleep with her in his arms.) Sometimes it is a system of hygiene with overtones of magic—as in the Tao, where he must learn to have joy of the woman without ever abandoning to her what is the principle of physical salvation and of immortality, without penetrating into her maleficent and fatal world (the world into which, precisely, Tristan longs to sink).[42]

How far was courtly love aware of these significations? Did the troubadours attribute them to the cult of the Woman and of the Virgin Mary or to the Sophia of the Gnostics? To the teaching of St Bernard tha ~*itas* is only a carnal urge transmuted? Or—in spite of Tristan —to the ancestral fear of Woman as representative of the pre-natal Night and of Death, against whom the ritual set up a protective magic? Did they establish a connection with the Cathar (and, still more, the Gnostic) idea that the carnal act is not immoral if it does not lead to procreation or involve the spirit? However this may be, that heroic but perilous chastity had little resemblance to the prudent Christian doctrine of abstention. Little, either, to the serenity of Socrates: true it existed in the same atmosphere of prowess, but Socrates *accepted* the ordeal of temptation—there is no evidence that he made a habit of it, still less that he sought a thrill in it. The pleasure of self-privation and the pride of resistance are evident in the courtly attitudes; but Socrates did not consider that to the philosopher chastity was anything more than a test. It enabled a man to see what stage he had reached in purification, in the critical separation of the pure from the impure, of real Beauty from sensory appearances; this was the reason for the interest he took in those confused, unexplored, imperfectly mapped frontier zones, where his adventurous nature was the better tested the more exposed it was. But Socrates never prowled round the edge of an abyss,

as did the Christian, whom the slightest miscalculation would plunge
into evil and damnation. Socrates was always able to correct his
position and his perspective. *Impurity* is only confusion. *Evil* is a power,
if not the Principle of this world. The dualism which underlies all
situations in the Christian world exposed the courtly hero to the danger
of suddenly overbalancing and hurtling down from the heights into
the abyss. This is what gave his exploits that heretical, occult or even
sacrilegious tinge, that taint of a recourse to magic and to the supernatural power of Evil opposed to that of Good.

This is the light in which the legend of Tristan should be viewed,
as is eloquently shown by the episode of the Judgment of God in the
version of Gottfried of Strasbourg:

> *Amen! said the lovely Iseult.*
> *In the name of God she took the iron*
> *And carried it, yet her hand was not burnt.*
> *So it was a manifest thing*
> *And averred before all the world,*
> *That the most glorious Christ*
> *Falls into folds like the stuff of a garment.*
> *He falls into folds and into place*
> *For the one who is able*
> *To fold in His way,*
> *As neatly and as perfectly*
> *As any could desire,*
> *He lends Himself to the wishes of all,*
> *Whether to sincerity, or to deception,*
> *He is always that which a man wishes Him to be,*
> *And denies Himself to no play, serious or light-hearted.*
> *Of this they could be certain,*
> *When they saw that clever queen*
> *Save herself by her duplicity*
> *And by the false oath*
> *Which she addressed to God.*

The love of Tristan and Iseult, far from leading them to God, opposes
them to God (even when they appeal to 'his courtesy'). It is not religion
but magic—*schrecklicher Zauber*, as Wagner puts it; and these legendary
lovers are not sinners, but accursed. Tristan was doomed to adversity
from his birth (hence his name, *le Triste*). He himself, in his confession

to the hermit Ogrin, calls his love *péchié*, and in old French, according to Vinaver, the word meant also misfortune. 'May God repent of having caused me to be born!' cries Brangien, because it is she who committed the fatal error through which the lovers drank 'destruction and death' in the love potion. This splendid love is from the start a fatal love. Tristan and Iseult never think that their love is other than sorcery and malediction. Or rather, they never *think:* they go through suffering and joy without discernment. Misfortune or happiness, it is all one confusion, that of a love shut in on itself. The great defect of passionism is that it is a hedonism, whereas Platonism strives towards eudaimonism. Plato desires to be at peace with his daimon, Tristan merely to put his to sleep.

This love, we are told, is the pagan *eros*.[43] But we know what *eros* was: from the start it was virtually a love of the divine, and it was aware of this, it was essentially lucid. *Eros* was a growing awareness, while passionism was a loss of awareness. In *eros* all is memory—a predestination that is a longing to go home, a beauty that is reminiscence, a wisdom that is a kind of faithfulness, an amorous madness that is grace: in passionism all is a forgetting, a sleep, a lie, in which predestination becomes inexplicable fatality and beauty is replaced by a spell, the divine madness by hallucination. So, while the one is attention and presence, the other is absence and refuge. It is escapist love—passionate love of a sort, no doubt, but one that shuts in upon the creature instead of opening out and expanding beyond in supernatural splendour. It may be a kind of *eros*, but it is one that repudiates and betrays its *vocation*. It commits itself to nothing, not even to lasting. We must not be misled by the delays which Tristan imposes on himself: in the two '*beaux amants*' there is no effort to explore to the full the destiny of a love which cannot, any more than the other things of this world, remain motionless—Tristan and Iseult remain at a fixed point. By incessantly renewing the obstacles to their desire they give themselves the illusion of movement, like the illusion one experiences in a train that is at rest, when the windows of a nearby train are seen moving past.

To labour the point seems hardly necessary: clearly the pagan philosophy of love was a doctrine of salvation, while the other was a

doctrine of perdition. Both desired ecstasy, but in the one it opened
on to what Diotima calls 'the real', and in the other to negation. And
not even a negation that tests itself, defining its insufficiency, but a
negation that is a thrill to be savoured. The worst error there can be
is to approach so close to the aim and to miss it. A 'Christian heresy',
it has been called: it was certainly an erotic heresy. Courtly love was
a literary *genre*, a code, a ritual, magic, an ascetic discipline—everything except the *way*. It was no more a mysticism than it was a philosophy. Such a continuation and elucidation of it was in due course
attempted, three centuries later, by Marsilio Ficino.[44] But he, a priest
who set out to bring the faithful back to Christ with the help of Plato
and who hoped to fire men's souls by means of the seductions of *eros*,
approached the subject with another prejudice—that of the identity of
eros and *agape*. Breaking faith with both, his philosophy of chaste love
was destined to come to grief.

The courtly doctrine of love, though incomplete and distorted, had
the merit of involving women. The great innovation of courtly love
was this exaltation of the Feminine; which caused contradictory feeling
in men—mistrust and terror, but also fascination and passion, indeed
a cult. In a world where the law of the Church weighed heavily on
women and on love (which had submitted to rules and regulations
extending even to the relations of husband and wife), extra-conjugal
courtly love established a fiction of equality. The *joi d'amour* conferred
on the woman a freedom which was the more wonderful for being
imaginary.

On the practical level, the consequences were less pleasing. The
ladies who had applauded the ennobling of love and the separation of
flesh and soul were not always able to benefit from them. Many of the
courtly poets were homosexuals. Some kept, side by side with their
metaphysical mistress or their *mystic* lady, another who was less so. In
practice the division of love usually ended in affairs on several levels
and with different persons. The courtly conception of love was
destined to precipitate the fragmentation of love and the dispersal of its
elements. This centrifugal tendency increased as courtly love grew
older: love spread itself more and more in fine shades and variations,
and ended by decomposing 'like light in a prism into its constituent

elements'. This fragmentation was the doom of *eros*, the negation of the philosophy of love as *liaison*, as a binding together. René Nelli has recognized that the courtly doctrine of love was powerless to unite soul and body in one and the same passion.

But the tendency of courtly love to fragmentation extended also to social matters. That hothouse fruit of a literary and wordly civilization could not ripen outside the circle of an aristocracy of class and its hangers-on. This became apparent in due course, when that culture degenerated into a literary convention. The posterity of courtly love was Mlle de Scudéry, *l'Astrée* and, taking the place of courts of love, the first *salons* of the *Précieuses*. The courtly phenomenon—with its tenacious notion of class privilege, its two moralities (one reserved exclusively for the aristocracy), its prejudice against marriage and its indulgence towards adultery—was to survive in the worldly gallantry of the eighteenth century and the heartlessness of stylized love.

Because it was a class culture, a clan culture, because it separated rather than bound together, and because, in addition, it stood for a love refined almost out of existence, the courtly phenomenon was bound, from its first appearance, to excite popular reactions against it, which on the whole were healthy. Already in the twelfth century there were the songs of the Goliards in praise of wine, gaming and girls. Abélard had been mixed up with these revolutionaries, who called in question the social order and criticized the clerks: he owed his first success and his real popularity to these songs, not to his theology. At almost the same period there was an outburst of jubilation in Germany, that of the *Carmina Burana*, a heterogeneous collection of drinking songs and love songs, written in a mixture of low Latin and German, and brought together in the thirteenth century by an anonymous collector: they celebrated with comic fervour *Venus Generosa*, goddess of Fortune, a kind of florid answer to courtly love. Turning its back on essentialist mysticism, this body of hedonistic songs also set out to sing the praises of the joy of life, wine and kissing. While the well-known *Jubilus*, with its popular song metre, naïvely calls upon Jesus with His 'kisses more tasty than jars of honey', the *petit cantique bachique*[45] depicts Him enjoying Himself among the roses in the form of Cyprus wine and invites us to empty the cups:

> *Videz, remplissez les coupes à la ronde*
> *Dans les roses.*
> *Qu'il nous soit donné de repartir joyeux,*
> *Et de passer, ô gué notre temps de vie*
> *Dans les roses.*

The broad Gallic reaction of the *fabliaux*,[46] *contes, bourdes* and *soties* was vulgar and cynical. To the great entertainment of the crowds, there appeared at this time a stock character, that of the sly and ingenious woman, a kind of opposite or negation of the *lady* of courtly love—together with her complement, the deceived husband, victim of many tricks. The word cuckold began to enjoy a favour that has not been eclipsed. Love, dragged down from its pedestal, was trampled in the dirt with a brutal, intoxicated vindictiveness. All that was left was the pleasure of the senses, and good housekeeping—and marriage, which the merchant class was determined to preserve from love. On this midden of unredeemed materialism we find, surprisingly, like a rare flower, the touching figure of Griseldis, an image of a distorted mysticism of marriage. In 1393 a merchant of Paris set before his young wife (fifteen years old) this *Miroir des Dames mariées*.

GRISELDIS, OR CRUEL EROS

The author of the *Ménagier* took the story from Petrarch who had derived it from Boccaccio (but, if Robert Guiette is right, Petrarch knew it before he read it in the *Decameron*).[47] The main lines of it are well known. The Marquis of Saluce was very much afraid of losing his liberty in marriage; nevertheless, under pressure from his barons, he resigned himself to taking a wife. But to make sure that his would give him total and blind submission, he chose Griseldis, a poor girl, the daughter of the old serf, Jehannicola. Physically she was beautiful, but still more so in her virtue and behaviour, humble, used to frugal living, having never tasted delicious viands or other delicacies, and continually at work with her spindle. The Marquis made Griseldis promise to obey his every wish in silence, '*sans résonance ni contredit, en fait n'en dit, en signe ni en pensée*'. He insisted that she bring with her no relic of her past life, and carried her off to the castle in her rags. There he ordered the ladies and matrons to strip her naked and to clothe her in sumptuous wedding garments. The first months passed by uneventfully. Griseldis won the admiration of all by her gentleness, wisdom and diligence. The day came when she gave birth to a daughter. For the first time the Marquis was tormented with the desire to test his wife. Simulating anger, he told her that his vassals, unwilling that he should have issue of a girl of low condition, were forcing him to 'do with his child in such manner than nothing could be more painful to his heart', and he said that he hoped Griseldis would endure this with the patience she had promised him.

Though pierced to the heart, the poor Griseldis gave no sign of sorrow. She said to her husband: 'I and this little girl are thine. Do with us as thou wilt'. The Marquis was filled with joy, but was careful not to show it. He had the child taken to his sister at Boulogne la Grasse. Four years passed by. Although the Marquis often observed his wife and watched her face and manner closely, he could not detect in her the slightest sign of grief. At the end of of these four years Griseldis gave birth to a boy of marvellous beauty. The Marquis was tempted again. But this time he would make the test still more cruel. He waited until the child was two years old before taking it away from its mother—treating her to the same speech again. She answered once more in the same way: 'Thou art lord of me and of my children. When I came into thy palace, I took off my poor clothes by my own will and affection and put on clothes that were thine'. The Marquis marvelled in his heart—was indeed somewhat ashamed, since he went away with his head lowered. He had his son taken to the same place as his daughter. And although she thought her children were dead, Griseldis' patience did not falter. The Marquis found her daily more loving and more obedient. If he still felt the need to test her, this was no doubt because he was committed to a path on which it is difficult to stop. Twelve years passed by, and then the Marquis of Saluce pretended to ask for and obtain the annulment of his marriage. Secretly sending for his children, he called Griseldis to him and, in front of his vassals, announced to her his intention of taking another woman in marriage. And Griseldis replied humbly: 'I always thought that between thy magnificence and my poverty there was no proportion. I thank thee for the time I have passed with thee. For the rest, I hold myself ready to return to my father, as poor as I came. Only, since it is not fitting that she who was thy wife should go home from thee entirely naked, I pray thee to give order that a smock be allowed to me'. In the face of such humility, the Marquis could not refrain from weeping, though he hid it. Nonetheless he did not give up his plan: he let Griseldis go, and she returned to her cottage and her rags while her husband prepared the wedding festivities. At length, when his daughter and his son drew near to Saluce, he sent again to fetch Griseldis, asking her to busy herself with receiving the maiden, her brother, and the lords accompanying them. And Griseldis returned to the castle in her poor clothes, which no one this time had thought of taking from her. She saw to the cleaning of the palace and the stables, the arranging of the rooms and the beds, the spreading of the tapestries and embroidered coverlets, so that all might be worthy of her lord's wife. The cortège arrived, and now everyone was exclaiming at the beauty and youth of the new wife, some indeed saying: 'The Marquis is making a wise change of marriage, for this wife is more tender and more noble than the Jehannicola girl'. And Griseldis, 'who was present at all these things, showed herself simply joyful, and fell to her knees to welcome the young girl and her brother. Then came the time to go in to table. The Marquis called his wife and asked her aloud, in front of everybody: 'What thinkest thou, Griseldis, of my wife? Is she not lovely and good?' And Griseldis, still kneeling, agreed and wished her lord a good and joyful life, begging him only not to test this new wife as she herself had been tested, 'for she is young and of great estate and could not endure it'.

Then the Marquis, conquered at last by Griseldis' love, could not contain himself any longer but gave utterance to his joy in the presence of all: 'O Griseldis, Griseldis, I see and I know sufficiently thy faith and thy loyalty. There is not a man under the sky who has so tested his wife. . . . Never will I have other wife than thee. This is thy daughter, and this thy son. *Let all who think the contrary know that my intention was curiously and strictly to test this my wife, not to bring her into contempt or drive her to despair*'.

At this the Marchioness of Saluce fell to the ground, overwhelmed with joy. They raised her up, they wept with her. They clothed her again in her fine clothes, and made much of her. After that, husband and wife lived happily for twenty years with their children and grandchildren. '*Ci finist le miroir des Dames mariées: c'est assavoir de la merveilleuse patience et bonté de Griseldis, marquise de Saluce.*'

This happy end has not prevented the husband's conduct from being considered cruel and even inexplicable. Petrarch already felt he must attenuate the cruelty of this marital circus-training by clothing it in a symbolic significance. So did the French poet who, in about 1395, told the story '*en vers et par personnages*'. But it was in the Low Countries, where the *exemplum* of Griseldis met with great favour, that it became the authoritative allegory of the soul married to the Lord, and submitting to those tribulations which were required to prove its fidelity. But Boccaccio, the first writer to treat it, laid stress on its 'beastly folly' and presented it as a true story. Whether symbolical or not, Griseldis' submission continued to be rammed down the throats of women as an example of wifely virtue.

This was the use made of it by the author of the *Ménagier de Paris*—that treatise on morality and domestic economy in which one is told how to make one's husband happy and how to cure sick wines, how to dress decorously and how to make chicken broth or milk of almonds. That the author of the *Ménagier* took the story literally, rather than symbolically, is proved by the fact that he accompanied it with other, no less edifying examples: of a woman whom her husband made jump three times over a stick like a clever dog; of another who was cruelly chastised for having refused to imitate her; of yet another who, learning that her husband had in the village a mistress who was poorly clothed and lacked fuel to warm her, sent linen, logs, a feather bed, shoes and clean clothes (and even offered to have her washing done for her regularly), so that her husband might be subject to no discomfort in his pleasures. The author of the *Ménagier* does at least reassure his wife that he has no intention of *trying* her: he is no marquis and has not married a shepherd girl. But, he says, he is old and she will marry again: let her learn to submit and, should it be her lot to marry a harsh and cruel man, let her not go complaining to anyone of the ill-treatment she might receive; rather let her withdraw to her room, weep quietly and address her complaints to God. 'This lesson is given', it has been observed, 'without raising the voice, in the modest tone of an aged merchant indoctrinating a young wife full of good intentions.' Indeed it is a tone with which we are familiar: this kindliness—so often praised in such ecstatic terms—is the same as that of Ischomachos, the husband in the *Economica*. The same loving care over the details of daily life. The same falsely debonair authority, the same hypocritical paternalism exercised over a very young woman. The same earth-bound, selfish morality, combined with precepts about everything that should be known *'pour le prouffit du mesnage accroître'*—from the art of engaging servants to that of conserving provisions, keeping the grain in good condition and airing the clothes and linen. All that was lacking in Xenophon was an allusion to those *esbatements et privetés* of which his Parisian successor seems to have been fond, just as he was fond of having his shoes taken off and his feet washed by his wife, being well fed, well served, well *seignouri* and put to bed in clean sheets with a good fur rug on top.

All this is remote from Griseldis. Remote also from *eros*. Not surprisingly, the *Ménagier* tells us a great deal about the marriage of a fourteenth-century merchant, but throws hardly any light on the terrible, far from charming story of the Marquis and Marchionness of Saluce. On the psychology of those two strange people we are reduced to hypothesis.

Why should not Griseldis' extreme, inhuman, sterile ascetic prowess, which is *not* the Christian asceticism (nothing is less Christian than this story in which God has so little place), have been an amorous asceticism? We are told that the Marquis of Saluce was young, handsome, rich, brilliant and all-powerful: how could the poor daughter of the serf Jehannicola not have fallen in love with him? The opposite would have been astounding. I wonder if the legend is not based on one of those erotico-mystical phenomena of real life, on which the sagacity of the profane exercises itself to no purpose. Only a form of *eros*—a tor-mented, painful *eros* stagnating and marking time for lack of issue, turning its energy back against itself and using all its ingenuity to prepare its own torments—can account acceptably for the conduct of that wife, monstrously sacrificing her children, and of that husband who, according to the story, turned aside to hide his tears but still did not give up his enterprise. His obstinacy in testing the love of which he was the object, in the hope perhaps of being filled with wonder and winning *knowledge*, was also a form of asceticism—for sadism can be asceticism. Perhaps all there was in him at the bottom of this experiment, was the curiosity, the question: just how far can love go? And in her perhaps the essential was this willingness to strip herself bare of any will of her own, to *denude herself* (as is suggested by the symbol of her parting with all her own clothes before the wedding)—to sink into purifying negation. If so, this sado-masochistic story—in which one might be tempted to see a kind of prefiguration (only a decent one) of the *Histoire d'O*[48]—would really acquire a mystical tone. But it is a false mysticism that fails to recognize its object. True, the conduct of this husband and this wife conveys the feeling of an adventure of the soul: both of them set out intrepidly upon one of those unbeaten, virgin tracks along which, as Rilke said, one goes 'alone like a mineral'. The 'mental cruelty' which the Marquis exercised against her love, provoking it in higher and higher degree in order to know it, not to enjoy it, was a kind of 'stripping bare'. So was Griseldis' blind submission, seeking, like all mystics, only to realize their absolute denudation, the inner emptiness which precedes union.

And yet what is the good of it all, if the final, the most opaque obstacle remains? Hadewych knew the true object of her hunger and her longing, even though she knew also that it could not be named and was definable only by negation; but Griseldis, perhaps even further from God than her husband was, called her object by a human name. In treating as the term of her love what was only its starting-point, she deceived herself. *Eros* must be lived right through. But the great Platonic lesson had been forgotten. And the story of Griseldis, deprived of its natural *dénouement*, should end in despair and death. Its happy ending is merely a concession to opinion.

Just as natural forms are distorted by a change of habitat and may give birth to new forms, so *eros* in the Christian world bore the marks of an *adaptation to environment*. All its embodiments reacted in one way or another against the failure to recognize its divinizing power. They all show some sign of having had their daimonic side repressed and of having found the way barred. In every case there was fragmentation. Human love, condemned to remain human, was unaware that it was also religious. Divine love, religious at the start, found itself obliged to repudiate its human ties—it deprived itself of its material, or made of it furtively. In every case there was a shutting in, instead of a communication.

But *eros* is, first and foremost, exchange and transport: it is *liaison*, a finding of connections, a binding together; this is the cause of its religious nature. The fragmentation was a desacralization. Certainly the reproach which can be brought against the pagan philosophy of love, that it was worked out in homosexuality, is a grave one and I have not tried to pretend that it is not; but in it, at least, love was not altered and reduced to impotence or to clandestineness: it was exalted as never before. And it was surely to be admitted that, when once this anomaly was removed, the Platonic conception of love applied admirably to the love of man for woman: this has been shown when it has been put into practice, here and there, in every age.

The real disaster was the desacralization: after it, instead of there being one love, there were sacred love and profane love. Profane love substituted magic for the sacred, the marvellous for the religious. Unfortunately the marvellous opened the door to romanticism and to the literature of escape. Of this escape, this self-absenting from the world, this defection intensified into a savour of death, the Middle Ages have left us the myth and the poison. But a myth of absence could not be a symbol of the Couple. There is also a great myth of integration, not of escape. This is the myth of the complementary nature of the Masculine and the Feminine—the Androgyne.

The androgyne:
a myth of the couple

THE ANDROGYNE IN MYTHOLOGY

'What? you say that God has both sexes, O Trismegistus?'
'Yes, Asclepius, and not only God, but all creatures, animal and vegetable.'
HERMES TRISMEGISTUS, *Corpus Hermeticum*

'That you are mine', said Heinrich von Ofterdingen to Matilde, 'seems to me like a dream; but it seems to me still more wonderful that you were not always so.' 'And I', answered Matilde, 'feel as if I have known you since unimaginable ages.'

After Novalis, Breton: ' "Before I knew you"—look, the words are meaningless. You know very well that, when I saw you for the first time, I recognized you at once.'

And again, 'In what world did we meet?' asks Nerval. 'There are moments when I think I can feel, through the ages and all the darkness of appearances, our secret connection. Scenes that happened before men appeared on the earth come back into my memory, and I see myself under the golden boughs of Eden, sitting beside her. . . .'

Those who love each other recognize each other. They have loved each other *from all eternity.*

I believe, my little girl, when people love as I love you, they have always loved each other. How would they recognize each other if the soul had not always contained an image, though a veiled one? We are divided into two halves the one open to the day, and the other plunged in night, unconscious. They live and move together and communicate: sometimes one feels this exchange without really knowing it. Where the springing stream goes to, where the wave which submerges us comes from, our weak sight cannot see. Until the other half also gradually lights up and is revealed. Then not only is the fullness of a whole life laid before us, but behind us we find that the dark barrier, which hid from us half our being, has been raised. And we see how what seemed distinct and complete with its own separate ways was already unconsciously in communication with the rest.

I greet you, my life, with all that I am, was and can be.[49]

The writer of this letter, whom love for his betrothed has turned into a poet and a psychologist, was a statesman, a legislator, who drew up the Dutch Constitution. His fateful meeting with the young and beautiful Adelheid Solger was enough to awaken him to the mythical awareness. The veiled yet recognized image of the beloved is Eve, whom every man, as a new androgynous Adam, carries within him: it is the epiphany of the myth of Genesis in the soul: it is also, a hundred years in advance, the entry of Jung's *anima* upon the scene. The nocturnal half of the self is Goethe's realm of the Mothers, and it is the collective unconscious. The dark barrier defending it is the *Shadow*, the encounter with which is the first stage in the Jungian initiation. Thorbecke's letter is evidence that a mythology of the couple is innate in us, and that it is in harmony with depth psychology.

The word *myth*, as is well known, has had a strange history equalled only by that of the now more fashionable *demythologization*. Originally a myth was a fabulous and usually symbolic story of events that took place *in principio*, in a primordial, sacred, non-historical time. Myths made their appearance at the dawn of the different civilizations, sometimes at thousands of years' and leagues' distance, and have circulated through the world with variations but, above all, with constants. To some people they constitute an authentic source of knowledge, while others treat them as merely fables and superstitions, nursery tales of a still infantile humanity. The former think—and the latter do not think—that there are aspects of the real which defy any attempt at rational expression, and that only image-making thought can include the complexity of these and their contradictions: this, they think, is the immemorial function of the myths. It is an opinion that has been singularly reinforced since the recent discoveries of psychology. To-day, indeed, opinion is divided not so much over the importance and present relevance of a mythology as over the problem of its origin. One school holds that the myths are a mere product of history, the residue of ancient but natural human experiences; the other school maintains that they also transmit and reveal the memory of some great supernatural and prehuman experience. To this school, myth has the significance of a sacred teaching, of a way, an approach.

The secularization of the myths by the historicists has resulted in the extension of the idea of myth to a whole series of phenomena of collective fascination. In this derived sense, we speak of a myth of Tristan or of Don Juan, a myth of Paris, a myth of surrealism—but also of a Bardot myth or a Sagan myth. Recently, somewhat ironically, Jean-Paul Sartre suggested there might be a myth of myth. When we remember that a myth, in the original sense, is essentially a mode of expression and transmission of a fundamental truth, while the new sense lays the stress on illusion, deceptive make-believe and imposture, two things become quite clear: not only the reason for the zeal devoted by our contemporaries to *demythologization*, but also the need to distinguish the false myths—legitimately subjected to this treatment—from the others, which must be preserved if we are not to be deprived of our most precious and rich heritage. Before discussing a mythical subject, it is important to distinguish clearly the great fabulous myths, whose principal feature is timelessness, from those effective crystallizations which form about a theme or an individual that has an assignable period, place, nationality, confession, social status or even date of birth. These are part of the specific luggage of a culture, a society or even, sometimes, a clan. They are in the air. They can only be transmitted from outside. But the other can also be transmitted from within: to know them it is not necessary to have read or heard them; they sleep and germinate in our deepest Self in the form of images, symbols, haunting ideas, aspirations.

Some men live immersed within their most subterranean self, as though in a diving-bell, and are sensitive to its slightest current. Others who live on the surface, in the historical present, see nonetheless from time to time, hooked up by some rather keen sensation, a fragment of the 'mythological deposit' rise to the surface. They carry this within them unawares and fail to recognize it, yet it awakens a longing, and so a memory. It is, in Eliade's phrase, 'the image of the lost Paradise suddenly set free by the music of a concertina'.

In this ancestral partrimony common to humanity, there is an erotico-sacred fable of origins, which radiates about the theme of the

Androgyne. In the beginning there was a being (or there were several—seven in the Gnostic myth, eight in those of the Dogon, ten thousand in Chinese tradition, innumerable according to the *Symposium*) possessing the attributes of both sexes. This being, divided—or dividing itself—into two halves (the one male, the other female, also to unite together), gave birth to men. 'It divided its body into two halves. The one was male, the other was female. In this female the male engendered the Universe.'[50]

In all versions, the Androgyne belongs to the primordial, non-historical times. In all of them the history of humanity begins at the moment when the Unity, represented by the Androgyne, gives place to duality in the form of sexuality. In all the great systems in which Unity is the beginning and the term of life, in which all has issued from that and all returns to that, this rupture of the original non-distinction, this coming of duality, is also a degradation. It is a degradation by comparison with a condition for which man still has a nostalgia, a homesickness, and to which he in fact returns—a return symbolized by the desire and union of the sexes.

One of the most impressive myths of the Androgyne belongs to the very old religion of Shivaism,[51] which has survived in India not only as a religion of the masses but also as the vehicle of the loftiest metaphysical speculations and of an esoteric doctrine, thanks to which the ancient wisdom of that civilization has been preserved and handed down. In the non-manifest, Shiva is sexless, as also bodiless, but contains the sexes by virtue of containing all forms and uniting the contraries.[52] But as soon as Shiva divides, there comes desire, which is the attraction of the contraries, and from desire the worlds are born. The union of Shiva and Shakti (his manifestation) is represented by the hermaphrodite, Ardhanâri-îshvara, half male, half female. Their separate existence is only a fiction. In the popular religion, as is well known, the eternal couple, Shiva-Shakti, symbolized by the *linga* inserted into the *yoni*, is still regarded as the perfect representation of the divine. It is the primordial axis, and, as Max-Pol Fouchet writes, 'the *linga*, joining with the *yoni*, shows that the Absolute develops in plurality but resolves in oneness. The *linga/yoni* relation brings out sharply the antagonism of the male and female principles and destroys it in a triumphant non-duality.' It could not be better put.

The Androgyne reappears, this time associated with the creation of the species, in the Brihadâranyaka Upanishad:

> In the beginning, in truth, nothing of all this existed. From non-being there issues being. This being changes into a Self. The Self existed first in the form of the cosmic Person (Purusha). He looked and saw only himself. He said: *I am.* . . . He desired another. He became as large as a man and a woman embracing. He divided into two. So there was a husband and a wife. This is why each man is only a half. The empty space is filled by the woman. He coupled with her. So it is that men were created.

And now the Androgyne presided over the creation of the animals:

> When the Creator had divided into a male and female, the female thought: 'How dares he copulate with me when he has just formed me from a part of himself? I will hide.' She became a cow. He turned into a bull and copulated with her. So the cattle were born. She became a mare. He turned into a stallion. She became a she-ass, he turned into an ass, and he copulated with her. So were born the hooved animals. She became a she-goat, he turned into a ram. So he created all, all which exists by couples, down to the ants.

Thus the symbol is associated sometimes with the universal multiplication, sometimes with the original and divine indistinction. The divine is the non-dual: it has been defined as 'that in which the contraries coexist'. As soon as a tendency to manifestation arises, this appears as a duality, which polarizes itself into two fields of force (positive and negative, active and passive) and extends to the whole creation in the distinctness of the male and female aspects. It is desire, the attraction between these distinct yet inseparable contraries, that provides the kingpin between the two implications.[53]

Still bound up with the problem of the contraries, the theme recurs in the sacred tradition of the Greeks. There arose Chaos, Gaïa (the Earth) and, side by side with Gaïa, Eros; he was the most beautiful of the gods. But after this the first births took place without him. Nyx (Night), the daughter of Chaos, is a twin, herself bisexual, born fissiparously at the same time as her male twin, Erebos. She herself gives birth by the same process to Day (Ether and Light). After this, still unaided, she engenders the generation of the Children of Night, among whom are Sleep and Death, a pair of twins, one black, the other white

Meanwhile Gaïa, without the help of Eros, gives birth to Uranus, crowned with stars, but with him the sombre Pontus.

So, in the cosmogonies, androgyny presides over a double line of contraries. These include the masculine-feminine pair Day/Night (or Light/Darkness), Odd/Even, One/Many, Right/Left, and so on.

In a people given to metaphysical speculation, this instinctive distribution of things into two lines could not fail to raise the ontological question. What was there at the start? One, or several? In other words, where should the One be placed in the tables of contraries? In one of the columns? Or outside and at the head of the columns? As Clémence Ramnoux has written in her fine book on Heraclitus,[54] this little arithmological problem in fact raised the problem of Evil and its irreducibility. The first hypothesis blocked the contraries, the second bound them together through the dialectical movement. The choice was between a world fixed in two categories, abandoned by God, a world of despair and, on the other hand, a world of hope, the religious world of continuity and communication. On the metaphysical plane this choice was between a static, definitive dualism and a functional dualism constantly in course of integration into Unity. Hesiod, by placing at the head of his cosmogony the irreconcilable couple—Chaos (the Abysmal Fissure) and Earth (Basis of Security)—as procreator of incompatible races, and by leaving to one side and all alone an Eros who, born to unite, was prevented from doing so, took his place in the clan of absolute dualism. Hence the reproach levelled at the master of the majority by Heraclitus: 'All believe that Hesiod knows more than anyone, he who did not even know Day and Night! For Day and Night is One'.[55]

Coming from that Sage whose enigmatic sayings constantly reaffirm the unity of contraries (and who himself seems to have placed the One, the essence of wisdom, apart by itself), this criticism seems likely to have been aimed at Hesiod's conception of a Love powerless to reconcile 'the progeny of Uranus with the progeny of Night', 'the powers of order with the powers of destruction'—the conception of an Eros 'incapable of remaking the unity of all'.

In a radical pessimism such as Hesiod's, the myth of androgyny could of course not develop all its implications. Only those systems which explain the mystery of the world and of life by the disintegration of a Unity that may always be reintegrated—Evil being originally no more than the decline from Unity into separation, into dualism—can allow love the power of raising us up from that decline and that duality; they alone give to the Couple, whose image is the Androgyne, its double significance, natural and supernatural—its terrestrial vocation and its vocation of salvation.

It fell to Plato to take up all these implications and to re-establish them within the fascinating perspective of a metaphysics of nostalgia. One may criticize him for devoting such ingenuity to extending the myth to homosexual love (though the fact remains that his explanation fits in with the latest sexological investigations), but this extension does not alter its content. In the marvellous story which Plato attributes to the lively imagination of Aristophanes, the proliferation of detail never obscures the original stock. Like Heraclitus, who called God the *great Re-assembler*, Plato is attracted by the polar relationship, dispersion and reassembling.[56] And so, in the *Symposium*, the myth of the Androgyne is not merely the story of something that happened to the species, as the result of which each of us is a complementary fraction, a human half severed from its whole—it is also a sacred revelation of an order of reality which cannot be attained except through the symbol. It is a myth of initiation. The whole passage turns on the opposition between a primordial, paradisial integrity, and the baneful coming of a duality. From that distant time dates 'the desire of one another, which is implanted in us, reuniting our original nature, making one of two and healing the state of man'.

Nothing is more Greek than this yearning for unity: it underlies both the Orphic dream[57] and the majestic procession of the thought of Plotinus. What Greek wisdom revered in bisexuality was, clearly, the symbol: it detested actual cases of bisexuality and encouraged the putting to death of children so deformed, although various rites of bisexuality, in particular that of dressing up as a member of the opposite sex, continued to accompany the initiation of adolescents and marriage ceremonies. Well after the beginning of the historical period, the theme of an indistinction of the sexes was embodied in a bisexual god, Hermaphrodite, the god of sexual union and marriage who provided an image, on the plane of popular imagination, of the conjunction of the dream of unity with love.

To study or even to list here all the variants of the Androgyne myth in different times and places is out of the question. Such a study would extend from the great 'historical' cultures to the so-called primitive tribes. It would run, for instance, from Chinese thought (with its couple emblems, Yin and Yang, governing the sexualization of every aspect of the world and constituting a symbol both of Unity and of multiplication, their reunion being venerated in many forms— hierogamies, musical metaphors, geometrical symbols such as the famous diagram of the T'ai chi) to the ancient Mesopotamian incantation, and to those used in the magical rites of Oceania and of Africa.[58] The wealth of material is overwhelming. Tempting though it be to pursue I must leave this subject to others, and confine myself to presenting a few particularly rich or interesting variants—though not without the hope that my suggestions may lead someone to map out a mythology of Androgyne.[59]

One variant that seems worth singling out is the Iranian myth of Gayomart.[60] Proceeding from the opposition of Ormazd (the power of Light) and Ahriman (the power of Darkness) the Mazdaean cosmology places Androgyne after 'the great catastrophe' and the invention of Evil. This is much the same as Hesiod's scheme. But the rigidity of the Iranian dualism is greatly mitigated by the continual intervention of the angels called Fravarti, whose function—a considerable one in the Iranian gnosis—to some extent corresponds to that of Plato's daimonism. Tradition has it that Gayomart, the primordial man, when Ahriman succeeded in introducing death into him, fell on his left side; then, since he was made of pure metal, the various metals issued from his body, each from the part of the body to which it corresponded. Gold, the most precious of all, which proceeded from Gayomart's soul and from his semen, was gathered up by Spenta Armaiti—that is, Earth, or rather the Earth Archangel. For forty years she kept it, and at the end of this time there grew from the soil an extraordinary plant: this plant was the first human couple, Mahryag-Mahryânag—two inseparable beings so alike and so closely united that in them it was impossible to distinguish, let alone to isolate, the male from the female. Upon this double, androgynous being there descended a soul. But a race issuing from a single being would not have been viable in a world dominated by Death. Mahryag-Mahryânag was split into two, to give birth to historical humanity.

The Iranian myth completes the corporeal androgyne of Mahryag-Mahryânag with the spiritual androgyne of the Saoshyant, the Saviour born of a virgin (and so a single being not subject to the biological conjunction of male and female). But historical humanity is also called upon to reconstitute the Androgyne by uniting with its celestial double. The Iranian conception is that the *Self* is only part of our total being: of its transcendent counterpart each man carries in him an image, in the form of the Angel Fravarti, a feminine figure (for the Avesta speaks only for the man. This Fravarti, who is his guardian angel, his guide and his celestial self, is the prefiguration of the Jungian archetype of the *anima*. Conjunction with this double, constantly longed for, is finally achieved after death—is indeed the great hope that is placed in death; but it can be realized in this life with real women, in whose beauty the Eternal Feminine of the divine Essence *shines through*. Sufism, the religion of love professed by the minstrels of Iran (whose prophet was Zarathustra) has lived on this feminine cult, the cult of the Fravarti, and on this love which 'gives to the human being the support of a light that transfigures him'.

Such a theophany—the divine shining through the human—implies a conspiracy of the sensory and the spiritual, the *ham-dami* of senses and spirit in a mysticism of love. Shi-ism and Sufism have raised androgyny so that it becomes the metaphysical conception of the Couple in a single essence. As Henry Corbin has rightly observed, every mysticism of Marriage rests on an experience akin to that of the Iranian Angel Fravarti. Hence the symbol recurs among the Christian mystics, with all sorts of allegorical variants derived from amorous union.[61]

The androgyne is represented in the Mosaic tradition by Adam before the creation of Eve. Eve was first contained in him, then taken out of him. She is, as Marie-Jeanne Durry has perfectly expressed it, 'the companion torn from his sleeping form, the feminine double who was there in his heart'. The book of Genesis makes the coming of sexuality coincide with man's satanic revolt against the divine Unity.

The first sin is connected with knowledge: 'Ye shall be as gods, knowing good and evil'. The Biblical story simply illustrates one of the consequences of unitive thinking: by reference to the absolute integrity of the divine, thought itself is degradation; it ventures outside the original simplicity: it severs itself from that by constituting itself. Of this separation the division into sexes is the symbol rather than the cause. And so it lasts as long as earthly life. 'There is neither male nor female, for ye are all one . . .'[62]

Thus, even in the orthodox Christian beliefs, there are traces of an original androgyne (another passage of Genesis—'male and female created he them'—is translated by some commentators: 'and he created them androgyne') and of a final androgyne. What is lacking is the link—the hallowed Couple as both memory and prefiguration of the Kingdom, the fleeting yet illuminating reconquest by Eros of a Unity that is both at the beginning and at the end of Time. The whole space was taken up by the Incarnation. True, the mysticism of the Marriage in due course exploited the myth of androgyny, but in a veiled way and as a symbol only of the union of the soul with Christ; there is here no sacralization of the human couple by myth, no initiation upon a specifically conjugal way of salvation.

In Christian Gnosticism the dualism of the two Principles again relegated the myth to a subordinate position. The radical separation of the world of darkness and the world of light held, like the theogony of Hesiod, to a double descendancy, one from the divine world, the other from the chaos of Tiamat, that ancient chthonic goddess borrowed by Gnosticism from Mesopotamia along with the myth of the Seven. 'There are seven, there are seven. In the depths of the ocean, in the habitations, have they grown. They are neither male nor female, they are those who shake the tempest, they take no wives, they engender no children. . . .'[63]

The Gnostic theosophy favoured also the idea of God as ambivalent, as both spirit (masculine principle) and nature (feminine principle). This ambivalence emerged in the stress laid on the distinction between God the Father and God the Son and on the androgynous nature of the Son. The Gnostic myth presents us with *Nous* (the Spirit) coming down to earth and being embraced there by *Physis* (Nature): from this couple are born the first hermaphrodites, from whom proceeds the human race. To this initial hermaphroditism there corresponds the spiritual androgyne of the Saviour, the Son of God—but also the real androgyne of Anthropos, son of Tiamat.

Alchemy, which Bachelard has called 'that vast sexual reverie', and Jung 'an undercurrent to the Christianity that ruled on the surface . . . as the dream is to consciousness', took up the Gnostic myth and modified it. After their copulation, Nous and Physis are not separate: they have become a single bisexual and devouring spirit, hidden in the *prima natura*. The symbolism of alchemy abounds in examples of androgyne, either as original indistinction or as final perfection. Symbolizing both the opposition of the contraries and their reunion (i.e. Unity), Androgyne dominates the whole alchemical vision of the Universe. The divine quaternary represents not only the reunion of the four elements but also the unit made up of odd (masculine) and even (feminine), according to the axiom: 'One becomes two, two become three, and from three issues the one as fourth'. The philosopher's stone (*rebis*, literally 'the double thing') is also bisexual; so is the *homo philosophicus*, corresponding to the Gnostic Anthropos. Borrowing from the Gnostic theosophy (which their conception of a world of continuity and harmony, in which the contraries balance, mitigated and improved when it did not contradict), the alchemists resuscitated the belief in a Chaos existing side by side with the divine world of the Unity, and in the real androgyne of a Son of this Chaos side by side with the spiritual androgyne of Christ. This Son of Chaos was regarded as of chthonic and feminine origin like Mercury, like Hermes Psycho-pompos from whom he proceeded.

The alchemists passed on their conception of a divine androgyne to the humanists of the Renaissance: the columbine, the snail, the stone, the double eagle, the unicorn and the Uroboros continued to illuminate symbolism with their double forms. Leonardo da Vinci joins this tradition when he draws a columbine or a snail in a corner or on the back of his picture, as also when he delights in depicting the ambiguous beauty of a Saint John or a Bacchus.

With Gnosticism and Alchemy the myth had entered the service of magic. Already in the twelfth century it had insinuated itself into *la courtoisie*, but as practical lore, not any longer as a sacred account of human origin. Troubadours and courtly lovers, by the exchange of hearts, were awakening the female double that was asleep in them: they then projected this image of the soul upon the real woman. As Nelli has said: 'Thus the couple was constituted: it formed a single being. Everything felt by one partner was at once felt by the other. The magical influence of woman was installed in the heart of the man, and *vice versa*'.[64] This rite was not unlike the Iranian cult of the Fravarti; but to the Iranian minstrels the evocation of the feminine double was essentially mystical, the preparation for a theophany, for the divine to shine through the human, while the aim of the courtly rite was usually profane and practical—or even prophylactic. The point was to exorcize the maleficent magic power of woman by assimilating it and converting it into protective magic—unless the courtly lover definitely chose, like Tristan, to abandon himself to that evil power and to sink into chthonic night. Dante has given an entirely animistic description of this magical operation in his *Vita Nuova*: in it 'the Lord Love' appears holding the Lady asleep in his arms, naked except that she is lightly covered with a blood-red cloth, and after a while awakens her, in order to present to her the poet's fiery heart; with his mind he 'made her eat that thing which flamed in his hand; and she ate as one fearing'.[65] The passage, for all its sumptuous strangeness, helps to reduce the myth to allegory; it is a prelude to the secularization of the myth.

From now on, the androgynous theme of the heart—exchanged, shared, offered or captured, swallowed or eaten (in proportion to the sadism of the various poets)—was a constant feature of literature. In vain Marsilio Ficino attempted to make the androgyne once more a part of philosophy by a transfusion of Platonic blood: his version remained anaemic. Bembo took up the theme again in *Gli Asolani*. But by his time these hearts, 'changing their dwelling-place', were merely rhetorical properties. The androgyne became a literary motif, a commonplace of the symbolism of love-making—sometimes a cover for homosexuality, as in Elizabethan London, where one might be accosted in the streets by young men dressed as women, and where the word *hermaphrodite* was both a favourite with the fashionable poets and an insulting epithet (the equivalent, Marston tells us, of *milksop*).

Sometimes, of course, a sincere passion gave fresh life to the symbol, as in the case of Louise Labé's famous sonnet,

Lors double vie à chacun en suivra
Chacun en soi et son ami vivra,

which, in defiance of the prescriptions of protective magic, applied it to a love that was not much *interruptus:* or again, in John Donne's splendid *Canonization*, a poem inspired by his love for his wife, Anne.

The glamour of the myth lived on in spite of wear and tear. An anecdote reveals its vitality: Frederick of Prussia, when he met Voltaire for the first time (a meeting long desired and often requested), chose, from among the many subjects on which he might have questioned the great man, Plato's androgynes. German romanticism, with its inclination towards unitive mysticism (towards the mystery of what Goethe calls the *All-One*) attempted to restore to the myth its full value. Novalis, Ritter and von Humboldt in turn tried their hands at this, but it was Franz von Baader who made it the basis of a sacred ethic of the couple. Borrowing the idea of a primordial and sacred androgyne from Jacob Boehme (and so, through him, from alchemy) Baader teaches that the aim of marriage as a sacrament 'is to restore the celestial or angelic image of man as he should be': sexual love must not be confused with the reproductive instinct—its true function is to 'help the man and the woman to integrate inwardly the complete human image', that is to say the androgynous condition. Balzac's *Seraphita* (which he wrote at the request of Eveline Hanska and under the influence of Swedenborg) turned out to be the last great work of European literature to treat of the androgyne from the point of view of *purification* through love. In literature after Balzac there is little trace of the mystical or metaphysical implications of the androgyne. Hermaphroditism was degraded to the level of *curiosa* and used by eroticism for ends that were as concrete as they were tortuous: by the crude substitution of the particular case for the symbol, it not only lost all significance but extended this lack of significance to love itself, deprived of its implications of complementarity. In fact, the myth was not so much degraded as reversed.

THE ANDROGYNE IN PSYCHOLOGY

It was under the auspices of science that, at the beginning of this century, androgyny staged a comeback—a brilliant one. Psychology, first with Freud then with Jung, took the theme of the androgyne away from literature and treated it as a basic nostalgia of the psyche. Coming from Freud, this rehabilitation may well seem surprising: his work was essentially one of demythologization, especially as regards love, which he tried to reduce to 'pure'[66] sexuality. But Freud had the courage to contradict himself sometimes, and to develop. The idea of the androgyne as essential to love appears in his work as early as 1900. Under the influence of the Berlin doctor, Fliess (who believed he had discovered the bisexual character of all living cells), Freud accepted the hypothesis of a universal bisexuality of organic matter. As far back as 1898 he told Fliess that he adopted his point of view and considered this conception a fundamental one for his work. In the following year he wrote to him: 'I am also getting used to considering every sexual act as one between four individuals'. He continued to apply this conception in his psychiatric technique.

The theme of Androgyny, tied up with that of the Return, made a later, still more spectacular appearance in his *Beyond the Pleasure Principle*. In that fascinating book Freud undertook a recasting of his theory of the instincts: up to then he had defined the instincts in functional terms and had based his system on the opposition of Eros and Thanatos (the instincts of life and the instincts of death), but now he set to work to express instinctual life in terms of direction (*Richtung*). It seemed to him that he had discovered a conservative, even regressive tendency common to all the instincts: he was on the track of a general property of organic life, of '*a tendency innate in living organic matter impelling it towards the reinstatement of an earlier condition,* which it had to abandon under the influence of external disturbing forces'.[67] In *Beyond the Pleasure Principle* Freud shows that his mind is made up: the tendency which dominates organic life is a tendency to return to the inorganic. True, the sexual act remains the place where Eros measures up to Thanatos; but the victories of life are never more than respites in the journey towards death, and life's provisional equilibrium always ends by distintegrating into the definitive equilibrium of death. The orbit of all the instincts is death.

Psychologically, this *Todestrieb* is expressed by the principle of *Nirvana*, which dominates our whole psychic life. Even pleasure tends only to plunge us back into it. With his usual honesty Freud at once faced up to his discovery. He went so far as to speak of an *elasticity* of organic matter, and to show surprise that only the great myths of androgyny in the Upanishads and in Plato have given a precise image of it. Referring to the speech in the *Symposium*, he asked himself whether living substance was not one and indivisible before being divided up into a multitude of small fragments which, it seemed, sought to *re-unite* through the sexual instinct.

This quite new conception of the *libido* as an effort to reconstitute a lost unity or identity, and of sexuality as an aspiration of the separated towards re-union (a tendency well expressed, in Freud's view, by the ancient myths), was put forward as a hypothesis which might also be a temptation. It appears to have been connected with the fascination that was exercised over him by death.[68]

Freud, as is well known, repented of having given way to the ascendancy of the myths. In *An Outline of Psycho-Analysis* he makes fun of 'the poets' fables, which the history of living matter has not confirmed'. But he went on to suggest a new vision of the mythic, androgynic theme of the Return. The coming together in love of the two basic instincts (the one driving towards life and the other towards death), and the paradox of an 'aggression tending to the closest union' (his last definition of the sexual act), leads Freud to situate the conflict on a plane where the destiny of the individual is distinct from that of the species. The act signifies sometimes multiplication, progression and life, at other times unification, regression and death, according to whether one is looking at the destiny of the species or that of the individual. It is always the cosmogonic Eros that enmeshes and involves man in the monstrous movement of the generations; but for the individual this clockwork signifies going round and round—involution—and for the species evolution.

Freud tried once again to extend his observation, to derive from it an explanation of the universe. This emerges from a passage in *An Outline of Psycho-Analysis*. After referring to 'this interaction of the two basic instincts with and against each other', Freud affirms that 'the analogy of our two basic instincts extends from the region of animate things to the pair of opposing forces—*attraction* and *repulsion* which rule the inorganic world.' In due course Jung took up this couple of contraries and connected it with the motif of the Androgyne.

Depth psychology, far from presenting itself as an operation of demythologization, rehabilitated the image-making way of thinking. Jung, as is well known, divides the psyche into three zones, the conscious, the individual unconscious and the collective unconscious—this last being a kind of hereditary reservoir in which the myths survive in the form of symbols and images. For the soul seems to conserve functional traces not only of its own experiences but of those of the species. The collective unconscious, a kind of cellarage of the psyche, appears to be a deposit of the most archaic human behaviour patterns: since man has lived through only a few thousand years of civilization but through far longer time of relative lack of culture, the imprints from that earlier time have remained strong and fresh, and a trifle can bring them to life again. This collective unconscious is always ready to project itself into the conscious. And it happens—the support which a mythic foundation of the couple gains from Jung's psychology is at once clear—that *the unconscious always has the 'colour' of the other sex.*

Neither the subconscious nor bisexuality was discovered by Jung—he was preceded by Freud, Fliess, Weininger and others; but Jung has exploited them admirably. Collecting an enormous quantity of references, he has studied theogonies, cosmogonies, religions, heresies, mysticism, magic, Gnosticism and Alchemy, and has succeeded in laying bare identical, or at least analogous patterns, which he came to call *the archetypes*. An archetype is always collective. It belongs to all people, or at least to a great many of them. And among them Jung was bound to come upon the archetype of the Androgyne. Not only did he unearth it in the myths of Genesis and the great fables of the Origins, not only did he find it also in many religions in the form of a divine syzygy, or in the androgynous character of the gods or of the Saviour, but he identified it in the workings of a man's psyche. Recognizing the presence in his subconscious of a complementary feminine figure playing a great part in the dream life, he suggested that this should be called the *anima*. According to him, this figure of the opposite sex represents that minority of feminine genes which the most virile man carries about in him. The hypothesis gains weight from the fact that this figure is not to be found in the subconscious of a woman: there Jung discovered a corresponding masculine figure, which he calls the *animus. Anima* or *animus* is, as it were, the double, belonging to the opposite sex, whom we carry in us, and who is an imprint of the sexual experiences of generations of ancestors and of the system of psychic adaptation which they have elaborated. Jung did not fail to relate this discovery to the question of the contraries, and to the human need to integrate these instead of fighting them. This is what he came to call 'assuming the totality of one's psychism'.

It is to the intensity of this dream life and the *anima* that Jung attributes the popularity of such books as Rider Haggard's *She* and Benoît's *Atlantide*—a conclusion which seems somewhat hasty when one reflects that this popularity is due mostly to women readers. But a novel like *Atlantide* cleverly combines the yearning for the *anima* with the yearning for the lost Paradise; and this combination fits in with the tradition which we learn from myths and from psychology.

Determined though Jung was to defend himself from the metaphysical temptation and from the generalizings of the visionary type of mind, he could not prevent this new science of the working and of the laws of the psyche from sometimes turning into a reflection on the destiny of man and a point of view about the direction of human conduct. Like Freud, Jung recognized in the human psyche a tendency to reconstitute a condition in which masculine and feminine coexisted: that is, he started along the same way as his master. But while

Freud tended to view this as a regression towards the inorganic, to Jung it appeared as an adoption of the primordial complementary contraries of the masculine and the feminine, psychically *imagined* as the anima-animus archetype.

Jung had a strong dualistic side to him: his weakness for Gnosticism and his persistence in looking at Christianity through the Gnostic theosophy are well known. He tended to regard Evil as a Principle, not only as a psychic reality, and recognized the existence of a Luciferian way. That he did not fall into Gnostic extremism is due no doubt to his having discovered in the psyche a self-regulating mechanism resting on the law of pairs of opposites. Jung was glad to acknowledge that he owed this dynamism of the contraries largely to Heraclitus, but it seems likely he owed it more to Freud, whose whole work is threaded through by a type of dialectical thinking, very characteristic of him and based on the reciprocal action of two opposed forces. According to Jones, the love of the *pairs* was constantly recurring in Freud: 'The fact of the existence in man's psychic make-up of a conflict between two opposing forces seemed to him fundamental'.

Jung's dialectic—whatever its origin, and in spite of some of his avowed predilections—placed him in the opposite camp to the Gnostics. His method is to seek a constantly increased awareness of the identity of the contraries, and relativity of their opposition, while the Gnostic attitude was based on the rigidity of this opposition. Jungian initiation—with its classical stripping away of more and more —consists in integrating 'the whole scale of possibilities that one carries in oneself': in Jung's own terms 'the old values are maintained, but one recognizes at the same time the value of their contrary'. The integration, that is, is mental. Evil is necessary—'the world continues to exist only because its contrasts remain balanced'—but loses its virulence, ceases to be Evil as soon as it is known, mentally separated from Good, discriminated. The therapeutic part of Jung's thinking is aligned with this conception. It is very close to that of dialectical and critical purification; and here again the heir apparent was taking the same road as his predecessor.

In Jung's work, then, the symbol of the Couple set ringing a wealth of harmonics. Its contribution, in that context, was that it brought out the idea of a bisexuality hidden in the human soul, and that it connected the mythic theme of the Androgyne with the psychical oneiric image of the *Anima*. As we have already seen, the existence of this double was not unknown. Gérard de Nerval's Yousouf says: 'I have a dream that constantly recurs, always the same and always varied. . . . As though in the bosom of the infinite, I see a celestial figure, more beautiful than all the creations of the poets, who smiles at me with a piercing sweetness and descends from the heavens to come to my side. Is it an angel? A peri?' But it is not usual to take seriously the intuitions of poets. By bringing to this one the support of fashionable science, by raising it once for all from that inferior rank to which commonsense degrades the objects of its envy, by giving a rational basis to Nerval's theme of the previous existence and the *already seen* (which scientific dogma believed it had well and truly crushed by labelling it *paramnesia*), Jung certainly contributed to the restoration of the great myth; and yet, beautiful and angelic though the figure of the Jungian *Anima* is, it remains an image, the representation of an aspiration that is itself above any form. The magus who evoked it was less advanced in his approach than was the visionary, who included sexuality in one majestic movement of universal integration with Unity, and who, in the deep night of human love, listened for the echo of the myth of Return.

The theme of the Couple, whether it be the residue of a historical but extremely ancient experience of the species, or an intuition of an ontological former state which the imagination represents to itself in temporal form, answers to a yearning for complementarity, which human beings cannot help feeling as though it were a memory: the myth of the Androgyne is also the myth of the lost Paradise, and love is a reconquest of a 'past happiness'. This is surely the meaning of the feeling of predestined love—we recognize a fate rather than a face. The beings who are fateful for us are those who announce to us that an original, remembered plenitude will begin all over again: androgyny is a myth of integration. As I have already said, only the great metaphysical systems in which everything comes from Unity and returns to it enable this myth to develop its full implications: in the beginning there is Simplicity, and evil is merely the decline that consists in going away from it; but with evil there appears the desire to raise oneself up from it again, with duality the longing to reconstitute the Unity, with the opposition of the contraries the attraction between them, and with the distinction of the sexes the yearning for their identity. In this world of continuity the contraries are always bound together: duality is only an *uncomposing* of the Unity, and sexuality is, at first, the division of the species into sexes, but then its necessary sequel, the attraction between the sexes. The Androgyne is not only the symbol of a time outside time, when two were one, but also that of a fusion within this world, a victory of the Unity over duality, this victory being signified by and embodied in the Couple.

In a rigidly dualistic system like Gnosticism there is none of this. In its impermeable world, where two remain two, the Androgyne can be used as a symbol of duality, of the opposition of the contraries, but never of the Couple. In the Gnostic world with its subjection to the powers of darkness, sexuality is radically evil: no distinction is made between the separation of the sexes and their reunion, before the fall into duality and the compensating, redeeming love—none, either, between voluptuous indulgence, marriage and procreation, all of which are to be equally culpable. The result is a morality of separation and rejection, not one of recuperation: logically it should have taught total abstention, and sometimes it has done so, but it has constantly been tempted to recommend, as a morality for the few side by side with the other, a perilous doctrine of illumination through sin, which has led some Gnostic sects to a frenzy of physical humiliation and debauch. This doctrine still exists: I have found a surprising but strangely precise confirmation of it in a recent book by Madame Schwaller de Lubicz.[69] According to this book, spiritual conjunction (which, the author says, is the only real one) cannot be achieved with the fleshly husband or wife, but only with the *spiritual witness*, a complementary psychic principle, passive in the man, active in the woman—in other words Jung's *anima-animus*. This brings us back to the conception of love as involving four persons, but the function assigned by Gnosticism, in this book, to the terrestrial partner is a limited, even a repellent one. Given the radical separation of body and spirit, there is no projection of the *anima-animus* into the physical person: the supreme sin is the sin of sublimation. 'The spiritual conjunction with each other, of which some lovers dream and go in quest, is an illusion that prevents them from realizing, each *for himself*, the conjunction with their own spiritual witness'—and the marital relationship can, we are told, be only an association. The only eroticism conceivable in such a marriage, according to this author, is the adoption of a sexual behaviour designed to arouse in one's partner an awareness of the animality of instinct and of the shame of being subject to it. Such shock-treatment love-making, aimed at bestializing sex, is love-making reduced to abjection: it is clearly a turning of love against one's earthly companion, male or female—but especially against the woman, who is insulted and degraded along with love itself. It is the negation of the Couple, of its primordial complementarity.

Over against this erotic of abjection there is the erotic of sublimation. Over against the pessimism of separation the optimism of liaison and integration. Over against an awareness of the soul's degradation, an awareness of its divine descent. Over against bestialized sex the divinizing Eros. It was not without reason that, in medieval and Renaissance symbolism, the Androgyne came to represent *perfect* love, a love adopted wholly. Every conjunction of masculine and feminine is already, no doubt, an allusion to this great Mystery, a mystery of incarnation, for in it duality is held in check for a moment for the sake of the Unity, which is both signified and recomposed. It is for us to decide whether we will content ourselves with this allusion or go on to recover our fabulous inheritance of myths and symbols. Shall we let this inheritance fall away again, like those dreams which, in the morning, for lack of courage, we abandon to sleep—grains imprisoned in their husks and not allowed to germinate? Or shall we choose to pull ourselves together, fight against slumber and keep our balance on the dividing line between the conscious and the unconscious, still sufficiently governed by the unconscious to feel its swell raising us up, but also firmly enough sustained by the conscious not to let ourselves slip back? There, on the crest of the wave (if we are attentive) we shall see the emergence of that nocturnal half of our self which Thorbecke described to Adelheid Solger. The seismic tremors of love raise it slowly, like a lost continent, from the depths of Night towards the Day.

THE ANDROGYNE IN BIOLOGY

After the science of the soul, the science of life: is androgyny, besides being a psychological reality, a biological one as well? What confirmation, if any, does the theme of a basic identity of the sexes encounter in the history of living bodies? In other words, what becomes of bisexuality when regarded from the evolutionary point of view?

A novice who consults any book on animal biology is soon struck by the fact that hermaphroditism is there treated as a natural phenomenon: clearly bisexuality is something other than a monstrosity to be exhibited in a fair. Whole classes of the simpler animals have male and female characteristics side by side: these animals are called *natural* hermaphrodites. Others are *accidentally* so—but with such frequency that it proves impossible to draw a firm line between them and the others.

Beginning with a simple sexual bivalence,[70] with the tendency for an individual to secrete both male and female products at the same time, bisexuality is sometimes, at a later stage (as functional differentiation soon expresses itself in differences of structure), encountered in the form of a single organ, the ovotestis, which already shows signs of the division into two sexes, for in it the male secretion takes place in one zone and the female secretion in another. Next the function is definitely divided between two different organs. Finally, it is divided between two distinct individuals.

Thus the facts observed at an early stage show us sexualization as one of the aspects of that expansion of the simple towards the complex, of unity towards differentiation, specialization and adaptation, which is characteristic of the evolution of species. To put it briefly, the first dualization is in the functions that correspond to the masculine and the feminine, then this difference of functions becomes extended to morphology, and then it is embodied in two distinct creatures: it is at this last stage only that we can speak of a real sexuality in the usual sense.

But this separation of the sexes (or gonochorism) does not end the dualization. Life goes on further into complexity and invents species with three or with four sexes, or again species in which the male and female genital organs are more or less completely unified. Indeed life produces or tolerates phenomena that seem to us fantastic: birds or insects made up of a male half and a female half, or of a whole sexual mosaic, crustaceans or polypi that begin their lives with one sex and end them with another, or even change sex periodically. These extravagances have their bearing on the human species, both in myth and in actuality. The prophet Tiresias, as is well known, was said to have passed from the male condition to the female and back again, and readers may know Ribera's strange picture showing a creature with a beard uncovering a swollen breast from which he is about to give suck. The popular press has exploited to the full certain cases of a change of sex in a champion runner or jumper. But these, at least as regards the human species, are anomalies. It is in the normal man or woman that we must look for traces of an original bisexuality.

Starting with anatomy, we see that the male and female genital organs in Man have likenesses as well as differences: structurally, each of the two sexes seems to have clung to a kind of sketch or plan for the other. It is, in fact, an abandoned plan. To understand it, one must go back up the course of ontogenesis to the earliest phases of the life of the embryo: one cannot help feeling wonder at the sight of the slow metamorphosis by which a genital organ, which starts the same in both the sexes, gradually becomes sexualized—in the male individual it develops a kind of genital bud which remains atrophied in the female, and in the female it leaves open the orifice which it closes in the male. Aristotle inferred from female anatomy that a woman is an unfinished or mutilated male. It is for the women to return the compliment.

This metamorphosis of the external organs occurs, in time, after that of the genital tracts, which itself comes after that of the gonads or genital glands. The normal course of things is that the embryo, passing through the same stages as the species (according to Haeckel's well-known law), first undergoes a condition of non-differentiation, with one and the same kind of organ in both sexes. This organ then develops either its central (medullary) part or its peripheral (cortical) zone, according as it takes male or female direction. This differentiation is governed by hormones, which are chemical substances secreted by the gonads. The bisexuality of the gonads is followed by bisexuality of the tracts. Every embryo, whichever is its genetic sex, has, to begin with, a pair of Wolffian ducts (the future male genital conduits) and a pair of Müllerian ducts (the future female genital tracts): as it grows it develops the one pair and not the other, and at a later stage it completes them by additions which help to produce the morphological differentiation of the external genital organ, yet leave still in existence, in a reduced and (as it were) degenerate form, all the organs of the sex which has been sacrificed. It is true, then, to say that every human being bears traces of an anatomical bisexuality of the embryo.

One is naturally tempted to ask if this bisexual character exists at other levels, particularly at that of the cell. As I have already mentioned, in about 1900 certain doctors in Berlin and Austria, Fliess, Freud, Weininger and others, believed that they had made a major discovery: the virtual bisexuality of every living cell. This theory, which stressed the importance of the part played in sexuality by the chemical[71] secretions, seemed of such consequence that scientists laid rival claims to its paternity and the friendship between Freud and Fliess did not survive the painful quarrels which arose. The theory is now, it seems, out of date, and more emphasis is laid on hormonal bisexuality, for which the evidence appears to be stronger. But this may still be largely a matter of interpretation.[72]

The growing importance of biochemistry soon drew the attention of men of science to the activity of the endocrine glands. Their secretions, as is well known, play a part not only in the differentiation of the primary and secondary sexual characteristics[73] but also in determining the sexual psyche. It is now known that a hormone injection suffices not only to develop the mammary glands but also to awaken the maternal instinct. At the same time, every individual secretes both male and female hormones: the males produce more androgens than oestrogens, but the proportion is constantly subject to modification; moreover, the chemical structure of the hormones themselves is such that, in certain cases, they are susceptible to radical change. Even when the individual has become adult, the hormones still keep up a kind of vacillation between the two sexes. Their regulating, equilibrating function implies a twofold sexual potentiality. It is on the hormonal level that the bisexuality of Man is most clearly evident. And the bisexuality of the human psyche is closely bound up with this oscillation of hormonal sexuality: it looks as if Jung was right in thinking that the *anima* represents that minority of feminine hormones which any man carries in him. The myth of the Androgyne is not only one of the great themes of story-telling, it is a profound reality of the history of life.

Androgyny symbolizes not only the original identity but its re-establishment. To what extent does science confirm the myth as a symbol of love and of the Couple?

In biology, a coupling is an act by which, impelled by a force that appears to animate all animals from the protozoa to man, two individuals of the same species and of different sex join together so that the male individual can transfer a part of his cellular substance to the female individual. This definition at once raises questions and objections. What is the nature of this force? To what extent is it bound up with sexuality? To what extent with fertilization? Must we cease to call it 'coupling' when a man and a woman come together without fertilization—that is to say, in most cases? Clearly it is important to think out afresh what the sexual mechanism is like at the two ends of evolution—in its simplest form and in its most complex, in the place of its broadest expansion (the human species) and in the place where apparently it is only at the start (the protozoa). Of the phenomenon in unicellular organisms I can find no more romantic example than that in Jean Rostand's account of the *paramecia*.[74]

The *paramecium*, a tiny inhabitant of freshwater pools, reproduces by binary fission : that is, from time to time the single cell of this infusorium splits and separates into two identical twin infusoria. This division repeats itself once or twice a day, so that—but for accidental mortality—a single *paramecium* could produce a million of its like in less than twenty days. Up to this point there is no sign of anything like love:

> But at longish intervals the *paramecia* stop feeding; they seem agitated, uneasy; swimming in all directions, as though in search of something, they collide, they strike one another with their cilia. And now two of them approach one another and unite, then two others, and soon the whole population is arranging itself in couples. Perhaps at this moment they give out particular substances, kinds of hormones which, diffused in the liquid medium, make them more attractive to each other. In any case the two *paramecia* that have joined—*conjugated*—now press close together, mouth to mouth. This coming together, this embrace, is followed by a still more intimate contact: the members enclosing their respective protoplasms blur, then fade at the forepart of the body, so that the two conjugant cells are now, so it seems, *open to each other, in each other*. This union takes about a quarter of an hour to achieve. The couple, which so far has been swimming, now sinks to the bottom of the water.

There follows a description of certain changes in the nuclei, at the end of which the *paramecia* are ready for the essential event of the *conjugation*, the exchange of genetic material.

> In each of the *paramecia* one of the two nuclei—the *sedentary* one—remains in place, but the other—the *migratory* one—passes into the *paramecium* opposite, across the thin bridge of flesh that now joins the two creatures. Then each migratory nucleus fuses with the opposite sedentary nucleus to forms a *mixed* nucleus, or nucleus of conjugation. These acts take about fifteen hours to complete. Having reconstituted their membranous frontiers, the two *paramecia* then separate, and each resumes its autonomous existence. . . . Nothing, in appearance, distinguishes the infusorium from what it was before the marriage. And yet it has become essentially different; it has expelled an important part of its nuclear substance (whence perhaps a beneficent purification), and, above all, having received from its partner exactly as much as it has given, it has become *half the other*.

Thus the force that drives two cells to join together must not be identified with the force that drives them to reproduce. It is a fundamental discovery, this, that even at that elementary stage of life the phenomenon of reproduction and that of conjugation are distinct. They may coincide, they are not the same. *The purpose of love is not procreation.* The multiplication of species did not require the invention of sexuality: we know that Life had found other methods—budding, reproduction by fission, parthenogenesis. Sexuality was not *necessary.*[75] Some have maintained that it is a biological luxury. Certainly it favours the rejuvenation of heredity, the elimination of the defects that gradually accumulate in a line: this is one of its advantages, but nothing justifies us in saying that this is its reason. Experiment shows that asexual reproduction can go on indefinitely.[76]

The force driving the *paramecia* to conjugate is not the reproductive instinct, but it is not the attraction of the sexes either: when these infusoria come together, the two partners are strictly alike, and they function as hermaphrodites. There is no tendency to compensate for a sexual difference, which does not exist, or to reconstitute a bisexual condition, which was there all the time. We are forced to conclude that the amorous phenomenon precedes sexuality. And here again sexualization is only *one* of the forms of dualization in living things; it leads us on to regard sexual conjunction as *one* of the ways of compensating for such dualization. It is this corollary that is so perfectly illustrated by the conjunction of the *paramecia*, which suggests that *love is not to be confused with sexuality any more than with the instinct for procreation*, and that the force which drives the sexes towards each other is only one means for accomplishing something that is far greater—a tendency to self-deliverance from any differentiation, any particularization, in order to reconstitute a lost identity. Though not the only one, this means of accomplishment is nonetheless the one specific to the Couple, the way laid open by love to Man and Woman towards a reconquest of their primordial condition. Whether it be a permanent or a passing fusion of two individuals, there is what appears to be an elementary type of love, not only in the infusoria, but in the bacteria, and perhaps even, if Rostand is right, 'in those infra-microscopic creatures the viruses, which are in some respects transitional between the world of life and the world of matter'. One even wonders whether a 'general propensity to unite is not part of the nature of a molecule . . . insensitive and inert though it be'.

'Principle of expansion', 'affinity of being for being', 'appetency for another'—the name matters little; what is there, so it seems, is a universal property, and it may be permissible to seek examples of it even in the cycles of transformation of matter and energy.

At the other end of evolution there is human love. The infusoria exemplify a kind of groping towards the love which is most completely fulfilled in Man. Evolution has moved in the direction of an always increased fitness or adaptation of one sex to the other. Bounoure is not afraid to say, of the higher species, that

> the male and the female, independently of the existence of each one as a *whole* individual, display a *reciprocal destination*. . . . In everything that touches reproduction, the two sexes are made not each for itself but one for the other, and the perfect co-ordination that renders them correlative is a true *external purposiveness.*[77]

To think at all deeply about human coupling is to find it much stranger than it seemed. It is always described as a process of fertilization. Yet, if even in the animal world the attraction between the sexes cannot be reduced to the reproductive instinct, this is also so, *a fortiori*, in the human species. In spite of this it is still essential, if we would understand the meaning of coupling, to consider its biological plane and the way in which the reproductive cells fuse together, though without forgetting that the act goes infinitely beyond this cellular conjunction—which yet remains, even when it is avoided, the model and the key to amorous behaviour.

In the protozoa like the *paramecia*, as we have seen, each of the conjugating cells is the whole individual; but in the metazoa, which are societies of cells, the conjugating individual delegates, as it were, one of its reproductive cells or gametes to act as its representative and operate the genetic transfer. This delegation is the result of selectivity. In Man, for instance, only one—the quickest and most agile—out of two million spermatozoa ejaculated will reach its aim and succeed in penetrating the ovule; and this is one of four hundred thousand female germinal cells, of which barely a few hundreds descend cyclically, one by one, into the oviduct, there to run the gauntlet of the chance of being fertilized. The morphology of the gametes corresponds to the part they have to play in this sexual scenario. The female cell is not very mobile—it is some ten thousand times heavier and larger than the male germ cell: this, which is called upon to compete with millions of its fellows in the frantic race up the oviduct, is tiny, extremely mobile and provided with a propellent organ, the flagellum. Only one gets to its object. What happens to the others? They die and are absorbed by the female's tissues. The male germ cell has two possibilities only— either to win the race or to die.

This one and only end is also a final one: the function of the spermatozoon is confined to penetrating the ovule with what is truly a rape on the cellular level (a replica, or rather a blue-print, of another sortie, which takes place on the scale of the individual) and transferring to this its genetic material—in other words, to fertilizing; this is all. For the ovule, however, this is the beginning of a long and stupendous activity. Once it has been fertilized, the ovule (now known as the ovum) takes up a fixed position; that is, becomes *embedded*. And then begins a truly marvellous metamorphosis. In the maternal element (prepared by the hormones to receive, shelter, nourish and develop it) the ovum, which has received from the spermatozoon not only its genetic material (including the sexual chromosome which determines its sex) but also the spur to an incredibly extended subdivision and multiplication, engenders both the millions of somatic cells (themselves diversified to form the organic tissues) and the germinal cells of a genital organ (which will gradually become sexualized in accordance with its chromosome formula). But the hormones will go on assuring this sexualization long after the embryonic stage. From child to adult, from primary and secondary sexual characters to physiological and psychological behaviour, they will extend the sexual differentiation over the whole individual.

A new cycle can then begin. The female hormones have prepared both the organs and the psychological make-up of the woman, not only for submission to the sexual act and fertilization, but for a considerable part of the development of the germ: they have also prepared her for being static and sedentary, and for gestation.[78] Parallel with this (or, rather, complementary to it), the male hormones have inclined the man to action, to movement, to the capture and domination of the female. The instinct for domination is governed by the male hormone, as has been shown by many experiments in the castration of animals.[79] These secretions condition, in each sex, the nature of desire and of love, which are always to some extent linked, in the man, with nomadism, conquest and aggression (sometimes also sadism), and in the woman with patience, passivity and submission (sometimes also masochism). *Probably it is the female hormones that produce the inclination towards a slow maturing of passionate love.*

The hormones by themselves would supply us with the proof that coupling takes place on various levels. In man this gradation involves infinite potentialities, from the most elementary rutting, the mere blind appeasement of an appetite, to the most complete awareness of the nature of love—from physiological fertilization to the fertilization of heart, imagination and mind.

One can only marvel at the constantly maintained concordance between the act, as it is carried through on the cellular level, and the act as it takes place on the psychic plane. At every moment the behaviour of individuals in love lets the biological plane shine through. The transfer of its material by the male germ cell—the giving cell—to the female germ cell; the way this receives it; the initiative taken by the former; the latter's submission to the violence: all these things are reflected faithfully in the normal behaviour of a man and a woman —in the man's tendency towards domination, polygamy and Don Juanism, and in the woman's (at least latent) disposition towards monogamy and faithfulness, as also towards monopolizing her man.

But the *abnormal* behaviour of men and women is no less amazing. It seems, in fact, that most of the human aberrations, perhaps all of them, have their precedent in the extraordinary evolution of love in animals. Not long ago, in one of his brilliant essays, Roger Caillois maintained that there is 'a kind of biological conditioning of the imagination', and that there are serious reasons for supposing that in man the make-believe or story-telling function does the work of instinctive behaviour in the insect. 'Man', he wrote, 'is not isolated in nature. . . . He is not exempt from the action of the biological laws that determine the behaviour of other animal species'. Yet in him these laws seem to be less imperative —not any longer to condition *action* but only *representation*.[80]

These views are attractive, but rather cut and dried. They fail to take account of a certain element of erotic make-believe in animals and of the human aptitude to *act out* the make-believe from fables, that is to give them objective existence in action. The truth is, there is no gap in the continuity between animal and human behaviour: everything happens as though man derived his most aberrant inventions from a kind of memory reserve or residue of animal experiences. What is the essential characteristic of sexual behaviour in animals? It is ambivalence. To them sex is both fascination and terror, it excites attraction but also antagonism. In the pages of Bounoure, Lorenz and Rostand we constantly come up against this contrast: side by side with a great diversity of rites of seduction (strutting, pre-copulatory play, display of colour, production of attractive or intoxicating scents, song and other noises) there is the most amazing repertory of tortures (beating, biting, infliction of mortal wounds, disembowelling, mutilation, decapitation, devouring).

Many have tried to determine the purpose of these forms of violence, and it has become clear that their effect—perhaps also their object—is to heighten sexual ardour: far from discouraging the partner, aggressiveness usually increases her frenzy tenfold. Combativeness is the motive power of love in animals. It remains remarkable that this combativeness conforms to the sexual scenario. In the male its tendency is to make the female submit more completely, to immobilize her and to penetrate her more deeply—hence, in certain Arachnids, the use of quasi-magnetic passes, the instilling of a philtre or an anaesthetic and the binding of the female; hence, also, the ferocious, deadly kiss of the lampreys, the stiletto blow inflicted by certain molluscs and, in some amphibians, embraces so violent that they crush the chest. Such violence is rare in the other sex: when it occurs, it usually takes the form of devouring, as with the female mantis and certain female spiders. In the female this cannibalism amounts to an excessive development of her function as the receiving partner: less ferocious variants are to be found in cases where the semen or the spermatophore is absorbed by mouth (there are locusts who chew this for a long time, devouring even the envelope).

These extravagances and many others, especially those whose effect is to break the monotony of the sexual act by variety of poses or by collective frenzy (as with the sexual chains of the Lymnaea), recur in human story-telling. So, for instance, a great many legends take up the ancestral theme of the devouring Woman. I have myself come upon the theme of the bound woman in Klossowski, Mandiargues and Proust: there is Roberte, bound half naked to a cross-bar in the basement of a shop in the Palais Royal; there is Vanina begging the 'young man of the pine-wood' to seize hold of her somewhat brutally and bind her hands behind her back with his tie; and there is Charlus, that monstrous female spider trussed up at last with iron instead of silk, caught and garrotted on the bed in the brothel.

The inventions of eroticism are *natural*. This, indeed, was to have been expected: they too are effects of the infinite diversification and inventive power of life. 'When we make love', wrote Rémy de Gourmont, 'we do it, as the theologians say, *more bestiarum*. Love is profoundly animal. That is its beauty.' Only the conclusion is false, and it is only half false: the distinction of human love is to be mental at the same time as it is animal, to bind the one to the other at every moment afresh. This is what gives interest to the similarities noted above, side by side with a biological continuity from the animal to man, they give us glimpses of a psychic continuity in man, extending from the animal to the mental. In animals there are all the elements of an *art of love* in the trite sense—that is, a collection of tricks for starting or intensifying desire: signals are given, which by association set in motion the sexual mechanism as inevitably as the sight of certain objects or a certain setting determines that of the fetishist or the sexual maniac; rites are practised which automatically provoke an eroticism, a trance, hypnosis or catalepsy. But these rites remain invariable in the case of a given species—they are the fruit of its invention, not of the individual's fantasy. Man alone has the power to choose from the repertory of natural inventions those that exalt him and those that please him. He can at will unfold the most diverse significations of sexuality; he can adopt them mentally, he can *imagine* them.

It is here—not at some dividing line between the normal and the abnormal, not in the extravagance of the forms and behaviour adopted —that perversion begins. It consists in abusing this *imagination*, in enslaving it to pleasure. For it is the same tricks that lead some to vice, others to that 'confusion of the limits', to that cosmic communion in which Vanina could feel that she was in communion with the whole of nature. In conforming to the rite of being tied up, Vanina was seeking—with that admirable, ancestral intuition possessed by some girls —only to prepare herself for a pure revelation. Her bare feet, her bound hands and her arms stretched backwards were only the outward signs of the rôle of captive woman which she had decided to *play*—so seriously that, before finally submitting, she sought to assure herself that her lover had really 'an aggressor's quality' by commanding him to untie her and let her go.[81] With Roberte and with Charlus it was a machination of pleasure, with Vanina it was *ceremony*. We have here the suggestion of a sublime play, designed to bring the *insignificance* of the particular case into harmony with the significations of the original and the universal. The simplest gestures, half simulated, half lived, become rites, and, when they mime aggressiveness, far from ruining the mythology of the Couple, stress its meaning and its mystery. The psychologist Baudouin has said that 'We must go down to the instincts if we are to understand something of the psychology of the contraries.' The other way round, appeal must be made to the psychology of the contraries if we are to understand the sexual instinct and to resolve that apparent contradiction, the antagonism of the sexes and of love.

Many enigmas are solved by an awareness that often, even in violence, love is merely seeking to affirm itself more spectacularly. And it is permissible to wonder if the same is not true of other aberrations, whose effect is to increase the distance between the contraries, between the low and the high, the ignoble and the sublime, or pleasure and suffering. The question will seem profoundly immoral to some people, strangely reassuring to others, according to whether, by doctrine or by temperament, they hold the contraries to be irreducible or to be inseparable, sexuality to be irremediably shameful and bad or merely mixed and therefore worth sifting out. The psychology of sexual aberration might in the end prove to be less painful than the moralists have led us to believe; it might turn out that love is trying to hold on to its function, which is to dig out and develop the least germ of spirit. But enough has been said to suggest that the evolution of human love is towards intelligence and an assumption of the primordial significance of sexuality by the spirit.

The upshot of this brief confrontation with science is, first, that in the history of Life sexualization makes its appearance as *one* of the modes of its expansion, of its dualization; and next, that the division of the sexes—necessarily preceded by a state in which the two potentialities are still identical if not united—is accompanied by a tendency of the sexes to *reunite*. This conception of sexuality (as a gap which tends naturally, indeed automatically, to close), relegates the function of procreation to the second place, in favour of some great physical, perhaps also metaphysical, Law of cosmogonic Eros. Side by side with Life's tendency to expansion, dilation and multiplication, the existence of a complementary tendency forces itself more and more on our attention—a tendency (which may be common to animate and inanimate matter) to fuse and regroup, to go back to a re-integration of its original condition, to return to Unity. Of this regressive property (or, in Freud's illuminating image, this *elasticity*) the attraction between the sexes may well be only one of the means of achievement—though it is the one specific to the Couple, its own way, the chance offered to it of compensating for the division of the sexes and repairing duality through love. If this is so, then the *meaning of love will lie not so much in yielding to sex as in mastering it.* This implies, nonetheless, that sexuality must be there, and it involves the condemnation of loves that are devoid of it: for what is, literally, insignificance.

The discovery of the hormones has given a solid basis to this interpretation of sexual love. Not only do these secretions sustain the hypothesis of a continuity between the physical and the moral, body and soul, matter and spirit (so ruining any rigidly dualist theory), but the existence of a real hormonal bisexuality supplies a striking confirmation for the myth of the Androgyne. What is more, the fact that the sexual characteristics determined by the hormones are labile and inconsistent, and subject to reversal in certain species in response to factors of temperature and nutrition, strongly encourages the view that sex is a provisional equilibrium always subject to revision, while the identity of the sexes is one instance of a basic balance in favour of which the provisional ones tend naturally to reversal. (In the same way, that strange, provisional equilibrium which is life, that knot of energies, is called upon to become untied and resolve itself in the basic equilibrium of death.) These new perspectives unquestionably provide a shining justification for the Couple. One cannot help recalling the Shivaite teaching: 'The union of the sexes is the only reality, their separate existence is merely a fiction'.

To represent sex as the result, always called in question afresh, of a latent conflict between the fields of force of the masculine and the feminine is to represent it as a bipolarity. (One should admire, in passing, the accuracy of the surrealist system of representation, especially in the case of Breton, who has so often spoken of love in terms of a vocabulary and system of images taken from the phenomena of induction and magnetism.) Our polarization into one sex or the other could be taken to represent our natures' coefficient of dualization. And perhaps it follows that individuals who are strongly sexed tend, in love, to be more closely dependent on sex, dominated by it and subject to the automatism of instinct, while the androgynic are more detached, therefore more gifted for those great acts of mental construction to which the sexual instinct serves merely as pretext and as motive force— more capable of projecting the Jungian *image* of the other sex (which they carry within them) into a physical manifestation. There are, indeed, many problems which can only be raised here. It sometimes seems as though the essential sexuality is still to be discovered.

These are a few of the reflections to which sexology can lead. The least one can say is that the material is overwhelmingly rich. Sexual attraction is, we have seen, not a simple need like hunger, and 'to make love' is not, as some have dared to put on paper, an 'act as indifferent as eating, urinating, defecating or sleeping'.[82] Nor is it the Marxist's 'glass of water'. All these simplifications contradict the findings of science. Even before Freud, Claude Bernard had divined that sexuality extends to the whole organism and that no part of the body escapes from its physico-chemical imprint. It depends on us whether we reduce love, I will not say to its animal function (for we have hardly any knowledge of the mysteries of animal psychology, and what we do know of the love of the lower species is not devoid of dignity), but to its organic function—or, on the contrary, determined to live through it on every level, set ourselves to adopt all its significations in a full awareness of *sacramental love*.

The recourse to chemistry in preference to other disciplines in order to describe the phenomena of love has, it is now clear, not impaired the standing of love but greatly reinforced it. Though shown to be reducible to a formula, sex has not been stripped of its mystery. It even invites us to think afresh about the notion of mystery. Unquestionably a revision of this notion is now going on. It threatens two extremist positions. The taboo mystery of the official religions—a mystery regarded as necessary, unapproachable, forbidden—is steadily being replaced by the idea of a mystery that demands to be approached.

In this approach, this *upanishad*, science itself is now showing the way. In opposition to the crude *scientism* which claimed to explain everything, modern science has learned to admit the inexplicable. In particular, during the last half century, it has become aware of the immensity of the mystery of sex. In biology as elsewhere, as the scientists elucidated problems, they saw fresh ones rising, more complex and more intimate. This gradual, never complete unfolding corresponds to the stages of the ancient initiation, in which, as approach is made to the *epopteia*, the Mystery is laid bare—but its light then becomes more blinding, its incandescence increases, and in the end one is face to face with something that is ineffable.

Einstein, in his wonder that the human mind should have been able to *understand* the world, deduced that the possibility of its one day understanding God is not excluded. Every critical approach, pushed to the extreme, does in fact come out at the same place, the place of Law (that is to say, the most that can be known of what man calls God): this is ultimate conquest of the Intelligible. But—on the way of science as on the way of love—there can be a stage above the intelligible, the one reached four times by Plotinus, of which it is only possible to murmur, like the Buddhist monk: 'Bliss unspeakable'. With this 'night of the presence' the mystic state begins, always preceded by a stripping away, a laying bare, an *asceticism*.

It was essential to make this clear. A philosophy of love as sacred will presuppose not unapproachable mysteries but a continual recourse to the critical stripping away. The characteristic of the new love must be both a deepened knowledge of sexuality and a consciousness of its fundamental mystery.

Towards a resacralization

SACRAL LOVE

Hardly anyone dares to face with open eyes the great delight of love.
ANDRÉ BRETON

To some people, as we have seen, the sexual act is essentially and irremediably vile, shameful, degrading, and nothing can raise it from this indignity. To others, it requires to be sanctified by a sacrament. To others again, it is naturally sacred, without the help of any sacrament; is indeed itself a sacrament—not only sacred, but able to communicate the sacred: this is what I mean by *sacral*.

To what are such differences due? As I have already said, both to doctrines and to individual temperaments. It goes without saying that those religions, metaphysical systems and doctrines of morality which teach the radical separation of body and spirit are not exactly favourable to sublimation through love. People whose natures are poor, inert, lacking in volatility, are no better placed. It is hard to see how souls deprived of the fundamental grace of connecting and harmonizing, of perceiving relationships and picking up signs, could be raised from their degradation: the real inability to love is an inability to connect. There are, unfortunately, two kinds of men—the daimonic and the others. It is the latter who condemn love as 'dirty'. Lack of imagination keeps them stuck in the organic, in the visceral, which shocks them all the more since they remain bogged down in it. Let us look at this squarely: what they find shocking in sex, as I have already said, is its closeness to the functions of excretion;[83] they find that 'sex has chosen its organs very badly'. In contrast to them the daimonic natures need little encouragement to regard as admirable a choice of organs which illustrates, better than they could have hoped, the conjunction of contraries. There are two ways of reacting to what is shocking: to make the most of it or to run away from it. One and the same poet, Marston, revels in describing the most nauseating aspects of love and then goes on to exclaim: 'O that we could encrease like roses by being slipt one from another . . .' The distance from cynicism to a bloodless idealism is less far than is often imagined.

The real lovers are equidistant from those two errors. They need no argument to convince them that love sanctifies. They know it: in love everything is possible, everything is permitted, everything is sacred, provided that sexuality is adopted in all its mystery, its gravity, its totality.

The first gift lavished by love is this sense of infallible certainty, this unequalled confidence, this ever ready rightness of choice—whether it concerns a gesture to be risked or some great decision taken, for instance between constancy or unfaithfulness. There is no better gauge of the greatness of a couple than its consciousness of its *sacrality*.

But this sacrality is not the product of affection, tenderness, esteem or other such edifying sentiments: it is by reference to sexuality that it will be decided whether a given conjugal union is sacred or profane. When, for instance, we read in *Les Mandarins:* 'We were too closely united for it to be possible for the union of our bodies to have great importance, in renouncing it we lost practically nothing', it is at once obvious that the Anne-Dubreuilh *ménage* will turn out to be an association, a collaboration, a pact, anything but a couple adopting its sacral significance. But neither would this be adopted by a couple that relied on sexuality without love. In the couple the division of the sexes must be both felt and resolved.

Nothing is easier than to exhibit in sexuality the essential features of the sacred—its absolute otherness, its ambiguity, its ambivalence, its polarity, its twofold character of positivity and negativity. Here, unquestionably, we are in that zone of extremes which is also, as a Catholic assures us, a zone of communication, 'because the sacred dissolves the determinations of individual beings and makes possible a fusion that is like a kind of liquid condition where there is no longer separate existence.'[84] Comparisons of this sort have already been used as images of love. The same words, the same images occur to those who would describe both *eros* and the powerful mystical experiences, their 'characteristics of excess, negativity, outgoing and fusion': even that tendency to lose oneself, to annihilate oneself (described by Otto in a still authoritative book),[85] which finds an amazing analogue in the consummation of the sexual act. If the relatedness of sex and the sacred were in doubt, the very nature of recent discussions on love would supply a fresh pointer to it. These discussions have taken the form of two campaigns, one for resacralization, the other for demythologization, and the second seems to me to be evidence of the sacral nature of love just as much as the first. It is noteworthy that there is an endeavour to find resacralization for sacramental marriage also, as though people are suddenly conscious of the need to recharge the sacrament itself with sacredness. It is to this reassumption of Eros by Agape that we are invited by a great Christian review, *Esprit*,[86] which declares that it is 'in search of a new sacredness in contemporary conjugal ethics' and hopes to find it in what it calls 'the marvel and enigma of sex'. But indeed, one cannot help agreeing with Paul Ricoeur: 'It is not possible, in point of fact, to understand the adventurous history of sexuality apart from that of the sacred among men'.

It might seem that, once this point is made, all that remains is to arrange the couples in two classes, those who attach great importance to sexual love and those who grant it only the indispensable minimum —the former being promoted to the dignity of that model Couple whose condition we have now to define. Nothing could be more false. It is true that there is a germ of the sacred in any and every physical love, and in this context it is unquestionable that even the brute is susceptible to a kind of cosmic *participation*—perhaps more so than the intellectual, who has too often succeeded in stifling his subconscious under bookish rubbish (D. H. Lawrence would certainly have thought so). But, in spite of this, the highest, most perfect, fully worked out love, the love that has gone furthest, is certainly the one that assumes the sacral quality; and assumption presupposes awareness. I have already said that love evolves towards the Spirit: a sacral philosophy of love must be mental, be *noetic*. This may disconcert some readers—they may be surprised to find themselves confronted sometimes with a rehabilitation of sexuality, next with a vindication of intelligence; after seeing me first uphold mythic thought and then a critical reflection, which side, they may ask, am I on? For the subconscious or for the conscious? For the body or for the spirit? At the risk of boredom I must repeat that I am for communication and exchange between them. Against a sexuality devoid of sublimation. Against an intellectualism or an idealism cut off from its roots. If it is true that 'the Spirit feels nothing except with the help of the body', it is also true that the body is called upon, is appointed to bring the spirit into the world, to be *delivered* of it. There can be no great couple without strong sexuality, nor can there be one that has not learned to fetch it in and master it. An erotic of assumption, it is already clear, will be always looking for new states of balance between sexuality and chastity.

Nothing is rarer than a love completely adopted. Camus thought that there are only two or three great loves per century. Nonetheless, the thing exists, it has been lived; and, if one cannot carry it through to the end, one can and should bear witness that there is a true greatness and dignity even in striving towards it. Do we blame the Christian for striving towards saintliness? At the same time, in the kingdom of Eros there are many mansions. There are some that cannot be recommended to the couple. These now require a word.

I have already mentioned an 'erotic of abjection': it regards sex as a defect, a degradation from which love cannot rise. It therefore presupposes the practice of a *detached* sexuality, a sexuality *hived off*, with the spirit refusing to be interested in what the body does—unless, pushing sex and degradation to their extremes, it urges the few (the elect) to give themselves up to the brutal satisfaction of a shock sexuality. This would be carefully preserved from the sentiment which might sweeten its ugliness; for the aim is to shock the conscious violently and so throw it back, in a kind of rebound, towards pure spirituality. With this method we must connect the art of love of the Marquis de Sade: 'it is impossible not to recognize in it', says Klossowski, 'the whole ancient system of Manichaean Gnosticism', and he finds in Sade's orgies a completely Gnostic hatred of the creation, including the body, and 'that frantic cult of the orgasm which was, in certain Manichaean sects, a form of the cult of the original light'.[87] In an impious century which had desacralized sexuality, Sade was attempting a resacralization in his fashion, by substituting for the discredited way of the 'heart' the way of profanation, outrage, bloodshed and orgy. Sade had in him, unquestionably, a longing for purity and even for humaneness (that great deviser of tortures had the courage to protest, in the midst of the Terror, against the death penalty and the guillotine). But that is not the point. Whatever one may think of his art of love (and I think it is a failure), it is clear that this 'Utopia of evil' goes directly against any conjugal fulfilment. The same applies to Baudelaire, who thought that 'the unique and supreme pleasure of love lies in the certainty of doing evil', and expressly condemned 'the spiritual intoxications based on the flesh', which he called 'that counter-mysticism'.[88] It applies also to Georges Bataille, with his idea that the only communication open to man is through laceration: it is evil, it is impurity that *opens* a man: the integrity of a being has to be attacked by obscenity or crime: one must *will* evil. 'I have need', says Bataille, 'of that element of infinity which belongs to the idea of sin.'

That the recourse to sin is a *way* is not in doubt.[89] It is the way of *the left hand*, which several great civilizations (India, China, Greece) have recognized and tolerated. But this is not the place for a considered judgment of the practices of hallowed obscenity: here we are concerned only to dispose of any attempt to involve the couple in a doctrine of love which is the negation of the couple. It is a negation not only of the theme of androgyny (of its complementarity lived at every level), but of love itself and of those attendant sentiments, tenderness, esteem, gratitude, which are not the whole of love—far from it—but without which love could not last. For a part of the disgust and contempt which, by definition, the 'erotic of abjection' is bound to provoke will inevitably rub off upon the lover himself and, above all, upon the woman in love. It is the woman who, one feels sure, will be vilified by these excesses: in spite of the cult of the celestial Sophia, all these Gnostics are fierce despisers of women.

What might be called the 'erotic of abstraction' must also be eliminated. In a type of relationship where the partner is of supreme importance and is rendered divine by passionate love, this method consists of a resorting to interchangeable partners, partners who *do not engage attention*. 'I cannot conceive', wrote Aragon with the inimitable seriousness of the 1920 generation (the book is *Le Paysan de Paris*), 'that one could go to the brothel otherwise than alone and grave. *I pursue, there, the great abstract desire.*'

Don Juanism is an analogous method: it, too, eliminates the partners, exorcizes them by their number. In kissing a woman's lips, Byron tells us, Don Juan was kissing all women. Don Juanism is a way of loving Woman, the Eternal Feminine, at the expense of the singularity of the individual. It amounts, on occasion, to a denial of the particular, of appearance—and even, yes, of beauty, youth, the flesh and what Plato called 'a thousand other mortal idlenesses': in fact to a pursuit of *l'amour pur*—always realized at the woman's expense because it concerns a masculine temptation.

But, once again, this is not the place for a detailed appreciation of the various kinds of love-making which exist: we are concerned here simply to weed them out for the sake of the kind of love that is able to resacralize the couple. This can only be the love that consecrates, instead of *abstracting*, the individuals—the 'love that takes absolute power, claims the whole length of life and of course only consents to recognize its object in a single being'. *L'amour fou*, Breton called it, and Benjamin Péret described it as sublime love, the hermetic philosophers as perfect love. It was Plato's divinizing love, and we have spoken of it as total and as unreasonable love. It is in fact simply love, the only kind that needs no qualification or description because those who come upon it recognize it without a second's hesitation. Why do they? Because it is like nothing else. Because it is a 'thing apart' and makes its appearance as an incredible privilege. It is with the feeling, so often described, of a privileged moment, of an instant set apart that the consciousness of the *sacral* of which I have spoken begins.

Anyone who is living through a privileged experience naturally desires to go on with it. Hence that fear of ceasing to love, of falling back into the common condition. There is no example of a man or woman truly in love having sincerely desired to stop being so. We are familiar with the irritation of people in love when someone tries to 'cure' them: these sick, mad, schizophrenic people do not envy the world of the healthy in the least. Is this stupidity, obstinacy, masochism, or play-acting? Or is it, on the contrary, an awareness of having been singled out for a noble and prodigious fate? This question is constantly being raised afresh (with a violence that reveals the bitterness felt by some at not being able to love), and on it I took sides from the start. But I have also, as we have seen, collected fresh data on the subject from mythology, psychology and biology, all grouped about the theme of bisexuality. It is by reference to these and in terms of present-day life that we must now try to clarify the conjugal condition.

Passionate love, with its slow gestation, is (as I have said) a feminine form of love, and instability, a virile tendency. The thought is a decidedly discouraging one at first sight, since it would confirm a permanent disharmony between the sexes, their deep-seated inability to fit together. But let us look a little closer. The sexual hormones govern the form of desire and love, the male hormones or androgens producing a disposition to wandering, conquest, the chase, assault and aggressiveness; the female hormones or oestrogens to passivity, sedentariness, receptivity and the slow maturing of the fruit. As we have seen, each of the sexes secretes also the hormones of the other sex, though in lesser quantity, so that it would be nearer the truth to distinguish between an 'androgenic' and an 'oestrogenic' form of desire and love.

But this is not all. Not only are individuals unequally sexed, but they are more and more pulled by their subconscious as they advance in age. This subconscious, we have seen, has a different sexual tonality: it contains the complementary image of a double who belongs to the other sex, and this image can be projected on to a living person. This tendency of a man to adopt his latent femininity, a woman her latent virility, and to be completed by it, amounts to the individual's adoption of his or her whole self in the form of a real bisexuality. According to Jung, this adoption shows that the individual has entered the second part of his or her life. This can happen more or less early. It can fail to happen: an elderly Don Juan is merely a man clinging, in some cases desperately, to his virility, his youth. It can also happen outside any amorous kind of projection, as is the case, it seems, with saints and sages.

'All the divine messages that have called humanity to true moral progress', writes René Nelli, 'have come from sages and from saints, whom men have been apt to take as gods, but in whom we see, above all, human beings who are *both supremely men and supremely women*.'[90]

If this adoption of the whole self takes place in a human love, then clearly, being a victory of bisexuality over sex, it will tend more than any other kind to the sublimation of passion. And in fact we see that, apart from adolescence, which is a period of sexual indeterminateness, passionate love usually arises in a man at the age when he is mature enough for this activation of the androgynous archetype—and likewise in the opposite direction, in a woman. It should be tempting to conclude that the loves of the mature are alone perfect, being alone built on this quaternary relationship; but we have to admit that tradition vouches for the validity of other formulae, for instance the love of a mature man for a very young woman. Such was the relationship between Rubens and Hélène Fourment, or again between Thorbecke and Adelheid Solger.

Thorbecke, who at the age of forty was a frequent visitor at the house of a beautiful widow in Berlin and is thought to have been courting her, fell suddenly in love with the young daughter of Madame Solger, took her away from her fiancé (the jurist von Savigny) and without too much difficulty married her. Their great love, even when its first ardour died down, continued to illuminate the lives of both of them. After twenty-two years of marriage, this Minister of State still wrote daily, when on his travels, to his 'little madonna', and they were real love letters: '*Adieu*. Never let an hour, never let a moment pass without loving the man whose highest joy is in this love'. Favoured by the difference of their ages, a relationship grew up which recalls the educational pattern of Greek love: Thorbecke never ceased educating his young wife. Yet this was a far cry from the marital circus-training provided by Xenophon's Ischomachos, or indeed by the author of the *Ménagier*: Thorbecke never preached at her, for he was trying to form, not a good associate, but a soul and mind (if we re-read the passage from a letter of his quoted on page 119 above, we are struck by its initiatory character). It was the supreme success in this type of relationship, where the man and the woman are equally ready for a love that is meant to be the only one to last; she from the simple play of the dispositions proper to her sex; he by the double play of his own sex and the sex he is psychologically adopting. To take up again and modify Freud's expression, such a love involves three people, not four —at the beginning, at least, since the initiation consists precisely in bringing the androgynous out of the subconscious into awareness. It is a solution for which there is a good case in a society where women remain infantile and rarely achieve their full growth. Perhaps one day a more evolved society will regard as more harmonious the love between a woman and a man both of whom are fully mature—a love that has flowered completely and is perfect. Instances of love between youthful partners will then appear simply as sketches for such a love.

Meanwhile, what view is to be taken of the union of a mature woman with a much younger man, whose initiator she makes herself? Letters from readers have convinced me that this formula is valid for some couples. I admit that I think it less exemplary, but I may be the victim of a very old prejudice. Simone de Beauvoir has ably argued that, by refusing to take seriously love in a mature woman and by showing such indulgence towards it in elderly men, society is merely completing its anti-feminist policy. We accept the sexual fantasies of Victor Hugo at the age of eighty, yet make fun of the agonizing love of Madame du Deffand (aged sixty-nine) for Horace Walpole (who, of course, more than anything, feared that it should become known) —or even the love of Madame du Châtelet (forty-two years old) for Saint-Lambert (who was twenty). It seems to me that we are sinning by mediocrity of imagination—for really these great passions that come late are signs of an exceptional vitality—and that we would do better to judge love not by its season but by its fruits. In short, in the matter of lovers' ages there is no rule, there are only special cases.

I do not agree with the view of Geneviève Gennari that the union of a perfectly male man and a completely feminine woman is supremely harmonious.[91] Apart from the fact that individuals so thoroughly polarized do not exist, I think that a union of this kind would hardly go beyond the lesser accomplishments of love, for in it the man and the woman would remain prisoners of their own eroticism. For the same reason there will seldom be a very deep harmony between a husband and a wife both of whom are very young. The harmony of a couple rests not on the perfect sexuality of a man and a woman but on their basic bisexuality.

It is time to say what we mean by lower and higher accomplishments of love. In the first part of life the aim of love is often physical union, and procreation, while in the second 'it is more a question of a *spiriual* union with the partner of the other sex in order to bear fruit—the spiritual offspring which confer the lasting quality to the whole spiritual existence of the united partners.'[92]

Both psychology and biology invite us not to reduce the object and meaning of love to procreation, to create a family is only the first of the couple's accomplishments—the first starting from below.[93] Even then it must not serve as a pretext for the partners to close up, to shut themselves away more narrowly instead of opening out, expanding, renouncing their preconceptions of themselves. Every love must be *gone through*, even that of parents: it is from unwillingness to do this that voracious mothers (often in search of a compensation for their disappointments with sex and love) have weighed down the destinies of their sons. Browning's mother, for instance, would not allow the communicating door between their rooms to be closed at night, and 'so closely mixed up were their lives', says André Maurois, 'that when she fell ill, he at once sickened, then recovered as soon as Mrs Browning was better again'. D. H. Lawrence became aware that to his mother he was both a son and the husband she did not love, and in due course he said of motherly love that it was a monstrous manifestation of egoism. But it would take another book to denounce the exaggerations of a feeling which has been the subject of as much indulgence—not to say connivance—as sexual love has been of mistrust and suspicion. The mother's instinct takes its right place and its true dimension (a dimension that is admirable when its significance has not been thrown overboard) within the deep and total love of a real couple.

But if procreation is only the first of the accomplishments of the couple, what are the others? Not everybody can write the *Symposium*.

And since a great love is one that is adopted completely, how can the husband and wife who are truly in love adopt the implications of the myth?

Depending on one's point of view, androgyny signifies either universal Multiplication or Unity represented by the union of the contraries; and according to whether a person is drawn to the lower or to the higher accomplishments of love, he or she is also drawn to the choice of a partner answering to this ambition. The choice of a partner in love depends on the meaning and range that one is unconsciously preparing to accord to love. Just as there are men, usually young, simple and healthy, who merely seek to have children and instinctively look for *une bonne pondeuse* (a good layer), others, whose yearning is for a passionate love, will be caught by a fine face or gaze, by a woman 'who has an air of destiny about her'.

In both cases the desire settles on a person with whom the chooser has a presentiment that love will take on its full sense and all its savour, on the being who will engage us the most compellingly in his (or her) movement—a movement of which, of course, one will often lose control. The sister soul is the one that will make us live—and die— most intensely. Sister souls recognize each other. But this idea of predestination in love must not be taken too literally: one thinks one recognizes a face—what one is recognizing is only one's own dream, which one *projects*, and could, no doubt, project on several other persons. Even the oneiric figure of the anima-animus is only an image of the powerful yearning for an ontological previous existence that we feel to have been happy—a previous existence that is also a destiny, a future, because we strive towards the condition from which we started out. In short, we allow ourselves to be fascinated by our own evolution. The movement that throws us into love is a greed, an impatience for our basic, eternal, supernatural condition, which is both germinal and final. From this comes that fateful character of the beloved individual, of which Nelli has written so well. 'Love is, in its essence, love of fatality.'

Sometimes this appeal is so strong that it works like a stream of energy, forcing the defences of a human being who fights against it and is, as it were, sucked by it out of his or her self. In such a case he or she is chosen rather than chooses. Sometimes hatred and repulsion are the advance signs of a great passion, the febrile symptoms of a violent but vain psychical defence. Alessandra di Rudini Carlotti detested d'Annunzio: though he was a friend of her brother's, she obstinately refused to meet him; she considered him ugly, vain and ridiculous; she made fun of his small stature, his baldness, his histrionic performance in the part of a man of letters, his scandalous reputation as a *donnaiolo*—until the day when they met face to face at a wedding. Immediately she felt her prejudices melt away. Less than a month afterwards she followed him, abandoning the world in order to join the number of those strange, scarcely orthodox nuns whom d'Annunzio initiated, one after the other, into the practice of 'the fugitive human act under the auspices of eternity'.

Nothing could be more incomprehensible, absurd and disappointing than such choice, if love were not at the same time love for something else. Love is, precisely, the miracle of a person, a human body, that has become wholly meaningful, and of a desire that branches out beyond all limits. For, whether it be kept down or flattered, desire remains the motive power of love: it is always the being who is most desired who will be the most illuminating and mediating. Let us here dispose, once for all, of what is called 'noble' love, with its false sublimations, with its 'narrow doorway' which is a condemned doorway. When a woman who seems to have all the gifts—beauty, sensibility, ardour —proves incapable of inspiring a strong passion in a man who seems cut out to appreciate these merits, and he then falls in love stupidly with the first green girl that comes along, the world simply cannot understand: 'after all, she had everything required to make him happy'. But what if he was seeking not to be happy but to love (for people make over and over again the Platonic discovery that to love is more divine than to be loved)? To give himself up to an activity of loving one person who is yearned for, singled out from all others, isolated in her shocking uniqueness?

On this sublime decision (Valéry has spoken with insight of 'love, that passionate attention', and Ortega y Gasset of 'love, that violence done to attention') the most misleading ideas prevail.

Confusion on the subject has been firmly established by the attractive but factitious image of crystallization. Crystallization is an image of addition, of accretion. Placed in a mother-liquid a crystal fattens; but all who have thought at all deeply about the working passion realize that, far from adding to the loved one, love digs out, scours, clears.[94] If the result is to bring together something like a mountain, it can only be a mountain of debris, like the slag-heaps in the neighbourhood of mines. It is at the same time true that to lovers everything is an occasion for bringing them face to face: a town that comes up in conversation, a season whose advance signs they notice, a piece of music to which they listen—the imagination seizes hold of many things to test love and to derive from them fresh perceptions of it. But these occasions do not cling to love—they do not accumulate, any more than do the acids or other agents used on a substance that contains a precious metal. In any case love disengages, strips and discovers: it separates what is worthy to be loved from what is not.

Alessandra di Rudini Carlotti was not mistaken in seeing d'Annunzio as short, rather ugly and in some ways absurd: she had succeeded perfectly in distinguishing what she loved from what she did not love. But from the moment of crossing a certain threshold her attention, letting drop the negative elements in order to concentrate on the rest, literally *dis-covered* in d'Annunzio what was truly beautiful, great and worthy of being loved, sympathized with and consoled—perhaps the look in his eyes, perhaps his forehead, perhaps his voice or speech, his infinite love of beauty, or the gift he had of converting the humblest thing into magnificence.

Far from producing illusion (as is so often believed) love has a pitiless lucidity. 'The passion of love is not blind', writes a great enemy of love, M. Robert Poulet, 'it sees in its object, with perfect clearness, two or three points, two or three signs which could, it is true, be seen just as well in a hundred thousand other people. *It refuses to see the rest.*' And another great enemy of love, Ludwig Klages,[95] maintains that, far from loving the exemplary, we love only the singular—often an irregularity, a defect: how indeed, he asks, could we love in anyone what this person has in common with the others? Is not the beloved person irreplaceable to us because of his particularity? 'To Kriemhilde there is only one Siegfried, to Tristan one Isolde, to Ophelia one

Hamlet, to Dante one Beatrice, to Romeo one Juliet.' And so on. Is there a contradiction here? No; for what love seeks is the *coincidence of the exemplary with the specific*, the meeting of existence and essence.

Yes, it is possible to adore a pout, a frown, a wrinkle or a slight squint in a face otherwise incomparable (a lover, as Molière said, loves even the faults of those he loves), it is possible to love an element of un-grace in grace (though it is rare for a wholly graceless creature to be loved), and it is indeed at this meeting-point provided by the singular that the de-singularising activity of love makes itself most sharply felt: this is the *daimonic paradox*. On what should a unitive activity exercise itself, if not on multiplicity and detail? So true is this that, as we have seen, religious mysticism sets to work in the same way. Most deeply spiritual people take some concrete detail as a starting-point for their prayer. St François de Sales teaches that the soul in love with God seeks out and chooses for herself motives for love: *she draws them to her* and then savours them. To seek out, to choose and to draw to oneself is to let the rest drop: it is to submit the object of one's love to a real critical activity. Yet love chooses only in order to adore better. All that is of God is by definition adorable and sacred, only human love consecrates, makes divine.

And so a relationship has to be established between the person and the divine, between the profane and the sacred. By holding back in its sieve some characteristics because they are exemplary and others because they are singular, love is merely bringing out clearly the two terms of this relationship. Probably, side by side with what d'Annunzio had in him that was most appropriate to the sublimation of divinizing love, side by side with what was unquestionably *adorable* in him, Alessandra di Rudini Carlotti chose to adore also some detail of his tone of voice or bearing, the way he had of carrying his right shoulder lower than the left, or the scar on his eyelid, or the smell of the toilet water he used, or some other incredibly profane and personal thing whose function was to represent the poet's singularity as clearly (though symbolically) as a badge or a flag: so that, by steering for this character-istic, the divinizing activity could always reassure itself as to the *integration of the person*. The real object of such loving consecration is to lay bare the divine kinship and to savour it in the mystical sense.

The unburying—rarely completed—seems to be one of the most admirable of the tasks of love. When it is achieved, there are no more 'illusions of love', there is no longer any deception about the beloved object. The person is really sacred, to the extent that it lets the sacred shine through.

In all this there is no dishonesty unless the attention is turned away from this shining through, unless the lover stays stuck in a complacent adulation of the beloved—instead of venerating in him or her the 'divine spark' which attests the true allegiance: this is the whole difference between a closed and an open love. Nor is there any objection to that work of sifting to which love proceeds, to that decision to keep one thing and forget another; for all it does is to fend off disorder (fleetingly and within the measure of the possible) and *ideally*, mentally, to remove the beloved from the mixture, from the impurity of Adam. Its aim is to restore the beloved to the original dignity, to raise the beloved from the *fall*, from the degradation which comes to a soul through leaving the One and becoming a duality. And so what we have here is not deception and abuse, but the generosity of love doing justice: not blindness, but the partiality of love cutting through appearance.

The truth is that every human being deserves to be looked at in this way at least once in a lifetime—loved and venerated for what is authentically divine in him or her. And every human being is called to this. It does seem, in fact, that where this discriminatory perception prevails it is not the most beautiful people, nor even the youngest, who offer the finest material to love, but rather those whose nature is rich, who have 'temperament', whose body and soul are gifted with a fine vitality. Perfect beauties can be discouraging, like souls dedicated to calm: they offer little purchase to the activity of loving, they leave it little to do. Graceless bodies and souls, which give it too much to do, are also discouraging. Plato—in spite of the Greek fanaticism for bodily beauty—regarded the love of a beautiful body as a stage lower than the love for a 'gentle soul in a body whose flowering is not brilliant'. Fortunately it takes less marked physical advantages to give profound delight to one person only, awakening in him or her a passionate attention, than it does to please many superficially. Our bastard ideas distorted by eroticism have overvalued the importance of physiological factors and of techniques of seduction: this is a regression of man towards sexual mechanics and animal eroticism. The only way in which the art of love in human beings can genuinely progress is towards an always greater awareness: it is a long elucidation of the spirit. But such a *purification* does not fit in with the brevity of desire; it demands the long, the infinite patience of true love. All the wiles of modern eroticism—which is, to my mind, already dated —remain inefficient at satisfying our real thirst, which is spiritual. And without a little of that love at which our world snaps its fingers (though such love can miraculously rescue the most unfortunate human being from degradation by establishing him or her in an incomparable dignity), the most beautiful, seductive and desired of women may die as lonely as a masterless dog.

One quite often hears it said that in divinizing *eros* the beloved is only a stimulus, a pretext for what is really a solitary exaltation. It is true that sometimes the activity of loving takes itself as an object for observation. All the great philosophies of love have set themselves this method, beginning with Plato.

To lovers who belong to this category the privileged experience consists in knowing that they are singled out as the place and instrument of a prodigy, and in laying bare, within the development of their love, its cause, its motive power, apprehending it as *Law*. In this case attention tends to shift from the loved person to the heart and soul of the one who is loving, in whom the experience is working itself out. Hence this attitude has been criticized as sacrificing of the person—but unjustly, because the experience could not be worth observing if it were not strongly felt, if the discriminating and divinizing activity were not an intense one, carried along by the passionate curiosity of a 'great love'. The androgynous fusion is so close that it ensures this: everything that happens to one partner proceeds from the other and benefits the other. Even when the object of love is felt to be situated beyond the person, the revelation of it is still received through the person. If this going-through is missing, we are off the way of *eros*.

This approach is, of course, rarely carried to completion. People allow themselves to be fascinated by mirages, such as happiness, which melt away as they try to lay hold on them, and by diversions, such as pleasure pursued as an end in itself. Love is abortive as soon as it becomes self-interested: when the loving discrimination described above serves only to mislead us about the advantages of the beloved, only to place at the disposal of the imagination a more convenient object or one better adapted to the pleasures we hope to extract from it (as Sartre shows in *L'Imaginaire*), then there is impoverishment of love. Whether the deception is in oneself or in the other partner, the danger of sinking into it and sticking there is equal. But if, on the contrary, a couple rejects the comforts of deception and succeeds, by force of lucidity, in outwitting all its snares and complacencies (and this involves triumphing over a formidable prejudice—that to be carried away by passion excludes lucidity), then it will be surely guided to its aim by the critical and mystical activity of love. This will either reveal to the lover the true kinship of the beloved; or it will lay bare his or her own loving activity—an activity that converts to unity, producing the conviction of being *governed by the Law*, by an image or idea of God that is itself submitted to critical purification. In both cases we are shown a world of continuity, of coherence, and are led back to Unity. This is the supreme accomplishment of daimonic *eros*. It is a method of knowledge as well as of salvation, and wisdom as well as of holiness.

The profound sacredness of love means that the couple, which decides to adopt this *sacrality*, feels bound by it from then onwards— and by the promotion which it confers on the humblest thing. It is altogether consistent with the economy of *eros* to hold that everything that is, has a share (though in unequal degrees) in the sacred, and that one of the essential tasks of love is to bring this out. Every woman in love knows instinctively that love extracts something authentically and primordially sacred from the humblest tasks—for instance, preparing a meal. But if the sacramental effect of love extends to that, how much more so to the husband or the wife in person: viewed in the perspective of the sacral, infidelity becomes a monstrous thing—it means that a body which has been divinizing is profaning and soiling itself. In this respect there is a legitimate jealousy, very different from the jealousy that is vanity and from the jealousy that is possessive-ness (these are off the line of *eros*). It comes to this: that, for a sacral couple, a pact or convention granting sexual liberty is inconceivable; the reservations implied by such a verbal 'gentleman's agreement' are negations of the sacral.

It is true that an androgynous union can reach a condition of saturation (by analogy with chemical saturation): one partner has so completely absorbed the other and taken the other's place, that this other lives in a state of total identity and so is benefited *spiritually* by the sexual successes of the former. But this is a sublime stage attained only in a love so great and disinterested that the lover is entirely lost in the beloved, possessing and enjoying through the beloved: it is a peak that can rarely be reached, and then only at the end of a long and difficult *asceticism* which cannot be treated as a rule, still less as a starting-point.

The worst of conventions or pacts of sexual freedom is that they reduce the importance of the sexual act, they deprive it of meaning. This is the effect of all licence. It is mixture and disorder. And, by its anticipation of consent it legitimizes lapses.

The accidental infraction is far less serious, for at least it does not strike at the status of the couple: a lapse may sometimes consolidate the union when it is covered by a generous and loving absolution. There is also the fact that great couples possess so firm a solidarity as to make it, in some cases, enough for one of the two partners to remain faithful; in the course of centuries how many women have acted for both partners in the rôle of the *egregoros*! Vigilant on behalf of the husband, they have kept his place for him, so that, on his return from his wanderings, he could take it up again as if nothing had happened. For, to love, all things are possible—including effacement in the marital mysticism. Nonetheless, one must not make a rule out of this unilateral-ism. Still less, a duty. Duty is as surely desacralizing as is licence.

Must one conclude that freedom and fidelity are irreconcilable? No. On the contrary, though a forced and conventional fidelity may have its moral and social advantages, only a spontaneous and loving fidelity, constantly renewed by being chosen in complete freedom, can strengthen the couple in its supernatural vocation. A couple must at least speculate on, bet on its ability to last. It must have faith in its love, faith in its resistance to time. If by ill fortune the love is extinguished, no duty or forced fidelity can give it back its sacral quality. What can happen then is a series of mutual adjustments in an atmosphere of association, of companionship; but it will do no good to deceive oneself —these adjustments will merely sanction the couple's passage from sacral love to profane love, and this must be held to be a falling off.

And so it is in the light of freedom that the practice of sexual life must be viewed. Nothing is more disastrous than the concept of conjugal duty; nothing is better calculated to desacralise sexuality than an awareness of being forced to it—with the fear of legal sanctions in the background. Obligatory sex has not only the disadvantage of taking away from love its incomparable spontaneity, it also deprives the couple of the benefit of chastity. All the great philosophies of love have recognized the importance of continence; all of them have taught a militant chastity, based not on contempt for the flesh but on an economy and storing up of sexual energy for the sake of a mystical transposition of physical union. It is hard to see why this noble way should be denied to people who are married. The pagan philosophy of love attained complete spiritual flowering, which has never since been equalled in the West, largely because of its right appreciation and heroic practice of chastity. As we have seen, in the case of Socrates these victories were hard won.

The wisdom then found has not been forgotten. In certain peoples (for instance in India) it is not exceptional for a young couple to commit themselves to chastity for a time. Christianity also tries to make it a part of conjugal practice; but such commitments, if separated from a doctrine of love, are apt to cause misunderstandings. When Madame Martin (the mother of St Teresa of Lisieux) extracts a promise of abstinence from her husband on the morrow of the first night of marriage, one cannot help suspecting that some disillusion or revulsion was the cause, and one is inclined to believe that in this case the flesh is not so much mastered as maligned. In contrast, the flesh is still present and held in high honour in the ordeal to which Homère Durand and Sophie, the characters in a fine and probably autobiographic story by Luc-André Marcel, submit.[96] Beyond any doubt the mortification there described, which is preceded by a scene of undressing that is ritual in its solemnity, is intended to exalt, not to humiliate, the value of the sexual act: it is in fact an effort to resacralize an engagement.

Possibly the spiritual adoption of androgyny requires that an experiment of this kind be made by some couples. Am I wrong in foreseeing that a new kind of sexual ethics will arise for the more adventurous among human beings? Freed as it would be from all external constraint (from tedious conjugal duty as well as from the conventionality of licentiousness), it would be an autonomous morality, which would set up chastity not as an ideal or as a moral standard, but as a practical rule—i.e. as a normal behaviour, whose result would be that, each time the couple allowed itself to be captivated by the flesh it would do so in fresh wonder at a thing not staled by use. What threatens marital love is the absence of freedom. In marriage, as convention regards it, sex is given a blanket permission, and so becomes desacralized by routine (when not by the blunders of marital authoritarianism).

To advocate married chastity is inevitably to raise a smile: not in vain have the mediocre, with their interest in confusing virility and womanizing, tried to discredit this discipline by ridicule. The time may have come to restore to it the considerable function and place it has always had in the philosophies of love. It alone can give back its meaning and force to that choice, which love constantly offers, between flesh and spirit, between perdition and salvation—and this by once more giving a kind of *play* to the sexual life. To achieve a meaningful sexual life, the practice of an erotic chastity is to be recommended—at least to some. As for the others, it is at least desirable to dissuade them from mixing up marriage and licence. No legal or religious confirmation can legitimize profligate and sordid behaviour.

One is, of course, ashamed of raising the great problems of fidelity and chastity only to treat them so briefly. I must say again that this book claims merely to call in question the current ethics of marriage, to show that a revision is needed and that possibly a rehabilitation of love should be started on all fronts at once.

To lay claim to the *invention* of a philosophy of love would be very naïve (not to say pretentious), unless *invent* be understood in its primary sense of *finding* or even *finding again* (as we speak of the

Invention of the True Cross). I have always thought that this is the right way to interpret Rimbaud's famous saying, that *l'amour est à réinventer*. Love seems to be a universal law (perhaps *the* Law) that may have undergone distortions in the course of history (even Platonism, for all the wonderful elucidation it achieved, took up its position in a false light), so that the most one can do is to *bring up to date* the doctrine of love, prepare for it forms that are adapted to the time and place. In our survey we have seen love constantly developing and putting forth fresh ramifications, as a salt does when dissolved in different media. In our world, as I have said, *eros* became marked by Christian and, even more, by Gnostic misconceptions, so acquiring dramatic qualities—agony or rebelliousness—that are specifically Christian.

But it must not be concluded that, after this happened, there was no one in the Christian West who lived through a complete experience of love. I believe that in all times, in spite of dogmas interdictions, prejudices and the warnings of the moralists, there have been men each of whom loved a woman—sometimes even his wife— with the love we have called 'unreasonable'.

Most of these experiences remain unknown to us: to come down to us, they would have to have been bound up with some great reputation or to have been closely studied and noted down. My reason for choosing John Donne's experience of love as the illustration for this chapter is that he analysed it and wrote it down with the cruelty of genius. Through his poetry—as through painting in the case of Rubens —we will follow the themes of *eros*.

Rubens owed his sexual and erotic feeling (we have seen that the two are inseparable) to what is often called his 'paganism', to his evident predisposition to apprehend the sacred in the stirring, energetic form of the cosmos as he saw it. Donne owed his to his *unitive* cast of mind—that readiness of his to catch relationships, *establish the connection* of all sorts of particular experiences with the universal, perceive eternity in the instant and infinity in a point, find the space of the cosmos in the space of a room where two lovers are, or of a bed, or even the pupil of an eye. Donne, the man with this passion for discovering connections, was thus supremely daimonic, exceptionally gifted for battling his way through the dialectic of contraries. Thanks to this gift, he came to adopt all the implications and contradictions of sacral love.

It must be said outright that his was not what is called a happy marriage: he and his wife had neither prosperity nor peace, but poverty, prison, sickness, death. That their love was still a success makes it the more exemplary. And any woman in love might well envy the woman who, after sixteen years of difficult life together, could inspire the exigent, pitilessly lucid, sarcastic John Donne to write an In Memoriam as wonderful as *Holy Sonnet xvii*:

> *Since she whom I lov'd hath payd her last debt*
> *To Nature and to hers, and my good is dead,*
> *And her Soule early into heaven ravished,*
> *Wholly on heavenly things my mind is sett.*

Leishman is right: what is peculiar to the poems inspired by Anne More (and often makes it possible to verify doubtful attributions, though this is not one of them) is the exactness of their tone, a certain way of lowering the voice and speaking *sotto voce*, and also the tempo, which reveals the contained emotion—fervour combined with modesty.[97] One cannot help recalling another expression of praise for the dead: 'Truly I have lost a very good companion, whom I could love and was bound in reason to love, for she had none of the faults of her sex. . . .' The tone, there, is the tone of profane love, and the profane does not last; but the love of John Donne for Anne More has remained marvellously alive in the poem which is so rightly called holy (just as the passion captured in the curves of the portrait of Hélène Fourment continues to shed its rays on the attentive visitor to the Vienna Museum).

Donne was not mistaken: the Couple lives on after itself. A certain constancy, a certain perseverance in attention, conferred by it on love renders it immortal:

> *If our two loves be one, or thou and I*
> *Love so alike, that none doe slacken, none can die.*[98]

How did their story begin? And first of all, what sort of people were they? She, unquestionably, was tender and gentle—more than once

to study and meditation. But after he met Anne everything changed: all his plans, calculations and projects crumbled away when, in December 1601, he secretly married her.

From the beginning Sir George More had fought against the idyll with pitiless energy: Donne could not be unaware that he was bound to make of him a dangerous enemy. If he did not see this, or did not deign to take it into account, the reason could only be that he was blinded or dominated by passion. But no one dreams of denying that John Donne and Anne More were frantically in love: it was this that led Donne to commit what his first biographer was to call 'the remarkable error of his life'.

From the temporal point of view, Walton was right. Donne's career was broken. At his father-in-law's request the poet was deprived of his post as chief secretary to the Lord Chancellor. His wife was taken away from him into Surrey—to get her back he was forced to engage on long and costly legal proceedings. He himself was thrown into prison, as were the two friends who had helped to bring about the marriage. He found himself without employment and without money. For years he had to go cap in hand in search of work and to live on the generosity of the king's favourites. He went through the humiliations of dependency and of flattery, the degradations of poverty and the remorse of having brought all this on his young wife. He was never destined to recover from the disaster. Holy orders, which he later received only with reluctance, were to him merely a last resort. This *metaphysical* had not the vocation for the priesthood, and he knew it. Paradoxically, the following fine definition of the divine is due to the erotic poet: 'Since all Divinity is love or wonder'. This great poet of human love was less outstanding as a Christian poet, but posterity has not been the loser.

What heights would he not have reached, his biographers wondered, if he had avoided that great mistake? A great statesman? An ambassador?

Instead of which, he was merely to be one of the greatest love poets—some think the greatest. Not one of the advertising kind who think they have done well enough when they have made an inventory and an expert appreciation of beauty—dull plagiarists of the *Song of*

Songs, auctioneers and valuers of love; but the greatest modern poet of loving union. As Leishman puts it so well, Donne's poetry is 'about the oneness of two persons who have become one, about what this oneness feels like'. He was the poet of the androgynous condition.

As we have seen, the theme of the Androgyne was far from unknown in poetry. The 'exchange of hearts' had become one of the literary commonplaces of the Renaissance, after having dominated the symbolism of courtly love. Donne in due course alluded to it in *Lovers Infinitenesse*—but to stress its insufficiency:

> *But wee will have a way more liberall,*
> *Than changing hearts, to joyne them, so wee shall*
> *Be one, and one another's All.*

And in *The Canonization* he is still more definite. Taking up the emblem of the Phoenix (as D. H. Lawrence did later), he found more meaning in it when applied to the Couple:

> *The Phoenix ridle hath more wit*
> *By us, we two being one, are it.*
> *So to one neutrall thing both sexes fit,*
> *Wee dye and rise the same, and prove*
> *Mysterious by this love.*

It is perfectly clear. The mystery, to Donne, is that double being in whom the sexes neutralize each other; and it is because they have attained it that lovers are *canonized.*

But to approach it, he needed the experience of conjugal union. Not that Donne's quest changed its object: he had never pursued anything other than those 'privileged moments' in which a fullness that is both existential and essential can be attained. Even in the midst of the most sensual joys (those 'whole joys' of 'full nakedness'),[101] he constantly speculated on the revelation given to him by those instants when the flesh comes into marvellous harmony with the spirit. But in facile love such instants are short-lived:

> *But oh, loves day is short . . .*
> *And his first minute, after noone, is night.*

Donne knew the melancholy of satiety: he treated in masterly fashion the theme of the sorry animal: poems like *Loves Alchymie* and *Farewell to Love* bear witness to his disappointment and deep dissatisfaction. Sometimes his libertinism seems like a subterfuge, to escape from the sadness of life by in some way taking it by storm. But, even if (as Ellrodt thinks) there is no real contradiction between the libertine making a case for inconstancy and the mature lover postulating the eternity of the Couple, there is at least a change of method. Donne replaced the Don Juanesque conception of love and its contempt for the individual by a philosophy of love which makes the individual holy; for vagabond love he substituted conjugal love. This meant a confrontation of *eros* with the formidable experience of a thing that lasts—and, as we know, the experience was not kind to him.

In the letters he wrote from his 'hospital at Mitcham', constantly disturbed by the cries of his children, he sometimes appears as a tormented, grief-stricken Hamlet-like person, but what hours of exaltation, revelation, illumination must be set against his periods of depression—which, Ellrodt suggests, were merely the price he paid for their intensity.

Donne was raised to a higher plane by his love for Anne More. It is a remarkable, indeed a consoling fact that the finest and most confident of his poems, those which glorify love as the supreme reality, date from the time when his love for her had just caused the ruin of his temporal hopes.[102] The cynic who had proclaimed (in *Loves Alchymie*) that love is 'imposture all', who to be rid of it had given (in *Farewell to Love*) the coarse advice, 'If all faile, 'tis but applying worme-seed to the Taile', turned his energies to proving that love is the highest value; everything else—honours, wealth, thrones—is merely imagination and pretence: 'Nothing else is'. The man who, with an even more cynical insolence, had advised lovers to disdain the face and go for the essential ('consider what this chace Mispent by the beginning at the face, Rather set out below'), now declared that sex was not the lover's object: 'it was not sexe'. The mocker, who had savagely made fun of

> *That loving wretch that sweares:*
> *'Tis not the bodies marry, but the mindes*

now wishes love to 'assume' the body. The word is marvellously chosen and strikingly modern.[103]

Donne was never what is commonly called a 'Platonic' or 'idealist' lover. Indeed, in his dread of seeing the material support of sublimation vanish away, he made the very most of the concrete, striving to give body to what seems most tenuous: hence those splendid metaphors of his, which give thickness and reality to his thought—the 'fast balme' that firmly cements the lovers' hands together, or the eye-beams that 'twisted and did thred Our eyes upon one double string'.

Donne never repudiated the body. In marked contrast to the cry of 'Beware of Lust' raised by his contemporary George Herbert, he took (in *The Canonization*) sexual pleasure as the image of initiatory death, the condition for a new birth—punning with genius so as to bring out the erotic sense of the word 'die'. He entrusts to the body the many tasks of mediation. And in *The Extasie*, that poem in which he sums up his conception of love, he gives to the body its letters patent of nobility:

> *Loves mysteries in soules doe grow,*
> *But yet the body is his booke.*

Donne—modern in this—maintains that there is no discontinuity between the ecstasy of the soul and that of the body:

> *And if some lover, such as wee,*
> *Have heard this dialogue of one,*
> *Let him still marke us, he shall see*
> *Small change, when we' are to bodies gone.*

True, as he matured he no longer spoke of the body with quite that joyful abandon, that insolent haste, with which, in the *Epithalamium for Lady Elizabeth*, he had hustled the young bride:

> *A Bride before a good night could be said,*
> *Should vanish from her clothes into her bed;*

with which, in *To his Mistress Going to Bed* (described by the solemn Ellrodt as a 'strip-tease'—wrongly, to my mind, since it is at the opposite pole from that rite's premeditated slowness) he tears off the clothes:

> *Come, Madam, come, all rest my powers defie . . .*
> *Off with that girdle . . .*
> *Off with that happy busk . . .*
> *Now off with those shooes . . .*

Licence my roaving hands, and let them go,
Before, behind, between, above, below.
O my America! my new-found-land.
My kingdome . . .

But what now made its appearance was a tenderness and respect for the body (which he called 'a great Prince'), a pity for the flesh doomed to death, a sorrow at having to abandon it to death.

Respect, tenderness and pity in the emphatically virile Donne—these feelings were indeed signs of a change. They answered to the poet's growing awareness of his own femininity, of the double of the opposite sex whom he carried within him. It is this epiphany of the anima that he is celebrating in the splendid *Good Morrow*—'And now good-morrow to our waking soules'. Naturally this awakening was accompanied by a sense of remembering:

> *I wonder by my troth, what thou, and I*
> *Did, till we lov'd? . . .*

> *If ever any beauty I did see,*
> *Which I desir'd, and got, 'twas but a dreame of thee.*

In other poems the theme of predestination in love crops up again; for instance:

> *Twice or thrice had I loved thee*
> *Before I knew thy face or name.*

In a poet so fascinated by knowledge this eruption of the subconscious could not fail to be accompanied by a strenuous, almost dramatic striving for lucidity: never losing sight of the woman who was its occasion, holding her before him by means of concrete points of reference which give purchase to the activity of loving, he focuses his attention upon the experience which has been granted to him and submits it to merciless criticism. With his great experience of love he was well aware that the activity of loving does not load, but eliminates.

It is often said that from the moment of his marriage his way of loving gained in depth. But this must be understood in its proper sense: love does not keep on adding, but digs deeper in: to go deeper is only a way of going further—going as far as possible. If Donne was constantly *refining* his love, this was because he was determined to reach the nucleus, the pure diamond which he could see shining through its matrix—and which he called by its true name, Spirit. To Donne, as to Plotinus, 'all desire is already desire for knowledge'.

Paradoxically this critical activity leads into mysticism. This is the reason for the many images of purifying, of laying bare and of penetrating. Images of passing through and shining through are repeated till they become obsessive, the only coined words used by Donne are 'through-pierc'd', 'through-sworne', 'through-light', 'through-shine'. When taken in connection with this poet's emphasis on undressing, such critical purification acquires the meaning of an initiation.

Donne, like all the mystics, was torn between his desire to keep out the laymen, to defend the Holy of Holies from their approach, and what he felt was his vocation of bearing witness. When he urges his wife not to weep for him when he is absent (in that admirable poem which Donne addressed to her in the eleventh year of their marriage, when he was forced to leave her and accompany his benefactor to France), this is because

> *T'were prophanation of our joyes*
> *To tell the layetie our love.*

In this truly exhaustive poem the idea of the sacred is once again bound up with the method that makes possible its attainment. In a love 'so much refin'd, That our selves know not what it is', their two souls 'are one', so that, though Donne must go away, they

> *endure not yet*
> *A breach, but an expansion,*
> *Like gold to ayery thinnesse beate.*

And to explain this mystery of the Couple he invents another image, the famous simile of the compasses which concludes this poem of perfect love:

> *If they be two, they are two so*
> *As stiffe twin compasses are two,*
> *Thy soule the fixt foot, makes no show*
> *To move, but doth, if the other doe.*

> *And though it in the center sit,*
> *Yet when the other far doth rome,*
> *It leanes, and hearkens after it,*
> *And growes erect, as that comes home*
>
> *Such will thou be to mee, who must*
> *Like th'other foot, obliquely runne;*
> *Thy firmness drawes my circle just,*
> *And makes me end, where I begunne.*

In spite of their beauty, these last verses contain a moral lesson—and the morality is the traditional one, which maintains that the husband may wander and the wife must stay put. For once, however, the greatness of the man justifies the effacement of his companion. Donne's debt to Anne is nonetheless inestimable: he owed her his fulfilment as a poet and as a man, his glory and his salvation. He was fully aware of the debt when she died, still young, leaving him in despair. But she died having accomplished her work: in her, Donne had been completely initiated, and now, having passed through all its stages, he could speak in one breath of the object of his love and the way which had led him there.

'Wholly on heavenly things my mind is sett', he says in *Holy Sonnet xvii*, and for this he gives the credit to her:

> *Here the admyring her my mind did whett*
> *To seeke thee God; so streames do shew their head.*

It was in vain that he tried to attain to God directly, as his ministry seemed to him to require; it was in vain that he asked God to batter his heart, and described the mystical ravishment as though by doing so he might provoke it. The poet of amorous ecstasy seems not to have attained to the supreme joys of prayer: Donne's faith remained tied to the experience of human love. Not that this great poet of the Spirit lacked a supernatural vocation, but rather that he was fated to reach the dimension of the supernatural by reference to the natural, to the concrete (it was this that made him so great a poet): and, though fascinated by the divine, he could not conceive of it except in the form of a coherence, or Order and Law. Establishing connections and eliminating—postulate and method these are the very conditions of daimonic and critical *eros*.

In short, the experience of marriage was to Donne a maieutic—just as it was to be for D. H. Lawrence, another great daimonic soul. (But Lawrence, unfortunately, was hindered by his fear of certain words: the word 'mental' seemed to him loathsome, and he tried to replace mental awareness by a 'phallic awareness'—an awareness, all the same.) In becoming a lover so refined by true love that he was all spirit and could understand 'soules language', Donne never treated salvation as an achievement reached in isolation, but said again and again that it was an achievement of the Couple, which gained from love—from a love stubbornly determined to bring to light its connections—a double soul, 'that abler soule' by which it would survive eternally.

CROSS PURPOSES OF THE SEXES

The man's privileged situation comes from the integration of his biological aggressive rôle with his social function as chief, as master.

SIMONE DE BEAUVOIR

There is an obstacle or, more exactly, a resistance to the achievements of the Couple—the antagonism of the sexes. Just as love and desire have both a masculine and a feminine form, so (allowing for the existence of a deep-seated bisexuality) has aggressiveness. Feminine aggressiveness, conditioned by the receptive rôle of the female, produces variations on the theme of monopolizing a man—and sometimes devouring him. (The unfortunate D. H. Lawrence was fated to attract several of these 'man-eaters.') Virile aggressiveness exploits themes of hunting, capture, rape and appropriation.

In love as I understand it—a love that compensates for the gap between the sexes—everything that attracts attention to this gap and concretizes it should, in principle, make the union still more exemplary. This observation both throws light on and sets limits to the part played by sexual aggressiveness. Only a certain violence—controlled, significant and, in a sense ritual or initiatory violence—can give love what Gilbert Lély has rightly called 'its stamp of perfection'. In short, to try to allow the antagonism of the sexes a proper place is better than to struggle to stifle or camouflage it—which indeed is absurd. The part played by the male in the act of love (rightly described in certain languages as the 'manly act', *männlicher Akt*), can never be prevented from being aggressive: such is the elementary pattern. However tenderly and considerately the man may treat his partner he cannot disguise this pattern or prevent the man's part in love from being, at least at the start, an outbreak, an act of violence, an attack on the woman's physical integrity. For women this element of suffering and subjection runs through and colours the whole of love. It recurs in the pangs of childbirth, in the normal position of human love, and in the fact that a woman can submit passively to love-making while the man must at least desire it.

What is required, then, is not so much to dodge this as to see that no misunderstandings poison it. But the sexual subordination of the woman to the man has constantly been poisoned, it has constantly been exploited in order to establish a social and moral dependence. Generations of men have made use of their sexual advantages to crush the married woman, to confine her not to the sacred world of sex but the profane world of practical life, with the result that the amorous relationship is completely distorted. Love demands the absolute equality of the partners, at least at the start: it is on this impartial basis that loving relationships can be improvised in all their purity.

As is well known, most of the Western countries have in recent years abolished—partially at least—the married woman's status of inferiority.[104]

But it may prove less easy to abolish the conviction that the man has a natural superiority, for this conviction is still deeply rooted in the minds of most men and even women, and education (by which I mean not only teaching and curricula, but also moral upbringing, culture and religion, the use of leisure, the choice of games, and even fashion) moulds people's minds to it from childhood.

Simone de Beauvoir was right when she stated that, if a woman is to be the equal of a man, she must *think* herself his equal. This movement of opinion is taking place inevitably, but it is slow, and meanwhile misunderstandings persist. Married women have always approached love with a minority complex. And so it often happens that adultery seems to her a kind of truancy, an escape from the schoolmaster's discipline.

To be sure, there are good marriages where the husband does not make the weight of his authority felt—and there are other, loathsome ones, ruled by a virago who takes it upon her to avenge her sex by intimidating a weak man. But on the whole, in marriage, the relationship between the sexes is rarely met with in its pure state. This is why I will take my first illustration from an illicit love.

All the women who have become examples of a great love have accepted the subjection of the woman to the man in love—not least the proudest and cleverest of them. There have been many cases where pride and the passion for liberty have suddenly been transformed to a passion for humility and sacrifice.

No clearer case of this loving submission can be found than the case of Juliette Drouet, who was a reigning beauty in Paris, an actress and courtesan surrounded with glamour. Kept magnificently by a fabulously rich prince, who lavished clothes, jewellery and silver on her and provided her with sumptuous apartments and a dazzling trousseau (thirty-eight dresses and more than twenty-four chemises were handed in to the pawnbrokers after Victor Hugo had forced her to do without Prince Demidoff's protection), Juliette renounced for the sake of love not only luxury but the ordinary comforts of life. She was soon leading, as Maurois says, 'the most surprisingly penitential and cloistered life ever accepted by a woman outside the monastic orders'. This apprenticeship was not always free from moods of regret or rebellion, from the resistance put up by the instinct to hold on to things; she did sometimes complain:

> 'Look, my Victor, this life of isolation, this stay-at-home life, is killing me. I am wearing out my soul longing for you, wearing out my life in a room ten feet square. What I want isn't society or stupid pleasures, but *freedom*, freedom to be, freedom to use my time and my energies in looking after a house of my own; what I want is to stop suffering, for I suffer a thousand deaths a minute, I am asking you for life, to be able to live *like you, in fact like everyone else.*'

This wearing-out of the soul, this slow consumption of a life is the terrible price of any great love, earthly or divine, when it postulates the absolute. And this abandonment of the most elementary rights of the individual does no more than meet half-way the lover's desires, if he is supremely virile; for a man possesses by supplanting and asserts himself by denying, in contrast to the woman, whose desire is to be possessed and supplanted, and who, to be more sure of this, will even deny her own individual existence. Juliette Drouet was well aware of this, aware also that her complaints and protests were no more than jolts in a surrender granted in advance.

It was a real immolation and eighteen thousand letters allow us to follow its clinical development. Some people, when they look at the one-sidedness of the sacrifice, will consider it monstrous; but did Juliette Drouet make such a bad bargain? She exchanged the facile pleasures of a brilliant but artificial life for the incomparable joy of a love which, in spite of the man's disloyalties (and these, like everything emanating from that Titan, were extraordinary), was preserved, eternalized. Juliette stands out as the perfect type of the wife who is an *egregoros*, staying at the sentry-post and keeping watch for two. And she succeeded. Victor Hugo loved other women (Adèle, Léonie) passionately, but it was with Juliette that he formed a couple. Posterity has made no mistake about this: with her alone he really adopted the sacral quality of love; and this sacral quality the two of them stressed again and again by all sorts of solemn celebrations, relics, pilgrimages and religious promises. On the night of 17-18 November 1839 (when their liaison had already lasted more than six years), Hugo entered into so solemn a commitment towards 'Madame Drouet' that, from that time onwards, the lovers looked on themselves as united by a secret and true marriage.

Juliette may have been deceived in the conventional bourgeois sense, but she was not cheated. She wanted to be Hugo's real wife, his life's companion, and this she was. Her subordination was always voluntary, a matter of consent. At every moment she remained the mistress of her destiny. And it was in order to lead her inner life more freely that she shut herself off from life in the world. For hers was a naturally mystical soul, which was bound to find its outlet in the divine. 'It is you that I adore in God and God that I adore in you', she wrote superbly. Her romanticism may sometimes have made her fail to distinguish between the two. This is of small importance. In any case, love surpassed itself and opened out supernaturally.

There is one sullen, singularly poisonous form of misunderstanding between the sexes. This is when marital authority is called in to cover up a failure in love, whether it be that the husband alone loves (or loves more than he is loved), or that he knows he is impotent (or likely to become so), or that he is aware of not having satisfied his wife. In general, when a man has been unsuccessful sexually and as a lover, he is tempted to make up for the damage to his manly dignity (Lawrence would have said, 'to his phallic consciousness') and make his mark by other means. So it comes about that perfectly kindly men are led to a forced sexual aggressiveness, even to the point of sadism or—far more frequently—into replacing the lover's domination by a husbandly or a merely masculine authoritarianism. The course downhill is a very painful one. Painful for the man as well as for the woman, for, as she tries to escape and to rebel, his thirst for authority becomes greater, therefore more and more odious, therefore more and more difficult to escape. Such cross purposes can only lead to hell. The woman married in order to be loved, and the lover has changed into a schoolmaster or a jailor, if not a torturer.

This was the kind of disaster that fell upon the famous couple, August Strindberg and Harriet Bosse. From the beginning, admittedly, things looked bad. What attracted Harriet (who, like Juliette Drouet, was an actress) was Strindberg's fame and glamour: she had a literary infatuation for him, and at first it took a romantic form—one New Year's Eve she prowled around his windows, pressed her lips against the glass and whispered prayers for 'the great man'. And he chose to fall in love with this young woman at a moment when he was going through a spiritual crisis: according to Harriet Bosse herself 'he had turned his back on the world and was striving towards the *life beyond*'. This movement of ascent was, unfortunately, not above stooping to details: a red divan cover was hastily removed from the young woman's room when Strindberg decided that it might draw his thoughts down an earthly slope. The moment, clearly, was a bad one for marrying a girl who was free, full of curiosity and zest for living, and by no means predisposed to ascetic discipline. But it may well be that Strindberg—a Puritan to whom physical love was scandalous, and a pessimist convinced that the world was fundamentally ugly and wicked ('a heap of filth')—was fated in any case to approach love in the wrong way. It is not surprising to find, even in Strindberg's own letters, evidence of a sexual failure. On the morrow of the marriage

Harriet actually told him that he was 'not a man', and a week later she brazenly announced to everyone that she was still 'not August Strindberg's wife'. Her sisters regarded her as not married. When she realized that she was pregnant she is said to have insolently exclaimed, 'How could such a thing have happened?' The cruelty with which Harriet Bosse applied herself to humiliating Strindberg and reproaching him with his sexual insufficiency was so great that it can only be explained by an equally great cruelty of Strindberg to her. And in fact this man of genius soon became a terrible despot. What has been said of his plays can also be applied to Strindberg's relations with Harriet: they were a ceaseless settling of accounts, a harsh book-keeping. On both sides: for Harriet also remembered and added up the tale of complaints, recriminations, scenes and failed or abandoned plans.

Strindberg's love for Harriet took, from the start, a pathologically obsessive form, as is proved by his strange way of proposing to her: 'Would you like to have a little child with me, Miss Bosse?' (Impregnation was always, to Strindberg, a sign and irrefutable proof of possession, of appropriation.) He put the question without any preamble, simply laying his hands on her shoulders and gazing at her long and ardently; and she, intimidated, could only answer, with a curtsey: 'Yes, thank you, Sir.' That is how they became engaged.

It had hardly happened before Harriet became frightened. Strindberg had told her that he was counting on her to reconcile him with humanity—above all with Woman and with sex (for he had terribly bad debts to recover, those of his two previous marriages). The task did not inspire her with any zeal. She was well aware also, that she was not really physically in love with him. But she was already subject to his will, and already he was taking advantage of this. He began to train her, to bend her to all kinds of obedience and renunciations.

What Strindberg was trying to obtain from Harriet was really no more than what Victor Hugo did obtain from Juliette Drouet. But Strindberg was a Puritan, and he would demand that this abdication, submission and effacement be made not in the name of love but in that of morality and the redemption of women. Was he the victim of his temperament, or was he trying to break Harriet's will? In either case he subjected her to some extraordinary vexations. When they went to a restaurant, he jumped suddenly to his feet because, he said, another guest had been staring at them—after that, they could dine only in a private room. If she felt like a ride in a victoria, he would choose the moment when she placed her foot on the step of the carriage to announce that they would not go. If they were making ready for a journey to Switzerland (to which she was looking forward eagerly) and had made plans, drawn up an itinerary, ordered tickets and made reservations, it would all be given up on the very morning when they were due to go, when the packing was done and the trunks registered. One gasps at Strindberg's attempt to console her for this—he urged her to replace the journey by reading Baedeker ('aren't the things we imagine always more beautiful than the real ones?') or learning a foreign language. Even her leisure hours were organized by her husband, and he decided what she should read. It was Strindberg, too, who chose the furnishings of the flat they were to share: Harriet was made to leave her personal possessions behind her, as if she were going into a convent. And so, two months after the marriage, all Harriet could think of was to recover her liberty and escape from the 'gloomy Kärlavâgen'. The flat where they lived (it is now the Chancellery of the Netherlands Embassy) can still be seen: it is not at all bad, but Harriet found it oppressive.

One day she took the boat to Denmark without warning her husband. Strindberg was overwhelmed. To go after Harriet and live with her in a country and a house not of his choosing seemed to him at first unthinkable. Yet he nerved himself to do so, for he loved his wife passionately. But the tyranny began again with the renewal of their life together. When someone tried to photograph Harriet bathing, their stay in the country was suddenly broken off; she was told to follow Strindberg to Berlin, and to this she resigned herself, only to find that she was forbidden to enter the 'City of Vice': she must live in lodgings at Grünewald, where she was bored to death.

When we realize that all these vexations were inflicted on an actress who had led an extremely free life and had already tasted success and popularity, the violence of her rebellion can hardly astonish us. Of course, there was the precedent of Juliette Drouet; but Victor Hugo's

authority was the radiant, almost royal authority of a superb lover—
in spite of infidelities and stormy scenes, their liaison was a complete
success sexually, and some of Juliette's letters are so clear about this
that no one has yet been permitted to publish them in full. The
authority which Strindberg was trying to impose under cover of love
was merely based on a thirst for vengeance against a woman whom
he had failed to dominate sexually and—beyond her—against the whole
of her sex. The predilection shown by this anti-feminist for women
of exceptional quality (Siri von Essen, Baronne Wrangel, Frieda Uhl,
the writer and journalist, and Harriet Bosse, a popular actress) has often
caused surprise. As Arthur Adamov has lucidly observed, what
Strindberg required was 'a woman of high quality who would allow
herself to be treated by him as a servant'. The unsuccessful lover wanted
vengeances that would be worth taking, but none of his wives loved
him enough to submit to the bargain, Harriet even less than her
predecessors. She made Strindberg's life a cruel torture—at least until
they decided on divorce. By this last the two fierce adversaries were
somewhat appeased: cross purposes over, they could meet as friends.

But meanwhile Strindberg stumbled from one extreme to another.
Sometimes he implored, sometimes he threatened. If Harriet ran away,
he begged her humbly to return to him. If she gave in to him, he began
to tyrannize over her again. It was his way of loving her, possessing
her: he had no other. There is nothing more painful than his letters
to his wife at that time. In them he lays down all pride and promises to
efface himself (for he was well aware that what drove her away from
him was the monstrous abdication he could not help demanding of
her):[105]

> I need not tell you that your home is waiting for you and that you can go
> into your yellow room and your green room without even noticing me,
> that you can close your doors or open them as you please, that you can call
> me if you wish, and that you owe me no explanation and I will be as little
> of a nuisance to you as I can.

With Siri also he had found that, when he resumed his 'virile determination, she withdrew her friendship'.

Poor Strindberg! One cannot help liking him in spite of his impossible behaviour—just as one cannot help disliking Harriet for being

right in so detestable a way. Why did she have to return a dishonest answer to that sincere letter, why resort to a trick?

> Cannot you understand why I went away? I wanted to save as much of a woman's modesty and dignity as could still be saved. The words you used to me on that unforgettable day in Berlin are still ringing in my ears. . . . No, Gusten, I cannot endure any more to be spattered with insults so shamelessly, especially now that I am expecting our beloved little child. It must be born in purity.

The tone is odious, but it arose quite logically: being treated as a servant, Harriet defended herself in a servile way. She went even further, and did not hesitate to throw doubt on the parentage of the child—the one joy remaining to Strindberg from his ill-starred love for her.[106] (The situation was used by him in *The Father*.) Light is thrown on this monstrous behaviour by the fact that Siri had already made use of the same treacherous weapon. The two women seemed to have reacted in exactly the same way, and one wonders whether it was not, in both cases, self-defence against Strindberg's odious idea of an appropriation ratified by fertilization. On the day when, meeting Harriet, he saw that she was obviously pregnant, the belief that this was his work made her seem to him 'glorious' (one feels that at that moment he was ready to forgive her everything). When each of the two women told him that her child was not his, she was trying to deny not so much his paternity as her own abdication.

The savagery of such a situation is that it can only grow worse, for it is automatically recharged by the force of a love turned into hate. Sex regains by aggressiveness what is refused to it. The result of baulking sexuality of what belongs to it is not to quieten it down but to envenom it.

Conjugal authority exercised within a union based on reasonable love is less heavy to bear—in proportion as less passion is involved; but it too leads to cross purposes. In practice, when people make a marriage that is not for love, they very rarely avow their real motives (self-interest, pride or vanity, competitiveness, imitation, the desire to have descendants, or simply the desire to find a manageress for one's home). The presence of love is so much more flattering, so much 'prettier'—and after all, 'a little sentiment does no harm'.

Public opinion supports this fraud practised on love by means of a whole collection of traditional pretences, such as the show of courtship, the allegory of the epithalamium, the honeymoon with its feigned abduction. The case of Paulus Merula, deliberately enlightening his bride on the austere way of life he has in store for her, is exceptional. Considering that 'reasonable' marriage bases the subordination of the woman on her inferiority, not on any loving submission, it requires some courage for a man to set it frankly before her, and for a woman to subscribe to it. Religion alone can give it an appearance of justification: submission then means, for the woman, basing her life on Order, on the Oath, on the Law of God. Some women, both pagan and Christian, have built up fine lives on this plan; yet these achievements, great as they may be, cannot be made into a rule, for the way is a purely religious one which suits only a limited number of individuals and can only discourage the others. It must be recognized that, apart from religion, the marriage of association is without dignity and shows up the cynicism of the system—with its simple mechanism churning on in the same old way. Rounded off by institutions which are merciless to any sexual straying on the part of the woman both before marriage and during it, this system practically excludes love from the life of any woman who submits to the rules of society. (There will always be some piratical women, like the great Louise Labé— and also some successful deceivers.)

To reduce the risks still more, public opinion subjects love in woman to a time limit—or rather, age limit—as well, and is always ready to use the weapon of ridicule against those women who flout it. But the system would not be complete if it did not include the division of women into two classes with two separate functions—wives and mistresses. Except in periods of decadence, men have always tried to maintain the separation between these two. As I have said, there is a long-standing policy of duplicity which consists in making use of the one without foregoing the enjoyment of the other. Love outside marriage is love limited in time and divided from reality: it is escapist love.

From it a woman emerges damaged, even when she seems to have benefited from it. A woman who falls in love seeks at once to build her life upon that love. The most independent women (such as Emilie du Châtelet) and the most cynical women (such as Lady Mary Wortley Montagu), as soon as they fall in love, hasten to offer their whole lives to men who would have been glad of less. A woman's love tends naturally to the conjugal. But women desire passion as well: Madame du Châtelet thought that with Voltaire she had 'found at last the deep and eternal passion she was seeking', but what she had found was merely a style of enjoyable living.[107] The divine Emilie soon had to pipe down, admit defeat, and aim at a less ambitious mode of loving. But the epicurean dilettantism of the *Discours sur le Bonheur* melted away when she met Saint-Lambert, with whom she fell madly in love —she who had flattered herself that 'after the age of thirty the passions no longer carry us away with the same impetuosity'. And at once cross purposes began afresh: 'I shall spend my life with you, that is certain', she wrote. 'Do you wish me to love you with all the fury, all the folly, all the abandonment of which I am capable?' She proposed again and again to devote her whole life to him, and that they should live together.

The naïveté of these women falling in love at forty is disarming. One could indeed wish that the sceptical Lady Mary Wortley Montagu might have kept a little of her cynicism to use upon Algarotti, for whom she waited in vain at Venice—not to speak of Palazzi, who despoiled her of her jewellery. But her letters echo those of Madame du Châtelet: 'What has become of that philosophical indifference which produced the glory and tranquillity of my past days?' And again: 'All that is certain is that *I shall love you all my life.*'

In a marriage or in a liaison the woman seeks both passion and permanence, while the man thinks these incompatible: here we have a collision between two radically different ways of love, and this is the most flagrant form taken by the cross purposes of the sexes. It is part of a woman's life to look upon love as a maturing, and of a man's life to consider his love satisfied when he has possessed the woman. Masculine love asserts itself in possession and concludes there: this self-assertion can, it is true, be repeated, but it loses some of its significance each time, while for the woman the significance constantly increases. As a result, when a man contemplates setting up a permanent establishment he prefers to give it what in his view is a more reassuring, more stable basis than passion. And he is the more inclined to do without passion in marriage since society allows him to enjoy it outside, in the form of 'brief encounters', of adventures without a morrow. Fantasies of this kind are considered attractive and even honourable— so much so that a man of a certain standing is obliged by his position to have mistresses, while a woman, if she takes lovers, is bound by her position to secrecy and furtiveness. The current collapse of morality has, of course, cut deeply into that social system, but—let there be no mistake about it—is far from having completed its ruin: one need only go into certain provincial circles to become aware that, especially in Latin countries, the mechanism is still working, condemning countless women to an incomplete and maimed life. Its effect has been not only to favour the husband's material interests and the protection of the patrimony: it has succeeded in imposing on society the masculine conception of love. The feminine conception of love has never been tried out in society. This should be done.

A policy that sacrifices one of the sexes so deliberately was obliged to offer it some compensation. Passionate love, from which society was anxious to expel the woman, had to be given back to her in an inoffensive form—or at least there must be a show of doing so. The trick has been considered by some people to be specifically bourgeois, and seems to consist in this: everything that threatens the institutions of society is compressed into a set of ideals, so that a purely verbal cult of it can be kept up while it is being secretly undermined. This view of things is appealing when we realize that tactics of exactly the same sort have succeeded in isolating and sterilizing culture, morality and religion, which have been reduced to their 'ideal' function, in the hollowest sense of the term.[108]

The bourgeoisie had no need to invent the ideology of passionate love, but found it ready-made in the arsenal of courtly love and of the Round Table romances. Society allowed people to 'dream of love', but secretly encouraged the marriage of interest. What it was bent on avoiding as much as possible was that love should mix itself up in 'serious matters' such as the founding of a family and, most important, the fusion of two patrimonies.

Served by a misleading literature, there arose an immense ferment of sentimentality and romanticism which favoured the exaltation of illusory love. The loves of royal personages and the loves of stars—more illusory than any others—today form the principal attraction of that branch of the press which is known to appeal to women. Countless women devour this and become intoxicated by a false image of love, which is always associated with luxury, wealth, exoticism and one or two special fantasies of the time, such as splendid motor cars. This is the kind of love known as 'romance', and it is not calculated to disperse conjugal misunderstanding: either the woman finds in marriage no more than reasonable love, and its down-to-earth quality soon repels her; or it may have been true love, and, still disappointed, she may even fail to recognize it. The strong taste of real love disconcerts her and makes her recoil. What is more, love—which always strives to be in some way a purification and a discipline—imposes trials and sacrifices on her; but she has been dreaming of a kind of fairy-tale in which the man, invariably chivalrous, never ceases to hand out the most delicate enjoyments—and now she finds that the man is an adversary before becoming a lover, that love is an antagonism and a combat before it is a harmony.

But not everyone is content with illusions, and the virulence of *eros* (to use for a moment language that its enemies might use) is not exhausted by relegating it to the ideal. Sometimes love overflows the bounds of artificiality and, proving to be very real, undermines the social structures; sometimes, then, one of their walls crumbles away, revealing to the astonished gaze of public opinion the intensity of a forbidden life which has been going on under the cover of middle-class respectability.

To disarm love, a defence mechanism even more efficient than false idealism was required, and so found. This was an invention of genius, produced by a society that is always busy perfecting its own adaptedness, and it consists in immunizing people against love by granting to the need of love a partial satisfaction. Commercial eroticism puts its trust (as Roland Barthes has warned us)[109] in a generalization of the principle of inoculation and vaccination. For the price of a newspaper, or of a cinema, music-hall or cabaret ticket, a dose appropriate to our

202 *Aspects of Love*

tastes and needs is sold to us, like a pill at the chemist's. It is not even necessary to pay: eroticism is given us free. It comes to us in fashions, in publicity, invading the streets and the motor roads, and immunizes us in spite of ourselves. Sustained by powerful means of mass diffusion, commercial eroticism gradually substitutes its abnormal satisfactions for the genuine relationship between the sexes. The habit grows of odd stimuli and brief pleasures, which are always isolated from love and here once more the masculine conception prevails, dispossessing the Couple.

A few efforts have been made in modern times to disperse the misunderstandings between the sexes and to give the relationship between them a fairer basis. I will mention two of these, which are in some ways alike: the Elisée Reclus type of anarchist free union, and the Sartre-Beauvoir type of pact. Both are cases of an association that is free but includes an intention to last, and in both of them the stress is placed on the work to be done together or side by side rather than on love. At the same time there is, of course, a great difference between the anarchist romanticism of Elisée Reclus and existentialism, between the optimistic faith in nature professed by the Volontaires and the lucid pact by which Sartre and Beauvoir have tried to reconcile commitment and liberty, *necessary love and contingent loves*.

There was a considerable naïveté and candour in the young geo- grapher who signed his letters *'ton brave Elisée'* and whose marriage recalls both Bernardin de Saint-Pierre and Rousseau. For he married his young and beautiful mulatto girl without any marriage settlement —a thing quite unheard of at that time. His tutor, who shared his ideal, exclaimed exultantly: 'Ah! you are a good young man! You are a man of nature!' Reclus became the promoter of 'the anti-marriage movement', and married off his children without any civil or religious formalities. He intended, certainly, to show his hostility to laws, but above all to rescue his daughters from 'the scandal of a contract that consecrates the man's right over the woman, the monstrous inequality of the sexes'. Marriage, to him, was a form of prostitution. 'It disgusts us that a woman should be declared a conjugal chattel, and that a man should be considered as the owner of such an object'. In anarchist marriage of this kind, husband and wife remained completely free:

'We have no right to ask you to make any promise', says Reclus in the marriage address. 'You are responsible for your acts. . . . Even today you are your own masters.' Such words do not even imply fidelity.

We must beware of exaggerating: in 1882 the woman's freedom to dispose of herself ran up against worse obstacles than the power of the law and the respect for contracts. Free union carried a restraint within itself and was based on the strictest morality. The whole of that revolutionary society (in many cases Protestant) was terribly puritan. So much so, that a man was taking no great risk by proclaiming the equality of the sexes, for any woman who had the bad taste to take advantage of it would at once be struck down by public opinion. In the matter of work, equality was no more effective: if a man and a woman collaborated, this was always in the man's work, in which the woman became at best his associate. In this respect there was no difference between these free unions and other couples—formally married, and indeed admirable—such as the Pasteurs or the Berthelots. At the end of the nineteenth century the woman still entered into a free union or into marriage as though into a religious community— *to devote herself to her husband.* Madame Pasteur copied out her husband's notes, studied the proceedings of the Académie des Sciences and initiated herself into the secrets of sodium tartrate or paratartrate. Madame Berthelot gave up her vocation as painter to become the scientist's secretary. A true equality is exceptional and does not run smoothly. It required the radiant genius of Marie Curie to achieve it and to triumph over what might have stifled her.

Very different is the society to which Simone de Beauvoir directs the message of *Le Deuxième Sexe:* her vigorous defence of the equality of men and women is addressed to a disintegrating world. What, in fact, is its bearing on the couple, or at least on those couples that intend to be lasting (for the others require no defence, since for a long time they have been coming together and coming apart in an atmosphere of indulgence or indifference)? In *Le Deuxiéme Sexe* we do indeed find the merciless criticism of current institutions and a revolutionary theory about the artificiality of the eternal feminine, but on conjugal status we can discover little that is new. Simone de Beauvoir would, it is true, like to see a new kind of feminine behaviour arise to complete the reform of established customs: 'Rare are those women who are able to create a free relationship with their partner'.

A new kind of behaviour? A free relationship? What does Madame de Beauvoir mean by this? It is very tempting to complete our information by reading a later book of hers.[110] When we do, we find some surprising things. We see, for instance, that the arguments of the Sartre-Beauvoir couple in favour of free unions are almost the same as those of Reclus, Grave and Lacour. 'Our anarchism was as healthy and aggressive as that of the old libertarians', writes Simone de Beauvoir 'it incited us, as it did them, not to allow society to interfere in our private affairs. We were hostile to established institutions because in them liberty is alienated'. But this liberty, it becomes clear, was chiefly that of Sartre. Simone de Beauvoir confesses as much, with her usual frankness: 'The anxiety to preserve my own independence was no great burden. . . . But I saw how much it cost Sartre to say goodbye to travel, to his freedom, to his youth, and become a teacher in the provinces and, finally, an adult'. As for the pact about incidental love affairs, not only does it seem to have been concluded chiefly for the man's benefit,[111] but the couple several times postponed its application. And Simone de Beauvoir was forced to realize that it did not exclude so outmoded a sentiment as jealousy.

Another thing we are struck by is the devotion of this feminist to her life companion: this adversary of marriage has, unquestionably, lived through a great conjugal love. The evidence shines out from passages of real eloquence:

> I knew that no harm would ever come to me through him, unless he died before me. . . . Neither of us would ever lie to the other . . . we would tell each other everything. . . . In my eyes, Sartre was superior to me, by virtue of the firmness of his attitude. . . . Far from being worried by this, I found it a comfort to esteem him more than myself. . . . To experience a radical harmony with someone is in any case a very great privilege; in my eyes its value was literally infinite. . . . I trusted him so completely that he guaranteed me final security, like my parents at one time, like God . . . All my wishes, the remotest, the deepest of them, were fulfilled; I had nothing left to wish for, except that this triumphant blessedness should never waver.

Simone de Beauvoir writes repeatedly of her vocation for happiness. Trust, security, tranquillity—these feminine words frequently escape from her pen, suppressing her earlier belief in solitude and freedom.

Clearly, then, this union, this couple is a success; but it is a success of the traditional type. Obviously the affection felt by Simone de Beauvoir for Sartre and described by her so movingly is not of the fatal or vampire kind: she is no Iseult, no Frieda Lawrence. Her love seems to fall rather into the category of 'absolute devotion'. It has been said of Simone de Beauvoir, sometimes in print, that she lives in the shadow of a great man; if this is so, the shadow has not harmed her work, which is perhaps the most monumental ever written by a woman. Yet the gap between work and life remains. There is a disagreement between the doctrinal position of Simone de Beauvoir and the impulses of her deeply feminine sensibility—the *values* by which in the last resort she is governed. The importance to her of happiness, of love, comes out all the more clearly from the determined restraint with which she expresses it. Happiness is to admire Sartre, to esteem him more than herself, to find the supreme tranquillity in him. Love is the superior kind of fraternity which they have achieved together. But there is also another love which they have kept apart from their union, and for which she still has a secret longing—the love described by her with a kind of exquisite naïveté in *Les Mandarins*, the love of Anne for Lewis in that book. It is a love that is both physical and romantic (with her habitual good grace and humour Simone de Beauvoir has admitted that she had a sentimental side to her)—in short, passionate love, which the heroine of the novel nonetheless prudently (one is tempted to say with bourgeois prudence) keeps apart from daily life. Week-end love. Holiday love. Escapist love.

It is fascinating to find that, on the whole, the behaviour of Madame de Beauvoir and of Anne, her representative, conforms to tradition. 'Serious life' is built on sensible love, a love that is, for all its merits, impoverished by the lack of its proper instinctive patterns and myths. Unreasonable love is still there, in the form of longing and—to use a dangerous word—of an ideal (in the sense of the word which Madame de Beauvoir detests); it is relegated to extra-conjugal adventure.

Roger Vailland's attractive theory of *l'amour-fête*—of love as a high festival or special occasion—is no less traditional: this, more than ever, is love isolated from life, escapist love. In *La Fête*, Duc reflects that 'a festival, a special occasion, can be long or short and can have all kinds of setting, but it requires a time separated from the rest of time and a place of its own—such limitation and separation give the festival its reality, just as the body gets its being from its form'. The book, which is a fine one, is ferociously anti-feminist. A man's high festivals are arranged at the expense of women—and first of all, at the expense of his partner, who takes hardly any advantage of the 'statute of sovereignty' which the man concedes to her in the name of reciprocity. 'I don't sleep with Duc any more,' says Léone to Jean-Marc, of whom she is fond. And the husband unquestionably finds this situation a comfortable one—just as he finds it convenient to impose the house-work on his wife:

> 'Duc', she said, 'prefers the house to be looked after by me. He says that sweeping, dusting, shifting things about, coming and going, turning the taps on and off, going up and down stairs, putting a window on the catch and the rustle of a skirt against his study door are the most intimate things in life, and he prefers that they should be done by me.'
> 'All the same', said Jean-Marc, 'if washing-up gets on your nerves. . . .'

Why does Léone consent to Duc allowing himself 'festivals'? For the same reason as countless women before her. To keep him. And besides, she was taught resignation. 'My mother taught me', said Léone, 'that a woman's duty is to respect a man's liberty.'

But this conception of love as festivity is nonetheless cruel to the woman who finds herself called upon to carry it out. 'I cannot desire without love', said Lucie; 'and if I love you, what will become of me?' They will give each other festivals, Duc explains to her. Nothing could be more melancholy than the one he prepares for Lucie, in spite of the trouble he has taken to choose the inn with the three gables: all his clever devices for loosening her up and extracting from her a con-fession of pleasure—one is reminded of one of the heroines of Simone de Beauvoir exclaiming, 'Look what they have invented now! Synchronism!'—would no doubt be superfluous if he were willing to utter the slightest word that would commit him. That would fill the girl with joy (she is a secret reader of the *Lettres portugaises*) but Duc avoids such words like the plague, for to him they belong to the 'mystifications of absolute love'.

Everything confirms the disharmony of these lovers. Duc, who is determined to be free and sovereign, thinks on his way to see Lucie: 'Must break it off in good time. . . . That is the art of living'. But Lucie, standing in front of a house covered with flowering creepers, sighs, 'If only I could live in it with you'. And yet Lucie is never taken in: she consents to love Duc in the way he wants, and falls in with his plan. The truth is that, by doing this, she is giving him a lesson in *sovereignty*, for a man is not sovereign who deprives himself of the freedom to give and to make sacrifices.

The pact or the statute of sovereignty are modern formulae[112] which have only replaced one misunderstanding by another. They claim to place the two sexes on the same footing by means of a kind of freedom which will in most cases remain merely nominal for the woman, either because she does not want to use it, or because, when it comes to the point, the husband refuses to grant it.[113]

More often than not, the pact merely regularizes and legitimizes masculine infidelity: all that the woman has done by accepting it is to lose her right to object and to protest. If, however, she does make use of the pact, if it is applied straightforwardly as by Anne in *Les Mandarins* (when she in turn attempts to treat herself to a 'festival'), the adventure at once turns into love. In that book, Anne comes close to death because she has tried to limit this love and separate it from real life: the last pages show her on the point of suicide—the cry of a child reminds her that there are people who need that she should live. Clearly we have still not emerged from bourgeois morality.

In short, either a conjugal union establishes itself on the traditional basis of inequality—in which case there is a grave danger of the natural antagonism of the sexes becoming vitiated or exploited (whether because the man, not having a lover's radiant authority, replaces it by an authoritarianism that no longer has anything to do with love, or because, without exercising it, he still takes advantage of it to extract from the woman a subordination that serves his interests under cover of a fiction of love). Or the union establishes itself on a basis of equality and of sexual freedom, but the woman is still harmed and even cheated (for she has given up the assurance or at least the hope of a lasting experience, indispensable to the maturing of love, in exchange for a liberty that is no use to her). Festive love and the conventions of mutual freedom sacrifice the woman's conception of love, just as much as do the marriage and the companionship of reason. A woman is bent on committing herself wholly to love, and this she cannot do under either system.

Two philosophies of love stand facing each other—one of separation, one of total adoption. The revolution that puts an end to the cross purposes of the sexes will not confine itself to establishing for these an equality of status, but will have to encourage a kind of conjugal union based on the feminine conception of love—on *eros* confronted with the test of lasting. When men become able to commit themselves honestly to such unions, which imply a re-evaluation of faithfulness, for the man as well as for the woman, then the concept of love as a diversion will have had its day, and *eros* will have become what it must be—an existential experience of the Couple, the maieutic experience through which it is delivered and fulfilled. A new relationship of the sexes will be created.

EDUCATION

Love is your last chance. There is really nothing else on earth to keep you there.
ARAGON

'Ah! poor love, ah! sad reality', exclaims Milosz's Pinamonte,[114] imagining that he has unmasked the face of love when he has merely seen fornication. Having caught out his mistress, Pinamonte decides that he will give up 'turning love into the vehicle of grace'. Poor mysticism, sad conversion. Pinamonte had to be confronted with another person's vice—his own vices were not sufficient—in order to feel 'his flesh quivering with the pleasure of prayer'. Offended, irritated and furious but not *purified*, he at once turns his resentment against Woman, 'whose body is a cross and her embrace a sponge filled with vinegar'. Haunted by two silly verses,

> *Ta femme, ô Loth, bien que sel devenue*
> *Est femme encore, car elle a sa menstrue,*

he cries: 'Why do we not break with the stupid routine of considering as our fellow-creature an Eve whose spirit and whose flesh we shall never know'.[115]

How does it come about that an experience which presents itself as an *initiation* ends only in such a false triumph of the spirit? From the fact that the narrator—a great poet—has remained prisoner to a type of love that refuses the test of time. True, the liaison between Pinamonte and La Merone is represented as lasting for several months, since they display ingenuity in adding to it new settings, fancy dresses, amusements and vices; but in spite of these they remain exactly where they were: they do not adopt an enduring love, they merely try to cheat time. Such is the fatal fault of a love that gives up trying to grow because it will not face growing old. An initiation of this kind lacks the essential—that progression in depth, purification.

My own programme may well have appeared severe. But I had no choice. When one goes into things deeply (and this had to be attempted, for there will be no loop-hole through which to escape from the crisis of the couple), one becomes aware that the choice is between love-as-discipline and love-as-licence.

Not that love has ceased to be incantation, enchantment and intoxication—*eros* would no longer be *eros* if it gave up captivating: because of this, it is grace. But *la grâce oblige*, and love captivates only to commit us more throughly. And this means that, in itself, it is education and training. But not everyone has the luck to meet with the great love at the start, as Adelheid Solger did. And so a preparation for love must be provided for. It can take the place of useless and costly experiments and can economize errors. For we live in a world where things have been wantonly confused: there prevails a misconception of love, to which literature has contributed not a little. A great deal of modern literature is indulgent towards libertinism and casual adventure, reserving all its contempt for 'sentiment'; in it a 'great love' is overwhelmed with sarcasms and treated with a form of mystification. Such a love is called 'a huge sentimentality' or '*cornichonnerie fabuleuse*' (by Poulet), an anachronism (by Nimier) and a neurosis (by de Rougemont, who recently wrote that 'A man who falls passionately in love with a woman whom he alone sees as beautiful is presumed to be a neurasthenic'. Even physical love is devalued[116]—for 'physical love' is still the right name for minor sexual gymnastics, hardly more exciting than the daily quarter of an hour of physical jerks. But conjugal love has been depreciated more than any other kind: it is regarded as edifying, straightforward love, that is to say stupid, absurd, *dishonoured* love. Not, it is true, publicly, for a sham of official honours is still accorded to it; but the *gens d'esprit* would be ashamed to be taken in by it, and it is good form to make fun of it.

Some writers have reacted against the degradation. D. H. Lawrence tried to be a priest of conjugal love. 'I am', he used to say, 'a deeply religious man.' But that fine poet was frightened of intelligence, which he attacked in the name of *life*. 'You make the horrid mistake of trying to put your sex into a spiritual relation', he wrote to Dorothy Brett. Because he underrated the value of any tie-up between sex and mind, of any sublimation of desire (and this although he was not incapable of such a thing, but suggested that sexual love should be used as a mediation and wrote that the war within the couple leads to *knowledge*), Lawrence failed. Perhaps the daughter of Baron von Richthofen, with her robust appetites, was not the ideal person to accompany him in the ultimate ascension: the couple held together, but the initiation stopped short. She did not lead Lawrence beyond a kind of communion with all things under the aegis of Pan. He came in the end to heap insults on love and *unity* (intuitive as ever, he could feel exactly where the shoe pinched: 'I detest unity').[117] Puritan dualism had triumphed.

The endeavour of the surrealists, especially André Breton, to restore sacral love was better inspired. The operation was aimed not only against the Cartesian tribe, but also against the 'specialists of pleasure', 'collectors of adventures', 'sexual dandies': it was from another kind of people that Breton said he hoped to win understanding—from those who, each faithful to a single person, pursue the truth which shines through that person's soul and body. The madness of this *amour fou* is wisdom, its experience is one of *communication*—a fusion of hearts and minds accompanying and even preceding physical union.

At the same time the defenders of Christian *agape* have made their attempt to restore to love its value. As far back as 1945 Jean Guitton was suggesting that Nygren's and de Rougemont's conceptions of *agape* should be broadened.[118] De Rougemont himself has recently pleaded for a 'paradoxical alliance of Eros and Agape within marriage'; his dream is 'a domestication of the energy of Eros, perhaps more important for the future of humanity than the domestication of nuclear and solar energy!' Paul Ricoeur, a leading advocate of a Christian reconquest of sexuality, also suggests a compromise between Eros and the institution of marriage. But no partial resumption of Eros is possible: *divinizing eros* must be taken along with the rest. Such a reconquest, if it is to do any good, can only do so by a regrouping of the dissociated elements of love: neither sexuality, nor an 'ethic of tenderness', nor forms of consecration can by themselves regenerate the couple, for what essentially constitutes human love is the constant exchanges taking place on all its different levels—its communication and liaison.

Is this regrouping impossible? The facts suggest that it is not. A fortunate concurrence of circumstances gives us ground for hoping that the whole question of the marital relationship will soon be raised afresh. There is the legal emancipation of women, which is bound to be followed by their moral emancipation. There is the continuing increase of knowledge about love—in all fields (biology, psychology, ethnology, mythology, comparative history of religions and civilizations): we are witnessing today the formulation of a complete science of sexuality and love, freed from the prejudices and taboos of Western provincialism. Art and the theory of art are making their contribution.[119] At the same time the raising of the taboos has multiplied the studies of the more secret regions of love: there are, unfortunately, countless books on eroticism in the narrow sense, but these also help to throw some light, if only a partial one, on the huge sexological landscape. And finally, the efforts now being made to meet Platonic and neo-Platonic thought in a new spirit have a bearing on the fate of love in the West, the importance of which has perhaps not been realised: this new attitude centres on the conception of purification, and so it may well contribute to a new ethical doctrine.

But even the great wave of demythologization (or 'debunking') must to some extent serve our purpose. That great clearing-away of false myths will also prove to have been a *purification*, a sifting. From it the myth of the Androgyne emerges in its granite strength and ancient *impressiveness*. Even what may be called the 'replacement myths' reveal, in their way, the basic longing: I find in those of my time encouragement for the belief that people are clinging to some pretext, no matter what, for resacralization. Marilyn Monroe, Brigitte Bardot, James Dean, Marlon Brando, Maria Callas, Princess Soraya— all these, in spite of and perhaps in proportion to their simplification and vulgarization, lead me to believe that the sacred has lost none of its fascination for the great mass of men and women. The halo of legend, the aura projected on to these figures by the popular imagination may be an impure and confused expression, but it is a really living and collective expression of something: it shows that some kind of impulse towards a consecration having sexuality as its starting-point has survived in modern man. These myths, it should be noted, always grow up around love stories, exhibitions of love-making or scenes of violence that are transfers of sexual aggressiveness. And so the communication between sex and the sacred remains open and the daimonism of Eros continues to function, even though in shameful ways.

In fact, as I have said, the world is ready to welcome a philosophy of love. And perhaps love—with its possibilities of embodiment in the couple—may be the only thing that can, in this day and age, convincingly offer to human beings a 'collective sacred'. Possibly it is our civilization's last chance: human love may, as Breton has already written, contain 'the whole of the world's power of regeneration'.

However propitious the ground may be, the regeneration of the couple will not take place unaided. It is senseless and absurd that Western education, which is so skilful at training scientists and practitioners in all branches of activity, prudishly denies itself the right to prepare people for the most important act in life, so that they are reduced to seeking such teaching in a few seamy books and in a few usually degrading experiences.

In our society, preparation for love is not merely left to chance but is deliberately doomed to ignominious failure. A vast majority of the men of the West approach the sexual act as barbarians might. The civilizing value of love can get the better of this barbarism, the practice and custom of love can refine and uncoarsen; but this is preceded by clumsiness, awkwardness, mistakes (sometimes irreparable), disappointments, irritations and revulsions, all of which an education in love would have avoided. The most sensitive and cultivated man may quickly lose his slender make-up of civilization when swept by the power of desire; and the woman cannot recognize—in this violent and raging creature, bent on clumsily forcing her submission and more possessed than possessing—the man whose delicate homage she received. She knows, of course, that the act to which she will submit for the first time is one that involves some violence, but she expects and hopes that it will be a controlled violence. If she feels real mastery in the man, she is happy, and it is then only that she can give herself to the wonderful joys of abandonment: the success of professional

seducers lies largely in the security they are so clever at providing—
their experience shields the woman from a loss of composure which
she fears. Love brings into play primitive, elementary and formidable
forces, which come down to us from immemorial ages and may easily
crush the lovers with their weight: if the man allows them to sweep
him off his feet, the woman's timidity may change into terror. But
terror produces a redoubling of violence; and so, on the margin of the
sexual instinct, there can arise the terrifying inevitability of an auto-
matic cumulative aggression—a kind of sadistic trance in which the
man, completely blinded by instinct, tries to get his satisfaction in no
matter what way. Sometimes this way may be murder.

The story really happened.[120] Its scene was a small town in Holland,
not unlike many others; cool, placid and reassuring, with the still
almost medieval line of its roof-tops at the end of a green expanse of
meadows; in short, Vermeer's view of Delft. Behind the town, at the
foot of a dyke on which geese strutted, the scene changed abruptly,
revealing a gloomy landscape under the vast sky of the Low Countries.
Peeled, gnarled, scarred and still bristling with lengths of barbed wire
and bits of rusting scrap iron, this had been an army shooting range.
In the middle there protruded a concrete shed, sheltering the butts.
There, on 20 November 1948, some school-children at their play
came upon a frightful spectacle. Attached to iron bars in the form of
a cross, which supported the butts, firmly bound to them with double
knotted cord at a height of half a yard above the ground, there hung
the naked body of a girl of fifteen, stabbed and with her throat cut.
She had disappeared from her home the evening before. All the
previously convicted, the sadists and the habitual malefactors of the
region were being questioned when a boy, also aged fifteen, gave
himself up. Asked why he had committed so atrocious a crime, he
would say nothing. The murderer, like his victim, belonged to a
respectable and strictly moral family. He was not mad, not a black
sheep: reports previous to the murder described him as a tender, gentle,
very sensitive boy, with an excessive modesty, both ignorant and
curious about sexual matters—and indeed the only thing there seemed

to be against him was a preference, somewhat abnormal for his age, for playing at Red Indians.

The authorities tried to find out how this had come about. An amazing diary, kept by the girl, was found: it disclosed the existence of a love relationship between Jan and Ada. They had walked and bathed together, embraced, quarrelled and fought, down there at the foot of the dyke. The dreamy, tender boy would slap the girl in the face, give her heavy blows on the back and strike her on the breast with his fist. At night he dreamed of undressing her, tying her to a tree and torturing her. He drew pictures of her lying on her back, and marked with small crosses the places where he wanted, as he said, to *prick* her. Far from being repelled by those oddities, Ada was fascinated. And this well brought-up little girl—her school report said that she had remained very much of a child and was rather too much inclined to sentimental dreaming of fairies and castles—wrote in her diary: 'Have a good rest, brute of brutes. I am mad on you. I love you. I cannot do without you'. And again: 'Goodnight, dear, I love you. Even if you kill me, I shan't say anything. . . . *Love is a hard thing to understand*'. The strange idyll went on, in between school lessons, P.T. classes and games of Red Indians. And now, when Ada was lying in the grass, she would find close to her head a note transfixed by an arrow: 'This evening Ada will be assassinated. The Serpent.' One day Jan, on his way to school, saw a Boy Scout knife in a shop window. It occurred to him that he could prick Ada with this weapon. He tried to resist, but the knife was 'always in his head'. He arranged to meet his friend: 'Put on your blue sun-top. We are going to catch the Serpent. Come even if it rains!' He took his small brother's skipping-rope and hid the knife under his jacket. He met the girl and took her with him on his bicycle. The time was 7.45 p.m. In the November darkness they rode along together, towards the shooting-range. The two children went in to the shelter and sat down on a cross-bar. Ada put her arm round the boy and kissed him. Jan asked: 'What shall we do?' She did not answer, but lifted up the jersey of her gym dress, so that he could see her body. Then Jan said: 'I am going to tie you up.' He tied her to the bars, first by the legs, then by the arms. He gagged her with a hand-kerchief. Till then, she had submitted quietly, but now she grew uneasy: she tried to move and to speak, and shook her head violently, but the more she struggled the more surely Jan lost control of the unknown force which had taken possession of him and was acting in his stead—the more strongly he felt that something had been set in motion which could not now be stopped. He tore off Ada's clothes and bandaged her eyes. The girl was now struggling with all her strength. Then, impassively, like a sleep-walker, Jan began to prick her with his knife—under the left breast as he had done in dreams, he said later (for eventually he was persuaded to speak). But he would not say any more, nothing could persuade him to tell what happened afterwards, except that he saw her neck moving and that a sob came from it. There was no explanation of how this novice murderer with a poor knife managed to cut that neck with the certainty of a professional criminal or butcher. Asked what he had felt as he struck his victim, Jan confirmed the hypothesis which the judge had formed: it appears to have been intense pleasure. The murder had been a monstrous enactment of coupling.

Such is the terrible story of those two child lovers. The enquiry established that Jan's sexual ignorance was amazing: he had absolutely no knowledge of what to do in order to make love to Ada. Unfortunately he solved the problem in the cruellest way. This shows that the pastoral loves of young innocents can have a different ending from the romance of Daphnis and Chloë.

In that horrible story it is frightening to see a child rehearsing, with an automaton's accuracy, the major effects contrived by the sadists. The tragedy of it is twofold—that of ignorance, and also that of the aggressiveness and antagonism of the sexes. Instinct, failing to find its natural outlet, brings up from strange depths of bestiality one of the dreadful forms sometimes taken by sex in animals.

The case justifies not only the teaching of the facts of life to the young—the need for this is now scarcely disputed—but also preparing them for love. The glaring defect of sexual education in our time is that it rarely takes any account of love—and, if it does, then of pro-creative love, never of divinizing love. There is no clearer sign of the degradation and fragmentation of love than the teachings about it which we dispense to the young.

The idea of an erotic initiation is, of course, old and venerable. But while, in the past, such preparation has always had a sacred character (both among primitive peoples and among the highly civilized), modern sexual education is primarily a form of demythologization. It is profane, rudimentary and disparaging, and it completes the break with the primordial implications of sexuality. Either it is a mere collection of useful precepts and hygienic precautions, a sort of handbook stiffened with pseudo-scientific notions (which are put forward with peremptory assurance). Or it takes the opposite line to pragmatism and attempts to drown reality in a welter of pseudo-poetical comparisons, in order to elude the embarrassing questions and bring sexuality within the infantile sphere by means of a power of lies and omissions.[121] In both cases there is a non-adoption of the fact of sex and a rejection of the erotic: physical love is still treated as scandalous, an object of shame and fear. But the fear is not avowed, and no warning is given of the existence of sexual aggressiveness (the rôle of love being precisely to counterbalance this aggressiveness): instead, it is hoped to disarm *eros tremendum* by denying it—either by putting it on the level of Snow White and the Seven Dwarfs, or by reducing it to the naturalist explanation. The false objectivity that claims to confine within the explicable the vast range of the reality of sex has been denounced before now: 'it is impossible to strip it of our amazement and our ecstasy. To neutralize it is to denature it'.[122] The naturalist explanation is grossly misleading. No explanation exhausts the content of acts that bring into play the basic mysteries of life and death, of perdition and salvation.

Sometimes these attempts to reduce love to insignificance go so far as to suggest sordid ways of preserving oneself from it. Many books on sexual education—and these not the least puritan ones—now contain a chapter in which the author tries to keep his readers from having a bad conscience about masturbation. But this is not unfamiliar ground: we have seen that one kind of puritanism is not so much against Eros as against the sublimation of Eros.[123] We are back among the old Gnostic errors, with their separation of things into compartments:

such people reject the ambivalence of love because they cannot resolve it. 'Man', we are told, 'finds it hard to resign himself to an act of love that is indissolubly a bestial act'—but suppose the rôle of love is precisely to adopt this contradiction and this task of sublimation? Love, as Saint Augustine (who spoke from experience) said long ago, carries the flesh even into the spirit, the spirit even into the flesh.

Neither Christianity nor even Gnosticism is alone responsible for the undervaluing of the erotic: the thought that shame attaches to the sexual functions and organs is as old as the hills. The Greek language had defamatory words for them, and the Greeks used these expressions at the very moment when they raised up the well-known *agalma* in the Dionysion of Delos. Their wisdom had found the way that leads, in love, continually from the lower to the higher, the dialectic that continually binds the flesh to the spirit, the sensory to the intelligible. What deprives love of its highest significance is our constitutional inability to conceive a binding together of the contraries. And so the degradation of love and of the Couple is part of the price paid for a puerile rationalism, a rigid cult of science. For a long time the chances of a philosophy of love making for restoration and sublimation have been stifled by men's inadequacy in metaphysics, by their lack of the power to move about among the paradoxes of a 'dualism constantly surmounted and constantly renewed'. But the last word has not been said. It is comforting to see a man like Teilhard de Chardin bringing love back into his labour of synthesis: he suggests that 'between a marriage that is always socially polarized towards reproduction and a religious perfection always presented theologically in terms of separation' there can be a third way, 'not a middle way but a higher one', leading to the conquest of the unfathomable spiritual powers still dormant beneath the mutual attraction of the sexes. Without any doubt Teilhard de Chardin is here laying the foundations of a new philosophy of love, one of sublimation.[124]

What future is there for a programme of this kind, which strives not to break completely with orthodoxy (whatever the liberties it takes with orthodoxy may amount to)? It does not look as if official religion, however great its power of rejuvenation, is yet capable of setting before men a 'collective sacred'. If conjugal love needs to be made afresh and thought out afresh (and the only ambition of the present book has been to succeed in convincing its readers of this), it will have to be done outside organized religion. The preparation for love will nonetheless have a sacral quality. At the same time it would gain, I think, if it were preceded by a non-sacred teaching, a kind of propaedeutic, which would include a historical and sociological section (comparative history of myths, of institutions and of legislation and policy concerning conjugal union) and a scientific section (a biological, physiological and psychological introduction to knowledge about sexuality and love). The real initiation would then follow. This would be progressive and gradual—many people, clearly, would be left by the wayside—and would present itself as a movement upwards (in contrast with present sexual education, which talks down to those whom it claims to be initiating) and as an *approach* to the Mystery of the sexes. Perhaps the decisive step in the regeneration of love will be this substitution of the idea of *mystery* for that of furtiveness. A mystery is something that lends itself to revelation, to a progressive unveiling —and yet in the end one is still faced with what Breton calls an 'unbreakable nucleus of night'. What is needed, evidently, is a whole new education directed towards respect—and to admit that there is a limit to human investigation. But indeed science itself has been taking a new direction, pointing out the insignificance of the known in comparison with what remains to be discovered—the Mystery of which recedes as it is pursued. Science has become once more a dispenser of wonder, and it gives to the gestures of love a greater significance than ever. Relatively few privileged men and women will achieve full awareness of these greater depths, but one may hope that in the others a salutary giddiness will arise and will sometimes bring up to the surface those data of the unconscious which are always ready to emerge, remembered rather than taught. In this case sexuality would recover its proper dimensions—fully adopted by some people, gazed at and counted on by the others. A climate of rehabilitation would be created. The rôle of science in the future of the couple will consist less in instruction than in raising sex up from its indignity.

Women will play a determining part in establishing this new life of the couple. It is in their interest to do so. And besides, they are needed. We are on the verge of a new period, when the woman's conceptions will at length prevail—of love as of other things, and before other things. The feminine way of loving involves both not separating pleasure from love and harmonizing passion with continuance.

In the hope that the world may be regenerated, women take their stand against techniques of pleasure and for a conjugal realization of love. The realization of love as total adoption and recovery in contrast with the masculine idea of it as separation and escape. A realization of love that is truly *existential* in the best sense. It alone can enable people to live love instead of dreaming of it: to assume all its ages including —after the initial turbulence—the wonderful tenderness and gratitude of partners who remember.

Essential as well as *existential*. With good reason Plato himself put into the mouth of a woman the most exalted words to which love inspired him. The eternal Diotima is essentially a purifier—and so a fisher in troubled waters, easily seeming *impure* to men who undervalue her zest as a washer of dirty linen, her 'shrewd anger'[125] her passion for triumphing over dirt. This passion is certainly not guilty of *idealizing:* it is a plant whose seed has fallen from heaven, whose roots are thrust deep into the earth—but if it succeeds in growing upwards, it will bind the two together eagerly and robustly.

Educative as well as purifying. The man may have the initiative in the ritual of sexuality, but the woman may well be called upon to reveal its meaning—a meaning that is only illuminated by love. She, more than man, is immersed in the night of sex. Out of the world of the *Mothers*, where the mystery is accomplished in the darkness propitious to all gestation, she emerges with a prodigious experience. If only she brings into it the disciplines of intelligence and carries lucidity into the heart of this irrational thing, she will even attain— through the sublime play of a sacral sexuality—to the great way of Knowledge.

NOTES ON THE TEXT

1. It seems hardly necessary to say that the kind of reason meant here is practical reason, not the spiritual reason, the νοῦς of the Greeks, of which it is the perversion.

2. The phrase is taken from Jules Monnerot.

3. Aragon, *Le Paysan de Paris*, Gallimard, p. 242.

4. Letter from Paulus Merula, advocate at the Dutch Court and professor *in spe* at Leyden, to Judith Buys (20 October 1589), *Het Hart op de Tong*, Hellinga, The Hague, 57.

5. Roland Barthes, *Mythologies*, pp. 50-51, Ed. du Seuil, Paris.

6. Women naturally develop a different and complementary symbolism of the arrow and the straight line. See Nelli's admirable book, *L'amour et les mythes du cœur*, Ch. IV, Hachette, Paris, republished 1952.

7. See Proverbs, XXXI.

8. *Life of Dion*, North's translation.

9. 'My soul, when I embraced Agathon, would come—the wretch—to my lips as if to fly away.'

10. 'I have still said nothing of Alexis, only that he is beautiful and draws all eyes to him. My heart, why do you show the bone to the dog? . . .'

11. *Essai sur l'amour humain*, p. 30, Aubier, Paris, 1947.

12. H.-A. Marrou, *Histoire de l'éducation dans l'Antiquité*, p. 60, Seuil, 1960.

13. On the difficult question of the chronology of the Dialogues I have followed Robin's learned exposition in *La théorie platonicienne de l'amour*, p. 90, 2nd edition, Paris, Alcan, 1932.

14. Plutarch, *Life of Dion*, North's translation.

15. This and the quotations which follow are taken from Jowett's translation.

16. In addition, if H.-A. Marrou is right (*op. cit.* p. 64), Euripides was the lover of Agathon, Phidias of his pupil Agoracritus of Paros, and the physician Theomedon of the astronomer Eudoxus of Cnidos.

17. Far from teaching, as Aristotle did, that 'suffering denatures and corrupts', Plato tells us in the *Gorgias* that a man can only amend himself by the way of pain and suffering.

18. *Phaedrus*, 256, c, d, e.

19. *L'amour en Grèce*, p. 159, Hachette, Paris, 1960.

20. *Femmes pythagoriciennes, Fragments et Lettres*, translated by Mario Meunier, *L'Artisan du Livre*, Paris, 1932.

21. Plutarch, *Conjugalia Praecepta*, XIV.

22. Ephesians, 4.

23. In spite of the charming *Banquet of the Ten Virgins* in which St Methodius, attempting to raise the standard, came to the conclusion that 'he who remains continent in the midst of the troubles of concupiscence is therefore better and more virtuous than the man who, not being stirred by any desire, remains calmly victorious in the camp of chastity'. But St Methodius, martyr though he was, has about him a whiff of heresy. The great Doctors of the Church always opted for prudence, not prowess.

24. St Jerome uses a curious argument against marriage: 'The Apostle Paul urges us to pray without ceasing, but the man who is accomplishing his conjugal duty cannot pray at the same time'. Clearly the *mysterion* of two human beings who are one flesh did not mean much to St Jerome.

25. Similarly St John Chrysostom: 'Marriage is the fruit of the disobedience of the first couple, of the curse and of death', and 'God did not institute marriage, he is only its *nomothete*'.

26. On the originality and genius of Hadewych, as also on the problem of a second Hadewych, see the works of Father van Mierlo, who devoted his life to this research. See also *Hadewych d'Anvers*, by J.-B. P. (Paris, Seuil, 1954), with his remarkable commentaries, and the intelligent, agreeably subversive essay by Marie-Hélène van der Zeyde (*Hadewych*, Wolters, Groningen, 1934).

27. S.P.C.K., London, 1932-9.

28. 'That which we can name *is not God*, for if men could understand Him with their senses and their ideas God would be less than they, and so we should soon cease to love Him.' Hadewych, *Letters*, XII, 33-37.

29. *Visioenen* (van Mierlo, Louvain, 1924).

30. On the orthodoxy of Hadewych, see the authorized opinion of J.-B. P. (*op. cit.*, p. 31): 'The spiritual doctrine taught by Hadewych, of which she gives the evidence in these visions and in the letters . . . has been found healthy and complete—rightly, in our view—by those judges who have studied it during the last thirty years, in particular by the Reverend Father van Mierlo, S.J., and the Prof. Stephanus Axters, O.P.'

31. Jean Trouillard (*op. cit.*) has drawn attention to the paradoxical coincidence of critical with mystical activity in unitive thought.

32. The theological term for this presence is 'natural' or 'prevenient' Grace: in those days—with St Bernard or with Guillaume de Saint-Thierry for instance—there was no such sharp distinction between nature and grace as came to prevail among both the Protestant and Catholic theologians after the Council of Trent.

33. On the possible attribution of this poem to a second Hadewych who came from the same circle, see Father J.-B. P., *op. cit.*, pp. 45 *et seq.*

34. It recurs in Rilke, in Henri Michaux and in many of the surrealists, but is also found in Plato and Plotinus; for 'the escape from this world below to the world above' is to flee into oneself—'it is not with our feet that we must flee', but we must 'shut our eyes, change this gaze for another, and reawaken that vision which all possess but so few exercise'.

35. 'Christian thought was familiar with only superficial forms, if not misinterpretations, of Platonism and of neo-Platonism, whether it looked at these as allies or as enemies. Its confrontation with the most important part of these doctrines is, for the most part, still to come' (Trouilliard, *Purification*, p. 131). A similar judgment is expressed by Gilson (*Le Christianisme et la tradition philosophique*, in *Revue des sciences philosophiques et théologiques*, 41-42, vol. II, p. 252).

36. More exactly super-essentialist: see *Supra*, pp. 145-6.

37. Denis de Rougemont, *Passion and Society*, Faber, London, 1940.

38. J.-P. Sartre, *Situations I*, N.R.F., Paris, 1947.

39. Denis de Rougemont, *Comme toi-même*, p. 12, Paris, 1961.

40. *Phaedo*, 68a; *Nicomachean Ethics*, III, 13.

41. René Nelli, *L'Amour et les mythes du cœur*, Hachette, Paris, 1952.

42. Tristan also concentrates his passion on Iseult alone, while the Tao teaches its disciple to defend himself from Woman by means of women: he is recommended to have recourse to several in the same night.

43. Furthermore, it is difficult to see how one can reconcile the thesis that passionate love was born in the twelfth century with that of its pagan origin.

44. On the connections between the courtly conception of love, Petrarch, and the philosophy of Ficino, see Festugière, *La philosophie de Marsile Ficin*, Vrin, Paris, 1947.

45. Little bacchic canticle of the Nuns of the Lower Rhineland, by Anne of Cologne: see Jean Chuzeville, *Les Mystiques allemands du xiiie au xive siècle*, Grasset, Paris, 1957.

46. Per Nykrog (*Les Fabliaux*, Munksgaard, Copenhagen) defines the *fabliaux* as a burlesque courtly *genre* in a popular style. In systematic opposition to courtly love, they were addressed to the same public as were the romances. But while the romances brought together everything the nobles regarded as aristocratic (courage, sublime love, physical beauty), the world of the comic *contes*—though no less *ideal*, no less artificial than that of the romances—took as its province

everything the nobility thought of as characteristic of the common people—'vulgarity, whoring, stupidity, low instincts, ugliness and filth'. In this case also the courtly *genre* worked towards the fragmentation of love, extending it to the social.

47. I have used as my source Robert Guiette's excellent text, *Le Miroir des Dames mariées*, Ed. du Cercle d'Art, Brussels, 1944.

48. By 'Pauline Réage', Ed. Pauvert (1954), with a preface by Jean Paulhan.

49. Thorbecke, *Lettres à sa fiancée et à sa femme*, Meulenhorff, Amsterdam, 1936.

50. Manu Smriti, I, 32, quoted by Alain Daniélou, *Le Polythéisme hindou*, Corrêa, Paris, 1960, p. 313.

51. *Ibid.*, pp. 371 *et seq.*

52. Shiva is represented in the androgynous aspect in a very fine carving belonging to the sanctuary of Elephanta; see Max-Pol Fouchet, *The Erotic Sculpture of India*, p. 33, George Allen & Unwin, London, 1959.

53. Compare Karapâtri Lingopâsanâ Rahasya, Siddhânta (Daniélou, *op. cit.* p. 347): 'Desire, the attraction of the contraries, which is born of the first dualism, of the distinction between the Person and Nature, is the supernatural Eros. Linked to nature by desire, the cosmic Person engenders innumerable Worlds.'

54. Clémence Ramnoux, *Héraclite ou l'Homme entre les Choses et les Mots*, pp. 373 *et seq.*, Belles-Lettres, Paris, 1959.

55. Like Pythagoras, who, according to Aristotle, assigned the One to the third place in the column of the luminous, not above.

56. The Anthology of Empedocles from which Plato afterwards borrowed (with its chaotic vision of detached limbs wandering at random—arms, legs, sexual organs, fragments of head or shoulder, tumbling over one another) also illustrates the theme of fragmentation and dispersal. What we have here is a kind of explosion of the original Simplicity. To this disintegration (which Plotinus later called a dilation—'the world is a dilation of the divine goodness') there corresponds a re-integration. *Exitus* and *reditus* are the complementary aspects of one and the same process.

57. The Orphic egg, germless and unfertilized, gives birth, by breaking in two, to androgynous Eros, who reconstitutes the non-duality.

58. For instance, sexual initiations, where adolescence is treated as an androgynic condition, to which circumcision puts an end. Or again birth rites, like those of the Dogon: on the ground where the woman has given birth the Nommo draws two outlines, one male, the other female, so that the two souls may invest the new-born child, making him one and alone in his body but spiritually two—for sex is only appearance, it is bisexuality that is real. Cf. Marcel Griaule, *Dieu d'eau, Entretiens avec Ogotommeli*, pp. 185-6, Éditions du Chêne, Paris.

59. This wish has already been realized in part by the following remarkable studies: *Méphistophélès et l'Androgyne*, by Mircea Eliade (Gallimard, 1962); *Hermaphrodite, Mythes et Rites de la bisexualité dans l'antiquité classique*, by Marie

Delcourt (Presses Universitaires de France, 1958); and *Contributions à l'étude de l'Androgynie*, by Halley des Fontaines, Paris, 1933.

60. See Henry Corbin, *Terre celeste et Corps de résurrection*, pp. 74 *et seq.*, Buchet-Chastel, Paris, 1961.

61. A curious example is the Fourth Vision of Hadewych, in which she describes herself as clasped by the wings of the beautiful incandescent Angel—especially the passage where the masculine Angel, reminding Hadewych that he is only deputizing for the real Lover, who is Christ (as the Fravarti deputizes for the celestial Daênâ), shows her 'those heavens entire, which she saw distinct and which are their double humanity before it was joined together by growth'.

62. More precisely still, a fragment of the Gospel of the Egyptians (a Gnostic text of the second century) teaches that the reign of death will last until the masculine and the feminine become one. Cf. Amadou, Table Ronde, no. 97, p. 48, *Les théories dualistes de la sexualité*.

63. Roger Caillois and Jean-Clarence Lambert, *Trésor de la Poésie universelle*, p. 40, Gallimard, Paris, 1958.

64. *L'amour et les mythes du cœur*, Hachette, Paris, 1952.

65. Rossetti's translation. The passage is quoted by Nelli in *L'amour et les mythes du cœur*, Hachette, Paris, 1952.

66. 'But sexuality has never been "pure", it has everywhere and always had a polyvalent function, whose first and perhaps chief valency has been the cosmological function.' Hence 'to translate a psychical situation into sexual terms is certainly not to humiliate it, for, except to the modern world, sexuality has everywhere and always been a hierophany and the sexual act an integral act (therefore also a means to knowledge)'. Mircea Eliade, *Images et Symboles*, Gallimard, Paris, 1952.

67. *Beyond the Pleasure Principle*, tr. C. S. M. Hubback, International Psychological Press, London and Vienna, 1922; pp. 44, 45.

68. A fascination accompanied by repulsion and fear, by *Todesangst*. This ambivalence is characteristic of the sacred. Ernest Jones thinks that to Freud death had an esoteric meaning. One day, when he came to from a faint, his first words (to the surprise of Jung) were: 'How sweet it must be to die'.

69. Isha Schwaller de Lubicz, *La lumière du chemin*, La Colombe, Paris, 1960. See the chapter *La Famille, Le Couple*, pp. 146–79.

70. It may be regretted that biology uses the same word *hermaphroditism* to designate both the sexual bivalence of elementary animals like the infusoria and the real hermaphroditism—genital organs of both kinds—of species such as the gasteropods. The first precedes sex and seems to be preparing the way for it, while the second presupposes sex.

71. In *Geschlecht und Charakter*, Weininger followed Fliess in defending the thesis of a potential bisexuality in every cell, but he laid stress on the tendency of the cells to divide into sexes—indeed independently of the sex of the individual to

whom they belonged. For instance, in the subject of Ribera's picture—a bearded woman with pronounced breasts—the male sex would be dominant in the cells of the epidermis and the female sex in the mammary glands. Weininger, like Fliess, attributed this potential bisexuality to the action of an internal secretion and a specific reaction of the cells to this secretion.

72. There is no evidence against the hypothesis of cellular bisexuality. As is well known, the cells of the human body contain twenty-two pairs of identical chromosomes, plus a twenty-third pair whose members are different in the male. It is generally thought that sex-determination depends on this twenty-third pair, known as XY in the male individual and XX in the female: these are called the *sexual chromosomes*. All the cells of the body conserve and reproduce this double set of chromosomes except, in fact, the germinal cells—which, when they mature, undergo what is called *reduction division*. This peculiarity recalls the distinction between *soma* and *germen*: the distinction may sometimes seem an academic one, since it has not proved possible to draw a hard and fast line between somatic and germinal; but the fact remains that there is a difference between the cells possessing a double set of chromosomes and the cells destined to part with one half of this double set. The latter, as they mature, are called *gametes*, and each male gamete (or spermatozoon) now contains only one sexual chromosome, either X or Y. Half the gametes carry the male potentiality and half carry the female. This choice of one out of two ways has necessarily been preceded by a state in which the double potentiality was still there without differentiation, and this indistinction is characteristic of all cells before their sexualization. It is noteworthy that it is on cells divided in this way that the active part in the sexual act devolves, its effect being, where fertilization takes place, to reconstitute the double stock of chromosomes by adding chromosomes belonging to the partner of the other sex. The impressive hypothesis of a tendency to reconstitute the pre-sexual state at the cellular level seems, then, not so fantastic.

The above reasoning is correct for the male gametes; but there must be another, analogous line of reasoning applicable to the female gametes, since parthenogenesis can produce males as well as females. In other species (butterflies, birds) the situation is the other way about: the male has the XX formation and the female the XY.

73. Some of the spectacular successes in producing hermaphroditism experimentally have been due to the injection of hormones into embryos of rodents or frogs.

74. See Jean Rostand, *Le Bestiaire d'Amour*, pp. 17 *et seq.*, Laffont, Paris, On the *paramecia* it is worth while also to consult Vivier: *L'Infusoire Paramécie*, in *Annales des sciences naturelles*, 12th series, vol II.

75. Brien's elegant experiments on the fresh water Hydrae have thrown light on this contingent nature of sexuality. A mere variation of temperature may provoke or stop it at will: 'Sexuality is not necessarily written into the biological cycle of an animal, it is determined by contingent factors', *Étude d'Hydra Pirardi*, in *Bulletin Biologique de la France et de la Belgique*, 1961, fasc. 2, p. 363, Presses Universitaires, Paris.

76. As has been proved by the observations of Carrel, Galadjieff, Metalnikoff and Woodruff on the infusoria, oligochetes and turbellaries. Woodruff's experimental work extended to over 8,000 generations of *paramecia*. Cf. Vivier, *Annales des sciences naturelles*, 12th series, vol. II, p. 393.

77. ᴵ ᴊᴉs Bounoure, *L'instinct sexuel*, p. 192-3, Presses Universitaires, Paris, 1956: '᷍ ᴄre can be no doubt', he concludes, 'that this view inspired the Platonic myth ᴏf love as uniting the separate halves of the real being, as well as the Biblical tradition of the creation of the woman as a part taken out of the man's organism.'

78. The only activity stimulated by the female hormones is that of provocation.

79. Bounoure suggests that, when in an animal couple the dominance passes to the female, this phenomenon is due to the male hormone secreted by the ovary. It has been proved that, in the female, it is the normal hormone of this sex that determines her submission to the male, her crouching down to accept coitus.

80. Roger Caillois, *La Mante religieuse, Recherche sur la nature et la signification du Mythe*, Aux Amis des Livres, Paris, 1937.

81. 'However, he merely smiled at this sudden change, as if to show that he had heard and understood, but his gaze had become so fierce and his expression so harsh that the absurdity of any prayer, promise or command was evident, since clearly nothing, short of killing him, would have prevented him from pursuing his aims'. A. Pieyre de Mandiargues, *Le lis de mer*, p. 190, Robert Laffont, Paris.

82. Dr Grémillon, quoted by Simone de Beauvoir, *Le Deuxième Sexe*, Book II, p. 209.

83. An essay by M. Jacques Sarano in *Esprit* (no. 11, p. 1850, *La Sexualité*, Ed. du Seuil, Paris) gives expression to this view: 'Is it not strange that the urine and the sperm go through the same channel, and that the act of generation is close to that of excretion? This must always strike the mind with amazement. Nobody and no subterfuge will ever be able to counteract such a neighbourhood'.

84. Jean Daniélou, *Discussion sur le Péché*, in *Dieu vivant*, No. 4, Le Seuil, Paris, 1945, pp. 91, 192.

85. R. Otto, *Le Sacré*, tr. Jundt, Payot, Paris, 1949.

86. No. 11, *La Sexualité*, *vide supra*.

87. Pierre Klossowski, *Sade, mon prochain*, Ed. du Seuil, Paris, 1947.

88. On the Gnostic sadism of Baudelaire, see Georges Blin, *La sadisme de Baudelaire*. 'Baudelaire', he says, 'seeks the pure woman in order to soil her, the impure woman in order to be soiled by her.' This acute judgment does not fit in very well with Blin's diagnosis (after Sartre) of the existence in Baudelaire of a 'pathological Platonism': Baudelairian love goes dead against the divinizing Eros.

89. This was conceded by Father Daniélou to Bataille in a well-known discussion entitled '*Discussion sur le Péché*', in No. 4 of *Dieu vivant* (Ed. du Seuil, Paris). 'Sin, awareness of our radical uncleanness, leads to God and is linked with grace: insofar

as it destroys sufficiency, insofar therefore as it is detested, and to the extent that it draws man to despair and forces him to the act of faith which transfigures the world'—a formulation which, with its Kierkegaardian echoes, seems not to have wholly escaped from the Gnostic contamination.

90. Nelli, *op. cit.*, p. 106. In the same order of ideas I should like to draw attention to a curious passage by Valery Larbaud. After mentioning a Catalan monk, Father d'Esplugues, who in *Le Vrai Visage du Poverello* sings the praises of St Francis and 'even suggests—though this cannot fail to cause irreverent amusement in a layman—calling him Mother Francis', Larbaud continues: 'A noble virility in a woman and an exalted femininity in a man are the counterpoises for the defects inherent in each sex. They mark the victory over the human beast and are joined together in sainthood'. Valery Larbaud, *Œuvres*, p. 719, Ed. de la Pléiade, Gallimard, Paris.

91. *Planète*, no. 4, p. 129.

92. Cf. Jacobi, *La Psychologie de C. G. Jung*, Ed. Delachaux, Neuchâtel-Paris, 1950, pp. 134, 135.

93. This book was already written when the author read Teilhard de Chardin's *L'Energie humaine* (Ed. du Seuil, Paris, 1962), with the amazing pages there devoted to the '*sens sexuel*'. Teilhard notes that 'religions as complete as the Christian religion have, till now, based almost their whole code of morality on the child', and he comments: 'From the point of view to which analysis of a Cosmos with a convergent structure has brought us, things are seen to be quite otherwise. That the dominant function of sexuality was at first to guarantee the conservation of the species is not in doubt—this was so as long as the condition of personality had not established itself in Man. But from the critical instant of Hominization another and more essential rôle devolved upon love—a rôle of which, it seems, we may be only beginning to feel the importance: I mean, the necessary synthesis of the two principles, the masculine and the feminine, in the building up of the human personality.' pp. 91, 92.

94. Jean-Pierre Richard (in *Littérature et sensation*, Ed. du Seuil, 1954) ingeniously carries further Stendhal's metaphor of the crystallized branch seen at Salzburg: he points out that the wood remains visible through the transparency of the crystals, which perhaps play the part of a natural magnifying-glass. The point that concerns us in his subtle analysis is that he agrees in thinking that love finally issues in truth. Significantly, he uses on several occasions the same metaphors as I have used—going through, shining through, digging out, setting free, discovering, defining—to describe the activity of love.

95. *Vom kosmogonischen Eros*, 4th edition, Iéna, 1941.

96. *Homère Durand* in *Cahiers du Sud*, no. 367, pp. 382-403. See in particular page 395: 'And I didn't have her that summer. No, I went back to my work, determined to subject myself to the test of abstinence in order to do her homage, yes, homage to my dear one. And for a whole year we didn't see each other and we didn't write—no, because that goes to one's head, and desire makes one say impossible bloody nonsense. And, to be frank, I wasn't spared the longing to get

out of that bloody situation: more than once I awoke in the morning covered with sperm like a pine with resin, and that afternoon in the hills obsessed me. Still I held good, even when splendid tarts accosted me as I came away from college. I have always loved whores, though I never touched them, or practically never ... I enjoyed in them a breath of ancient Rome or the bacchanals—to give more reality to the atmosphere of our lectures on classical antiquity, of course.' Clearly, in this experience (which is as traditional as can be) it is chastity and fidelity that are seen as existential, and marriage as 'idealist' and 'literary'.

97. On the delicate problem of the inspiration of these poems, I have felt able to follow the conclusions reached by J. B. Leishman in a remarkable book, *The Monarch of Wit* (Hutchinson, London, 1951). While he considers that the auto-biographical element in Donne's poetry has been exaggerated at the expense of an element of dramatization and play, Leishman nonetheless considers that about twenty of the finest poems or songs and sonnets were inspired by Donne's wife. Joan Bennett (*Four Metaphysical Poets*) comes to a very similar conclusion.

98. *The Good Morrow.*

99. *Op. cit.*, p. 231, n. 2. In the introduction to *Poèmes de John Donne*, tr. Truzier and Denis, Gallimard, Paris, 1962.

100. *Poètes métaphysiques anglais*, Corti, Paris, 1960.

101.   *Full nakedness. All joyes are due to thee,*
        As souls unbodied, bodies uncloth'd must be,
        To taste whole joyes.

102. I cannot understand how Michel Butor, in his article *Sur le Progrès de l'âme de John Donne* (*Cahiers du Sud*, no. 321, p. 276), can attribute the misogyny of *Metempsychosis* to Donne's marriage and the ruin of his career. That strange poem, which is a satire against the Queen, was written in 1601, at a moment when Donne may have been already in love with Anne but had not yet married her: the marriage took place in December 1601.

103. Donne was also, according to the *Oxford English Dictionary*, the first to use the word 'sex' in its usual modern sense.

104. France, by the law of 1938; Holland, by the van Hoven law, 1956; Belgium, by the Lilar law, 1958.

105. Arthur Adamov, *Strindberg*, L'Arche, Paris, 1955.

106. Letter from Strindberg to Harriet Bosse, 28 August 1901 (*Letters of Strindberg to Harriet Bosse*, p. 49, Nelson, New York, 1959).

107. Delightfully described by Hénault as follows: 'I also visited Cirey. It is a rare sight. There they are, the two of them alone, with everything they could wish. One of them is busy making verses and the other triangles'.

108. Attention has been drawn to a similar separation between ideals and practical morality as regards the problem of labour and wages. The bourgeoisie preaches respect for labour and for poverty in such slogans as 'labour ennobles', 'there is no such thing as a pointless employment', or 'poverty is not a vice', but bases its

acts on quite different values, such as money, power and honours, and 'at the same time institutes a morality of example and insinuation, in which practice preaches what doctrine condemns'. (Albert Lilar, *Eloge de l'Humanisme*, p. 45, Buschmann, Antwerp, 1936).

109. In *Mythologies*, Ed. du Seuil, Paris, 1957.

110. *La Force de l'Age*, Gallimard, Paris, 1960.

111. 'Sartre had not the vocation for monogamy', she says in *La Force de l'Age*. Cf. *Les Mandarins*, where it is said of the character Robert Dubreuilh that 'he considered it normal to pick up a pretty tart in a bar and spend an hour with her', and on page 71 Anne says: 'During those five years I had lived chaste, without any regret, and I thought I would always remain so'. Cf. also *L'Expérience vécue* (p. 536): 'The nature of her eroticism, the difficulties of a free sexual life, incite a woman to monogamy'.

112. Less modern, though, than is often admitted. High society in the eighteenth century made use of such arrangements, perfunctorily disguised by the conventions. Respect for marriage was left to the lower classes. A pact of this kind applied in the case of the quasi-conjugal liaison between Voltaire and Madame du Châtelet. Voltaire accepted that Madame du Châtelet should love Saint-Lambert—'she will merely see to it that these things do not take place before his eyes'. When Madame du Châtelet became pregnant, they held a council of three. And since, in that century of lightness and wit, it was above all important to show that one was not deceived, Voltaire wrote a charming one-act play about this mischance.

113. The autobiography of another famous couple shows us the writer Lüdwig Nordström, taking advantage of such a pact without any scruples, but finding it hard to endure Marika Stiernstedt making use of it. (Marika Stiernstedt, *Kring ett äktenskap*, Bonnier, Stockholm, 1953).

114. O. V. de L. Milosz, *L'amoureuse initiation*, André Silvaire, Paris, 1958.

115. Significantly, after this licentious scene La Merone is called the Initiatress, and the 'illuminated' narrator makes the discovery that 'to attain to the Love of God, one must *deny* human love'. The reader will have recognized in this the erotic of abjection.

116. To get an idea of this devaluation, which has occurred in the space of a generation, we need only compare two avowals by Anne and by her daughter Nadine in *Les Mandarins*. Anne, speaking of her lover, says that 'between us, from the start, desire was always for love'—sex was not dissociated from sentiment. To Nadine, on the contrary, love was scarcely, if at all, pleasure, and she invited her lover to make love to her on the beach because 'out of doors it might be a little less boring'.

117. 'To me it is life to feel the white ideas and the "oneness" crumbling into a thousand pieces, and all sorts of wonder coming through.' (From a letter to Rolf Gardiner, 4 July 1924.)

118. Jean Guitton, *op. cit.*

119. A good instance is the sensation caused by the 1960 exhibition 'L'Art amoureux des Indes', and by Max-Pol Fouchet's fine introduction to the catalogue. See also Alain Daniélou's recent books, Le Polythéisme hindou (already mentioned) and L'Erotisme divinisé (Paris, 1962), as well as Max-Pol Fouchet's The Erotic Sculpture of India.

120. See J. H. Wiggers, Nederlandse Jurisprudentie, no. 22, 1952.

121. I recommend to the consideration of my readers a small book of Danish origin, which has a large circulation in England and is called Peter and Caroline. In it they will see how the attempt to strip physical love of its secrecy, its formidableness, and to reduce it to the pretty, leads straight to obscenity.

122. Jacques Sarano, L'esprit, le sexe et la bête, Esprit, no. 11, pp. 1848 and 1852. It is this that renders the sexual education of our sons and daughters difficult. Either we feel the ineffableness of that strange act from which after all we were born, and so we keep silence. Or else we take it upon ourselves to overcome the ineffableness, and so adopt the pose of objective seriousness, the air and tone of deceptively naturalist explanation. Objectivity itself is here a lie and a betrayal.

123. See Roland de Pury, Eros et Agape: 'Eros is not sin, what is sinful is the sublimation of Eros'. This stands in contrast to Teilhard de Chardin, who comes out strongly in favour of the sublimation of sexuality, for instance in his Le sens sexuel, pp. 91-96 (Ed. du Seuil, Paris, 1962).

124. Teilhard de Chardin, op. cit. The whole chapter on sexual feeling should be read. It is a fully-fledged theory of amour-passion (he is not afraid to use the word), with the aim not of happiness but of spiritual fulfilment. Warning us against the dangerous tendency of the Couple to close in on itself, he urges us to choose open love, not a closed love. And by this he means: to pass over a world of two in favour of a world of three—which is not, as might be expected, the man, the woman and the child, but the man, the woman and God. 'Without going outside itself, the couple can find its balance only in a third that is in front of it.' That is a love that is lived through. Such love develops and its later development would be towards a gradual diminution of what, though still admirable, is a transitory part of the sexual: towards a gradual lessening of the importance given to procreation, in favour of a 'full flowering of the copious love set free from the duty of reproduction'. What is proposed includes a new conjugal ethics of purity, an erotic chastity. But one can only urge readers to study these truly revolutionary pages.

125. Bachelard's phrase. And Simone de Beauvoir (preceded by Ponge) has devoted some fine pages in Le Deuxième Sexe to woman's vocation for material purification (Book II, pp. 229 et. seq.).